The COLT Observation Scheme

Language Learning & Language Teaching (LL&LT)

ISSN 1569-9471

The LL&LT monograph series publishes monographs, edited volumes and text books on applied and methodological issues in the field of language pedagogy. The focus of the series is on subjects such as classroom discourse and interaction; language diversity in educational settings; bilingual education; language testing and language assessment; teaching methods and teaching performance; learning trajectories in second language acquisition; and written language learning in educational settings.

For an overview of all books published in this series, please see benjamins.com/catalog/lllt

Editors

Nina Spada
Ontario Institute for Studies in Education
University of Toronto

Laura Gurzynski-Weiss
Indiana University Bloomington

Volume 60

The COLT Observation Scheme.
Digital versions and updated research applications. 2nd revised edition
by Nina Spada

The COLT Observation Scheme

Digital versions and updated research applications
2nd revised edition

Nina Spada
University of Toronto

John Benjamins Publishing Company
Amsterdam / Philadelphia

TM The paper used in this publication meets the minimum requirements of the American National Standard for Information Sciences – Permanence of Paper for Printed Library Materials, ANSI Z39.48-1984.

DOI 10.1075/lllt.60

Cataloging-in-Publication Data available from Library of Congress:
LCCN 2024016459 (PRINT) / 2024016460 (E-BOOK)

ISBN 978 90 272 1482 9 (HB)
ISBN 978 90 272 1481 2 (PB)
ISBN 978 90 272 4690 5 (E-BOOK)

John Benjamins Publishing Company · https://benjamins.com

Table of contents

Acknowledgements

In this second revised edition, much of the material from the original COLT book is included. I remain grateful to many people who contributed to the preparation of the first edition and who were acknowledged in the book at that time. I would like to reiterate my thanks to those who played particularly important roles, and this includes Victoria Murphy, Patsy Lightbown, Roy Lyster and Leila Ranta. My deepest thanks go to Maria Fröhlich, my co-author of the first edition.

CHAPTER 1

Introduction

This book describes the *Communicative Orientation of Language Teaching* (COLT) Observation Scheme – an instrument used in the observation of teaching and learning in second language (L2) classrooms. It is intended for use by anyone involved in L2 classroom observation. This includes both novice and experienced classroom researchers, graduate students working on course projects or theses, novice and experienced teachers, and teacher educators. Depending on the user's goals, the scheme may be used to describe specific aspects of instructional practices and procedures in L2 classrooms, to investigate relationships between teaching behaviours and learning outcomes, to sensitize novice teachers to different aspects of the instructional process, and to guide more experienced teachers to reflect on their teaching practice.

In 1995 I co-authored a book about the COLT scheme (Spada & Fröhlich, 1995). The book's primary purpose was to describe how the observation scheme works so that potential users could make informed decisions about whether it might be useful in their own work. Over the years, COLT has become well established as a research instrument in L2 teaching and learning and is "highly influential in L2 classroom research due to it's elaborate category system and the high-profile research it has been used in" (Dörnyeii, 2007, p.181). Based on COLT, an observation scheme was designed to measure the multiple dimensions of the Motivational Orientation of Language Teaching (MOLT) (Guilloteaux & Dornyeii, 2008). Given the wide recognition and extensive use of COLT, one might wonder why the need for a second edition of the book. The motivation (after almost 30 years!) is because new digital versions of COLT (Part A and B) have been developed. These adaptations of the original COLT scheme have resulted in more efficient ways to employ COLT in both the coding and analysis of data. The digital advancements also provide opportunities to use COLT in more expansive ways including the use of automatic speech recognition for faster transcription, and the use of artificial intelligence (A.I.) in the coding of L2 classroom observation data. When I became aware of ongoing work with these digital innovations of the COLT scheme, I was motivated to make this information available to as many current and future users as possible.

This second edition has a similar organizational structure to the original COLT book. Two of the main differences are a new chapter on Digital COLT (Part A) (Chapter 6) and an expanded final chapter that includes updated research summaries reporting on the use of COLT (manual and digital) in different L2 contexts (Chapter 7). As with the first edition, Chapter 1 describes the history and development of the COLT scheme with updated information, perspectives, and references to relevant work in the intervening years. The next 3 chapters are virtually identical to those in the first edition, which describe the main features and categories of COLT (Chapter 2) and the original/manual coding conventions for Part A (Chapter 3) and Part B (Chapter 4). Data analysis remains the focus of Chapter 5 with the addition of a new section describing a numeric coding system for COLT Part B. As with the first edition, the material is presented in a way that is as 'user friendly' as possible. Because some of the contents can be rather technical and require precision and detail in their specification, efforts have been made to provide the reader with examples, illustrations and 'hands-on' activities wherever possible.

The COLT scheme: Historical influences

COLT was developed in the early 1980s within the context of a large-scale research project investigating the nature of language proficiency and its development in L2 classrooms. This project, referred to as the Development of Bilingual Proficiency (DBP) project, was carried out at the Ontario Institute for Studies in Education (OISE) at the University of Toronto, Canada, and was organized around four general issues: (1) the nature of communicative competence, (2) the influence of social context on its development, (3) the effects of instructional variables on L2 learning, and (4) the influence of individual learner characteristics. A model of communicative competence consisting of grammatical, discourse and sociolinguistic competence was proposed, and it provided the framework for all studies within the project (Harley, Allen, Cummins, & Swain, 1990).[1]

Since a major component of the DBP research project was to investigate the effects of instructional variables on learning outcomes, a classroom observation scheme was needed to systematically describe the instructional practices and procedures in different L2 classroom contexts. Furthermore, given that one of the central research questions was whether instruction that was more (or less) communicative in its orientation contributed differently to particular aspects of L2 development, there was a need for an observation scheme that could describe as precisely as possible the characteristics of instructional input. Importantly, we wanted to identify features of instruction that were derived from theories of communicative language teaching and from relevant research in second language acquisition.

Three major themes in the L2 teaching and learning literature that influenced the design of the COLT scheme are discussed below:

- the widespread introduction and acceptance of communicative approaches to L2 teaching
- the need for more and better research on the relationship between teaching and learning
- the need to develop valid psycholinguistic categories for classroom observation schemes

---

1. Funding for the development of the COLT observation scheme and its use in the DBP project was provided by the Social Sciences and Humanities Research Council (SSHRC) of Canada.

Communicative language teaching 'fever'

In the early 1980s communicative language teaching (CLT) had reached its peak, particularly in North America and the United Kingdom. Professional meetings were replete with presentations on designing curricula based on communicative objectives, developing communicative activities, and evaluating communicative programs. Just about every applied linguistics book and ESL text published at the time was almost guaranteed to have the word 'communicative' in its title. There was no doubt that the theory of communicative competence, originally proposed by Hymes (1970), had had an enormous impact on the field of L2 teaching and learning. His theory was based on the claim that knowing a language includes much more than a knowledge of the rules of grammar (i.e., linguistic competence). Hymes drew attention to the importance of a knowledge of the rules of language use (i.e., communicative competence) and this view was enthusiastically adopted and led to several developments of both a theoretical and applied nature. Models of communicative competence were proposed (e.g., Canale & Swain, 1980) and efforts were made to empirically validate them (Allen, Bialystok, Cummins, & Mougeon, 1982; Bachman & Palmer 1981). Communicative language teaching curricula (Breen & Candlin, 1980; Munby, 1978; Yalden, 1983) and notional functional syllabuses (Wilkins 1976) were developed, and these provided a framework for the specification of the communicative needs of L2 learners. There was also considerable work in the creation of classroom techniques and activities to encourage more realistic use of language in the classroom (e.g., Littlewood, 1981) and proposals were made for an overall methodology of communicative language teaching (Brumfit, 1984; Widdowson, 1978).

Although CLT was widely accepted and implemented, there were early indications that it did not mean the same thing to everyone. There were also different interpretations of how CLT could be applied in L2 classrooms (Johnson, 1982). Several models and frameworks were proposed some of which did not include attention to language form while others included attention to both form and meaning. For example, Allen (1983) made a distinction between 'experiential'(meaning-based), 'structural analytic' (form-based) and 'functional analytic' (form-and meaning-based) instruction and suggested how one might incorporate these components to different degrees, depending on the learners' needs and program expectations. Similarly, Stern (1983) introduced an analytic and experiential dimension which characterizes CLT as moving along a continuum from form-based to meaning-based instruction. Others, however, viewed CLT only as message-oriented practice and argued strongly against the inclusion of attention to language forms within a communicative approach (e.g., Newmark & Riebel, 1968; Prabhu, 1979). Although there was considerable debate about some aspects of CLT, virtually everyone agreed that previous approaches to L2 instruction, which focused exclusively on the isolated presentation and practice of grammatical rules and/or memorization and rote-learning, immediate and frequent error correction, and accuracy, had not been successful. The prevailing view was that instruction emphasizing opportunities for learners to communicate ideas, to express a greater variety of linguistic functions and intentions and to interact in more natural and spontaneous ways would lead to more successful learning. Unfortunately, there was little in the way of empirical research which had investigated these claims, and the research that had been done was quickly interpreted by many as support for exclusively meaning-based instruction even though the research provided evidence that a combination of form and meaning was more effective (e.g., Savignon, 1972).

While these developments were taking place in applied linguistics theory, research, and pedagogy, there were developments in second language acquisition (SLA) research which also provided support for the movement away from a focus on language forms to a focus on communication and meaning. Advocates for a communicative approach argued based on SLA research findings, that L2 learning was similar to L1 learning and that efforts were needed to create environments in L2 classrooms which more closely approximated the conditions of LI acquisition. For example, Krashen (1985) hypothesised that if L2 learners were exposed to 'comprehensible input' and provided with opportunities to focus on meaning and messages rather than grammatical forms and accuracy, they would be able to acquire their second language in much the same way as L1 learners (see also Krashen, 1981, 1982).

Other developments in SLA research provided further support for communicative approaches to L2 teaching. While Krashen's proposal for successful L2 learning emphasized input, other researchers claimed that interaction and output were crucial. They argued that when learners engage in conversational interaction, they are forced to 'negotiate meaning'; that is, to express their meanings and clarify their intentions so that they can arrive at a mutual understanding. It was claimed that by engaging in this process, learners would also develop the language forms which carry the meaning (e.g., Hatch, 1978; Long, 1983; Pica, 1987; Swain, 1985).

The impact of SLA research combined with applied linguistics theory and research in CLT led to recommendations for radical changes in L2 classrooms. Yet, because these changes were described in rather general terms (i.e., a shift away from discrete point grammatical presentation and accurate production to communicative interactions, comprehensible input, and a focus on fluency), it was not entirely clear how this was to be accomplished. Furthermore, given that there were also different interpretations of CLT, it was likely that there were variations in the ways in which individual teachers implemented it. Therefore, in the early 1980s it seemed useful (and timely) to develop an observation scheme which could capture differences in the communicative orientation of L2 instruction and to examine their effects on learning outcomes.

The need for process-product research

When the COLT scheme was initially developed, the field of L2 teaching and learning was in a period of primarily process-oriented research; that is, research which focuses on the description of instructional practices and procedures in L2 classrooms. A call for more process-oriented research had been made approximately a decade earlier by several researchers (e.g., Allwright, 1972; Jarvis, 1968; Politzer, 1970) who had been discouraged by the results of the 'global method comparison studies' in the 1960s and 1970s which were heavily product-oriented (i.e., focused on learning outcomes as measured by language tests). These studies, which attempted to determine for example, whether audiolingual instruction was more effective than grammar-translation, led to inconclusive results (Chastain, 1969; Scherer & Wertheimer, 1964; Smith, 1969). They were due in part to the fact that little effort had been made to systematically observe the classrooms to describe differences in instruction. This was a serious drawback since individual teachers can vary greatly in the ways in which they implement a particular method even though they believe they are teaching according to the same one. Furthermore, even though teaching methods have different labels, they overlap in several ways (Krashen & Seliger, 1975; Long, 1991), making it difficult to identify the truly important or effective characteristics of a method. This lack of information about the instructional practices inside L2 classrooms led Long (1980) to refer to the L2 classroom as a 'black box' and to liken it to the unobservable mechanisms of the human brain which are believed to be responsible for first language (L1) acquisition.

Partly in reaction to the discouraging results of the 'global method comparison' studies, a proliferation of L2 classroom observation schemes began to appear and considerable efforts were made to systematically observe what goes on inside the L2 classroom. Approximately twenty-five classroom observation schemes were developed in the late 1970s and early 1980s and they differed along several dimensions (e.g., recording procedures, type, and complexity of categories, focus and range of behaviours). While some focused primarily on descriptions of pedagogic events, others focused on linguistic behaviours and several included both (see Chaudron, 1988; Ellis, 2012; Long, 1980; Spada, 2019, for reviews of L2 observation schemes). In addition to the increased use of observation instruments in L2 classroom research, other approaches to describing events in L2 classrooms were undertaken. These included detailed discourse analyses of teacher and learner speech (Allwright, 1988; Coulthard, 1977) as well as ethnographic approaches to classroom observation (van Lier, 1988, 1997; Watson-Gegeo, 1997).

The investigations of classroom processes led to a much better understanding of the complexity and variety of instructional events in L2 classroom settings. We learned much more about how classrooms differ in terms of the variety of activities and modalities used, the proportion of teacher talk to student talk, the way in which conversations are structured between teachers and learners, the ways in which teachers respond to errors, the kind of language that learners produce in pair and group work, the kinds of questions teachers and students ask one another, the types of verbal interactions which take place within different activities/tasks, and much more. However, in the early 1980s, there was some concern that the pendulum had swung too far (Long, 1980). That is, while research on language teaching in the 1960s had been almost exclusively product-oriented with virtually no attention to instructional processes, classroom research in the 1970s and early 1980s focused almost exclusively on instructional processes with little attention to learning outcomes. Clearly, there was a need for research which investigated both process and product and, more importantly, relationships between the two. COLT was developed to contribute to this endeavour.

Our goal was to design an observation scheme that could be used to describe classroom processes and to examine them in relation to learning outcomes. In doing so, we hoped to discover what instructional feature or more probably, clusters of features, contributed to more successful learning. Although there were several observation instruments available when the COLT scheme was developed, none of them was rooted in a theory of CLT and SLA research.[2] Given that our research questions were specifically directed to the potential effects of CLT on L2 learning, we needed an observation scheme that could capture features of communication that had been described in the existing theoretical and pedagogical literature on CLT. We were also motivated to develop an instrument that included variables hypothesized to be important predictors of success in second language acquisition.

The need for psycholinguistic validity in observation categories

In a seminal paper on L2 classroom observation research in 1980, Mike Long raised several concerns about the nature of the work. One of the problems he addressed was the tendency for developers of observation schemes to include categories that were without psycholinguistic validity. That is, many of the categories did not measure those features of instruction which 'current theory would suggest [are] relevant to classroom language acquisition' (Long 1980, p. 20). Part of the reason for this shortcoming was because several of the L2 observation instruments had been designed primarily for teacher training purposes (e.g., Fanselow, 1977; Moskowitz, 1970) and, as a result, their implementation had greater pedagogic than psycholinguistic value. But as Long pointed out, 'observational instruments are, in fact, no more (or less) than theoretical claims about second language learning and teaching yet little has been done to test those hypotheses' (Long 1980, p. 12).

The development of COLT was an attempt to respond to this concern. We wanted to identify those features of instruction which communicative theorists and L2 researchers consistently referred to as contributors to successful learning. We also wanted to identify fea-

---

2. It is not the intention to compare the COLT scheme with other L2 observation instruments. For an overview, discussion, and comparison of several L2 observation schemes, (see Allwright, 1988; Chaudron, 1988; Ellis, 2012; Long, 1980; & Mitchell, 1985).

tures of communication and interaction which were believed to be important contributors to successful language learning in the L1 and L2 research literature. Importantly, we wanted to define our instructional categories in such a way that these hypotheses could be tested in process-product research. In 1984 we published a paper describing the rationale, the overall organizational framework, and the specification of the COLT scheme (Allen, Fröhlich, & Spada, 1984). A year later we tested COLT in different L2 programs to determine whether the categories could capture the information intended, and whether the overall scheme permitted distinctions between more and less communicatively oriented instruction (Fröhlich, Spada, & Allen, 1985).

In the Fröhlich, Spada, & Allen study, COLT was used to describe the type of instruction provided in three French second language (FSL) programs and one ESL program for school-aged children. The FSL programs included core French classes in which students received 20–40 minutes a day of FSL instruction; extended French in which students received instruction in one school subject through the medium of French in addition to their regular core French classes; and French immersion classes in which students received most (or all) of their subject-matter instruction through the medium of French. The ESL classes in this study were ones in which students received all-day English language instruction with varying amounts of subject-matter instruction in English. Prior to observing the classes, we had predicted that some of them would be more communicatively oriented than others. These predictions were based on previous observations in these programs, on an examination of textbooks and other teaching materials and on discussions with teachers, consultants, and school board officials.

According to the COLT categories, classes described as more communicatively oriented were those in which teachers spent more time focusing on meaning (i.e., topics and themes rather than language forms) and group work interaction. More communicatively oriented classes were also those in which teachers (and students) asked genuine questions and where students were given opportunities to use language in creative and unrestricted ways and participated in the negotiation of topics and tasks. Less communicatively oriented classes, on the other hand, were those in which the instruction focused primarily on language forms and error correction and where teachers tended to ask questions to which they already knew the answers and placed restrictions on the variety of language forms that learners could produce. Early research to examine the validity of the COLT features and categories indicated that they succeeded in distinguishing between the types of instruction provided in more and less communicatively oriented L2 classrooms (Fröhlich, Spada, & Allen, 1985).

Using COLT over the years

Since our initial work in the development and use of the COLT scheme, much has changed in L2 theory, research, and practice. In the early 80s, the prevailing view, particularly in North America, was that L2 classrooms in which the focus was on meaning-based instruction, group work and creative language-use opportunities were likely to be more effective for L2 learning than teacher-centred classrooms with a focus on language forms, correction, and restricted language use. Since then, a growing body of research has investigated the effects of communicative approaches on L2 learning. This includes research in communicative L2 as subject-matter classrooms where the focus is on topics and themes relevant to the learners' age and interests. It also includes research in content-based language teaching (CBLT), that is, in classrooms where language learning occurs via instruction in the regular school curriculum (i.e., geography, history). The findings have indicated that while an exclusive focus on meaning can lead to higher levels of fluency and communicative abilities in the L2, it does not lead to high levels of linguistic accuracy or more developed language knowledge (Lightbown & Spada, 1993, 2015). One early process-product study using COLT to investigate the effects of CLT on adult L2 proficiency provided evidence that a combination of form and meaning was more effective than an exclusive focus on either meaning or form (Spada, 1987). Other research using COLT in French language programs with adolescent learners revealed minimal differences between more and less communicatively oriented classes and learning outcomes (Allen & Carroll, 1987, 1988; McKay, 1994). Summaries of these studies are presented in Chapter 7.

Over the past 3 decades, extensive research has been conducted to investigate the effects of different types of instruction on L2 learning. Particular attention has been devoted to the contributions of implicit (i.e., meaning focused) and explicit (i.e., form focused) instruction on L2 development. This domain of research is referred to as instructed SLA and the overall findings based on hundreds of studies can be found in several synthetic reviews and meta-analyses. The results indicate that both types of instruction are beneficial and that stronger effects are evident for explicit instruction (Ellis, 2001; Goo et al., 2015; Norris & Ortega, 2000; Spada, 1997, 2011; Spada & Tomita, 2010). However, these findings are likely related to two facts: (1) in most studies learners' progress was measured using controlled written grammar tests and (2) there is an inherent bias in the research literature with a larger number of studies investigating explicit as opposed to implicit instruction (Doughty, 2003). Fortunately, in recent years there has been an increase in research to investigate the effects of implicit instruction on L2 learning that include tests to measure learners' use of language in more natural, unrestricted, and communicative ways. Preliminary findings indicate greater benefits for implicit compared with explicit instruction over the long term (Kang, Sok, & Han, 2018).

It is important to note that little of this research has included the use of COLT to describe instructional practices. This is because most of the studies have been carried out in laboratory or quasi-laboratory contexts to investigate relationships between instructional input and learning outcomes that are more narrowly focused. Even instructed SLA research that has been conducted in L2 classrooms tends to concentrate on a smaller range of instructional variables. This movement away from broad-based comprehensive observation schemes has been referred to as a shift from macroscopic to microscopic description (Spada & Lyster, 1987), from generic to limited (McKay, 2006), and from global to single issue research (Mitchell, 1985). Such an approach has enabled researchers to concentrate on more detailed studies of specific instructional features (e.g., corrective feedback, teachers' questions) and examine their impact on different aspects of L2 development.

This does not mean that broad-based observation schemes like COLT no longer serve a useful purpose in L2 classroom research. On the contrary, as I have written elsewhere, "the strength of comprehensive instruments is precisely in their capacity to provide the big picture" (Spada, 2019, p. 198). A good example of how the use of COLT helped to explain the perplexing findings of a study focused on a single instructional feature (i.e., corrective feedback) is included in Chapter 7 (see Lyster & Mori, 2006). Furthermore, the use of the new digital and online versions of COLT facilitates the use of this multi-category, comprehensive scheme making macro-analysis more feasible as a complement to micro-level observation research.

One of the concerns that has been raised about COLT is the labor intensive and time-consuming nature of using some aspects of the scheme. This is particularly the case with Part B, which involves detailed coding of the linguistic interactions between teachers and students. Thus, the digital versions of COLT are a welcome development and advancement for the scheme. As readers will discover in subsequent chapters, COLT coding and analysis are greatly facilitated when using the digital versions of Part A and B. Ongoing work to explore ways of transcribing classroom speech using the latest speech-to-text technology and the use of A.I. to enable Automatic COLT coding, are ambitious and promising developments. This work is described in Chapters 6 and 7.

Since the publication of the first edition of the COLT book, the observation scheme has been increasingly used in teacher education research. As noted earlier, this was the principal reason for the development of the early classroom observation schemes, which were intended to evaluate L2 teaching practices (e.g., FLINT by Moskowitz, 1970). In contrast, to evaluation, COLT has been recently adopted as an instrument for reflective practice in pre-service and in-service education programs. In fact, all the research that has employed the new digital versions of COLT has taken place within teacher education research (see Chapter 7). One research summary describes how teachers access an online portal where they upload videos of their classes and examine their instruction using COLT and discuss their observations with colleagues. Using COLT in this way is considered a powerful self-reflection tool because it gives more control of professional development to the teachers themselves (Sano et al., 2017).

A few caveats

It is important to emphasize that the COLT scheme offers one way of looking at instructional practices and procedures in L2 classrooms. Depending on the user's purpose and needs, it may be more appropriately used in some contexts than in others. For example, if one is interested in undertaking a detailed discourse analysis of the conversational interactions between teachers and students, another method of coding and analyzing classroom data would be preferred. Similarly, if one is interested in carrying out ethnographic research in classrooms, the COLT scheme (or any other scheme with a set of predetermined categories) would not be suitable given the differences in theoretical and methodological perspectives between ethnographic and interaction approaches to classroom observation. Since it is not our intention to describe the use of other classroom observation schemes here, we refer the reader to the references at the end of the book for reviews and critiques of the use of L2 classroom observation instruments in general, and of discussions specifically related to the COLT scheme.

It is also important to note that depending on the user's purpose, there is scope for adaptation in the categories of the COLT scheme. For example, the user may find that a category (or set of categories) is not relevant to their research and in this case, the category can be discarded or adapted. Similarly, if the scheme fails to capture a feature considered to be important to a particular study, it can be added. As long as consistency in the definition and coding of the categories is maintained, there is considerable scope in the revisions one can make to the scheme. It must be remembered that observation schemes are simply tools for research and should serve rather than direct it.

A comment concerning the degree of subjectivity that enters any approach to classroom observation is warranted. As you will see in the definitions and coding conventions chapters which follow, some of the categories are relatively easy to code because the behaviours they capture are explicit and overt (e.g., student repeats utterance). Other categories, however, are more difficult to code because they capture more implicit, covert behaviour (e.g., student requests clarification) and thus lead to more judgment and inference on the part of the observer. This is an inevitable problem in classroom observation. One method of reducing the element of subjectivity is to ensure that at least two observers code the same classroom events independently and to verify that they make the same coding decisions for classroom behaviours. This is referred to as inter-rater reliability.

Finally, an important consideration in the development and use of observation schemes is the establishment of the validity of the categories. This process requires evidence to demonstrate that the categories are measuring the intended theoretical constructs that they represent. With COLT, reliability was determined by identifying a relationship between "programmatically defined degrees of communicative language teaching with categories on the scheme designed to measure the communicative orientation of L2 programs" (Spada, 2019, p. 191). To increase the validity of the scheme, the developers of COLT also calculated a 'global score' based on the frequencies of five selected categories that determine the degree of communicative orientation across the programs (see Chapter 5). Efforts such as these are useful but not without their limitations (Chaudron, 1991). These issues will be evident as you become more familiar with the COLT categories, coding conventions, and adaptations that have been made to the scheme with digital COLT.

In Chapter 2, the structure and organization of COLT is described. This includes a detailed description of the main features and categories in Part A and Part B along with a rationale for their inclusion in the scheme.

Category descriptions and rationale

The COLT observation scheme is divided into two parts: Part A describes classroom events at the level of episode and activity; Part B analyzes the communicative features of verbal exchanges between teachers and students and/or students and students as they occur within each episode or activity.

This chapter provides definitions and descriptions for each of the main features and categories in Part A and Part B of the COLT scheme. Some examples are provided in this chapter, and many more examples and illustrations are presented in Chapters 3 and 4. Also included in this chapter is a brief description of the rationale and theoretical motivation for the main features of the observation scheme. More information and discussion of the theoretical framework of COLT can be found in Allen, Fröhlich, & Spada (1984).

A few changes have been made to the definitions of some of the categories since the original conceptualization of the COLT scheme. There are also a few categories which have been deleted or added, as well as a few minor changes in the organization. These changes are acknowledged and explained either in the text or in the accompanying footnotes.

Part A: Main features and categories

As shown in Figure 2.1, the Part A categories describe classroom events at the level of activity and episode. Coding for all categories on Part A of the scheme is done in 'real time'; that is, while the observers are present in the classroom (or viewing a video) as the lesson unfolds. The following seven main features are differentiated in Part A:

1. *Time*
2. *Activities and Episodes*
3. *Participant Organization*
4. *Content*
5. *Content Control*
6. *Student Modality*
7. *Materials*

A definition and rationale for each Part A feature is provided below. They are presented in the order in which they appear on the scheme, starting with column 1 at the extreme left-hand side.

School: _____
Teacher: _____

Subject: _____

Date of Visit: _____
Coder: _____

COLT Part A
Communicative Orientation of Language Teaching Observation Scheme
© Spada & Fröhlich 1995

TIME	ACTIVITIES & EPISODES	PARTICIPANT ORGANIZATION								CONTENT									CONTENT CONTROL			STUDENT MODALITY					MATERIALS								
		Class			Group		Individual		Manag.		Language				Other topics					Type									Source			
																				Text											
		T↔S/C	S↔S/C	Choral	Same task	Different tasks	Same task	Different tasks	Procedure	Discipline	Form	Function	Discourse	Sociolinguistic	Narrow	Broad	Teacher/Text	Teacher/Text/Stud.	Student	Listening	Speaking	Reading	Writing	Other	Minimal	Extended	Audio	Visual	L2-NNS	L2-NS	L2-NSA	Student-made
		3	4	5	6	7	8	9	10	11	12	13	14	15	16	17	18	19	20	21	22	23	24	25	26	27	27	29	30	31	32	33
	1																															
	2																															

Figure 2.1 COLT Part A

Column

1   *Time*
The starting time of each episode/activity is recorded.

Rationale
Each activity and episode are timed so that a calculation of the percentage of time spent on the separate (and combined) COLT features can be determined.

2   *Activities and Episodes*
These are separate units which constitute the instructional segments of a lesson. *Activities* are larger units, and they can encompass *episodes*. The distinction between them is marked by changes in the categories of the main features of COLT. Separate activities would include such things as a drill, a translation task, a discussion, or a game. Three episodes of one activity labelled a dialogue would be: teacher introduces dialogue, teacher reads dialogue aloud, individual students read parts of dialogue aloud.

Rationale
All Part A features are coded within the context of activities and/or episodes; they are the basic units of analysis for Part A of the scheme.

Participant Organization
Participant organization refers to the way in which the teacher and students are organized. Three basic patterns of organization are differentiated in this category: Class, Group and Individual.

Class

3   *Teacher to student or class* (T↔S/C)
One central activity led by the teacher; the teacher interacts with the whole class and/or with individual students within the central activity.

4   *Student to student, or student to class* (S↔S/C)
One central activity led by a student or students (e.g., a group of students acts out a skit and the rest of the class is the audience).

5   *Choral work*
The whole class, or individual groups, participate in choral work (e.g., repeating a model provided by the textbook or teacher).

Group

6   *Same task*
Groups/pairs of students all work on the same task.

7   *Different tasks*
Groups/pairs of students work on different tasks.

Individual[3]

8   *Same task*

Students work on their own, but on the same task.

9   *Different tasks*

Students work on their own, but on different tasks.

Rationale

In the literature on communicative language teaching, group work is considered essential in the development of communicative competence. In group work, learners can be encouraged to 'negotiate meaning', to use a greater variety of linguistic forms and functions and to develop overall fluency skills. This contrasts with teacher-centred instruction which may restrict learners in their use of language and their opportunities to engage in more than a few words. In teacher-centred classes, learners tend to spend more time responding to the teacher's questions and rarely initiate discourse. Group work is more likely to focus on the expression and negotiation of meaning and less likely to focus on the accuracy of utterances. Thus, classes which engage learners in more group work are often described as being more communicatively oriented. For these reasons the feature *Participant organization* was developed to describe distinctions between teacher-centred and group-work interactions in L2 classrooms.

Content

Content refers to the subject matter/theme of activities; that is, what the teacher and students are talking, reading, or writing about, or what they are listening to. Three major content areas have been differentiated: 'Management', 'Language', and 'Other topics'.

Management

10   *Procedure*

Procedural directives (e.g., "Open your books to Chapter 3 and do the first exercise")

11   *Discipline*

Disciplinary statements, directives (e.g., "I am getting more and more frustrated with the noise level in this class.")

Language

12   *Form*

Reference to grammar; vocabulary, pronunciation etc.

13   *Function*

Reference to functions/communicative acts (e.g., requesting, apologizing, and explaining).

14   *Discourse*

Reference to the way in which sentences (spoken or written) combine into cohesive and coherent sequences such as describing a process (e.g., how to plant a herb garden).

---

3. In Allen, Fröhlich, & Spada (1984), columns 8 and 9 referred to a combination of group and individual work. A separate column for combinations is not necessary, however, since two columns can be checked off simultaneously to indicate combinations.

15   *Sociolinguistics*
Reference to forms or styles (spoken or written) appropriate to specific contexts (e.g., the difference in the use of 'tu/vous' in informal/formal contexts).

Other Topics[4]
A binary system is used to represent the potentially vast number of topics that can arise in classroom discourse. These topics are categorized as either narrow or broad depending on their range of reference.

16   *Narrow*
Range of reference: topics which refer to the classroom and the students' immediate environment and experiences (e.g., personal information, routine school, family, and community topics).

17   *Broad*
Range of reference: topics going well beyond the classroom and immediate environment (e.g., international events, subject-matter instruction, and imaginary/hypothetical events).[5]

<u>Rationale</u>
One of the crucial issues in second language learning and teaching is whether the primary focus of instruction should be on meaning or form. Traditionally second languages were taught with a strong emphasis on grammar and correction. This, however, was not proven to be successful in terms of the development of either linguistic or communicative competence. In the 1970s, some theorists and researchers began to argue that L2 instruction should be exclusively meaning-oriented because this is the way that children successfully learn their first language. This resulted in the considerable growth of content based, subject matter-based and meaning-oriented instruction – all of which were described as communicative. More recently, researchers and theorists have argued that a combination of meaning and form is more useful since many aspects of L2 learning in classroom settings differ from L1 acquisition. This category was developed to measure the extent to which a focus on meaning and/or form may contribute to differences in L2 development.

---

4. In Allen, Fröhlich, & Spada (1984) a tripartite system was used to describe 'Other topics' (i.e., Narrow, Limited and Broad). We have changed this to a binary distinction because our experience has revealed a tendency for observers to categorize most topics as Limited thus failing to distinguish between them. Although there are still some problems in categorizing topics as Narrow or Broad, we have had more success with this binary system since the original conception and use of the scheme. This is an example of a high inference category where establishing inter-rater reliability in the coding is very important.

5. If COLT is used in subject-matter classes (e.g., French immersion), the observer may want to make further distinctions regarding the range of reference within the subject matter. This scheme has not been developed to respond to characteristics of content-based/subject-matter instruction but see Chapter 3 for further discussion of this issue.

18–20   *Content Control*

Content control refers to who selects the topic (or task) that is the focus of instruction – the teacher, the students, the textbook, or a combination of them.

18   *Teacher/Text[6]*

The topic (or task) is determined by the teacher and/or the text.

19   *Teacher/Text/Student*

The topic (or task) is jointly decided by teacher; students, and/or the text.

20   *Student*

The topic (or task) is determined by the student/s.

Rationale

In the communicative language teaching literature, it has been argued that if students are encouraged to become more involved in their learning as co-participants, and are encouraged to negotiate methods, tasks, materials, and the content of instruction, this will contribute more positively to their learning. This feature was developed to describe the extent to which classrooms may vary along this dimension.

21–25   **Student modality**

This section identifies the various skills involved in a classroom activity. The focus is on the students, and the purpose is to indicate whether they are listening, speaking, reading, or writing, or whether these skills occur in combination.

21   *Listening*

22   *Speaking*

23   *Reading*

24   *Writing*

25   *Other*

This category is included to cover such activities as drawing, acting, or arranging classroom displays.

Rationale

Traditionally, L2 instruction isolated the teaching of not only grammatical features but skill areas as well. This meant that learners were often engaged in listening practice activities separately from speaking activities etc. One of the arguments made in the communicative language teaching literature is that students should be encouraged to integrate their skills practice to reflect a more authentic use of language. This feature was developed to determine whether a differential focus on the skill areas contributed differently to learners' use of these skills.

---

6. Allen, Fröhlich, and Spada (1984) referred to teacher only, however, since the topic can also be determined by the text used, text has been added.

26–33   *Materials*
This feature describes classroom materials in terms of Text type and Source of materials.

Type of material

26   *Minimal text*
Written text: captions, isolated sentences, word lists etc.

27   *Extended text*
Written text: stories, dialogues, connected sentences, paragraphs etc.

28   *Audio*
Recorded material for listening.

29   *Visual*
Pictures, cartoons etc.
Note: Films, videos etc., would be double coded as audio and visual.

Source of material[7]

30   *L2-NNS (L2-Non-native speaker)*
Material which is specifically designed for second language teaching, such as course books, teacher-prepared exercises, material etc.

31   *L2-NS (L2-Native speaker)*
Materials originally intended for native speakers of the target language (e.g., newspapers, brochures, advertisements, etc.,).

32   *L2-NSA (L2-Native speaker-adapted)*
Native speaker materials which have been adapted for L2 purposes (e.g., linguistically simplified, or annotated stories and other texts).

33   *Student-made*
Materials (stories, reports, puppet shows, etc.) created by the student/s.

Rationale
On the one hand, certain advocates of communicative language teaching argue that authentic materials should be used wherever possible so that learners will be better prepared to deal with 'real' language outside the classroom setting. On the other hand, research in second language acquisition has shown that simplified and/or adjusted input increases the learners' ability to comprehend. This category was developed to describe the different types of materials used in L2 classrooms with the purpose of investigating in what ways this might affect learning outcomes.

---

7. The categories were changed from Pedagogic, Semi-pedagogic, Non-pedagogic (Allen, Fröhlich, & Spada, 1984) to L2-NNS, L2-NS, L2-NSA and student-made to more closely indicate the source of the materials used. Another category in the original COLT scheme, Use of materials, is not included here nor its subcategories (i.e., high control, semi-control, mini control). They were deleted after the pilot phase as they led to problems with inter-rater reliability.

Part B: Main features and categories

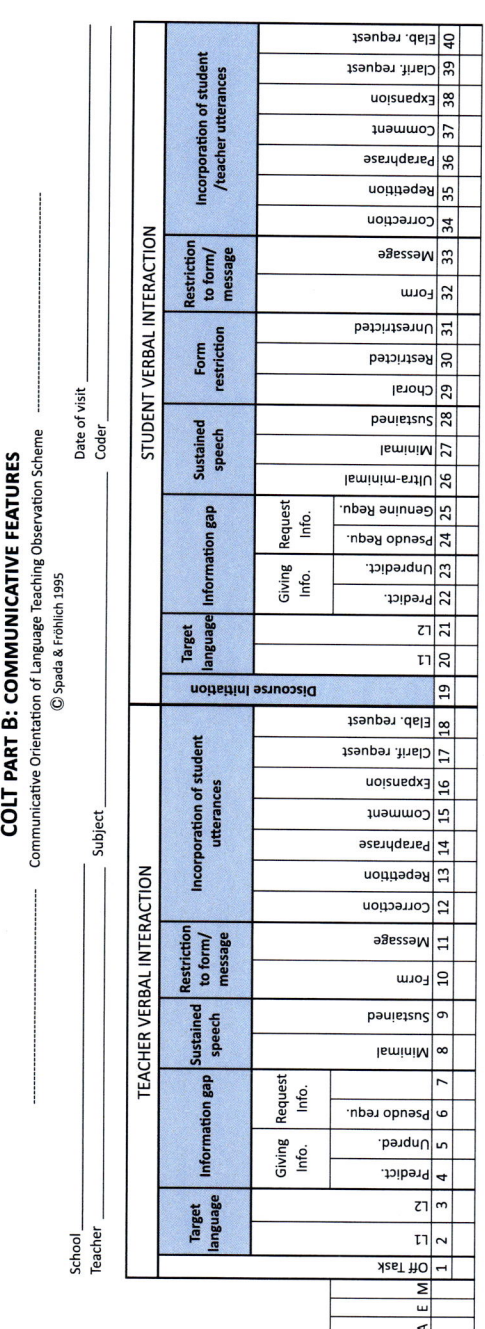

Figure 2.2 COLT (Part B)

Part B of COLT illustrated in Figure 2.2 describes the communicative features of verbal exchanges between teachers and students and/or students and students as they occur within each activity or episode. Because this level of analysis is more detailed than Part A, the coding for Part B is done after the observation, from transcripts made from audio or video recordings.

A definition and rationale for each of the COLT Part B features is provided below. As with Part A, these features are presented in the order in which they appear on the scheme. The following seven major communicative features are differentiated in Part B:

1. *Target Language*
2. *Information Gap*
3. *Sustained Speech*
4. *Reaction to Form or Message*
5. *Incorporation of Student/Teacher Utterances*
6. *Discourse Initiation*
7. *Form Restriction*

In Part B of COLT, the number of communicative features and their categories varies slightly for teacher and student verbal interaction. Columns 2 to 18, on the left-hand side of the grid, refer to Teacher Verbal Interaction and columns 19 to 40, on the right-hand side of the grid, to Student Verbal Interaction. At the extreme left-hand side of the grid are three columns labelled A for *Activity*, E for *Episode* and M for *Minute*. The use of these categories is described in Chapter 4.

1   ***Off Task***
This additional category, which is not a communicative feature, is reserved for verbal interaction unrelated to the regular curricular activities (e.g., teacher announces a parent meeting).

2   ***Target Language***
The categories used to measure this feature are quite simply the use of L1 versus L2.

2&20   *L1*
Use of the native language

3&21   *L2*
Use of the second/target language

Rationale
This category is based on the obvious assumption that for L2 development to occur, the target language must be used. It also permits an investigation of whether, in classrooms where the students share the L1, more communicative interactions tend to take place in the L1 rather than the L2.

Information Gap

This feature refers to the extent to which the information requested and/or exchanged is unpredictable (i.e., not known in advance). The two main categories designed to capture this feature are: 'Giving information' and 'Requesting information'.

Giving Information

4&22   *Predictable*

The information given generally follows a request, is easily anticipated, and is known to the questioner. The information given in such instances by different respondents is identical, although there may be different ways of saying it (e.g., the teacher asks about the weather and the students answer "It's nice" or "It's warm").

5&23   *Unpredictable*

The information given is not easily anticipated in that there is a wide range of information that can be provided (e.g., in response to the question "What did you do on the weekend?" a variety of unpredictable information is possible).

Requesting Information

6&24   *Pseudo requests for information*

The speaker already possesses the information requested (e.g., "Who is the author of the book that we are reading today?"). These are also referred to in the L2 literature as display questions.

7&25   *Genuine requests for information*

The information requested is not known in advance by the questioner (e.g., "Where did your parents come from?"). These are also referred to in the L2 literature as referential questions.

Rationale

Theory and research on the nature of communication have shown that in natural discourse speakers do not typically ask each other questions to which they already know the answer, nor do they provide each other with information that is easily anticipated or known in advance. Yet this happens a great deal in L2 classrooms. Teachers often ask students questions that they (and other students) know the answer to and, as a result, students may not be motivated to engage in communication. Proponents of communicative language teaching advocate classroom interactions and activities in which the answers are not known in advance. This feature was developed to measure the extent to which instruction allows for the giving and receiving of unpredictable information in the learning process.

Sustained Speech

This feature is intended to measure the extent to which speakers engage in extended discourse or restrict their utterances to a minimal length of one sentence, clause, or word. The categories designed to measure this feature are Ultraminimal, Minimal, and Sustained.

Rationale
Traditionally, L2 instruction has restricted the amount of speech that learners produce, and they are rarely given the opportunity to engage in extended discourse. This is not typical of the language produced outside classrooms where speakers engage in both extended and minimal speech. Some researchers have argued that learners will benefit from opportunities to stretch their linguistic repertoire further in extended discourse. This feature was developed to characterize instruction along this dimension.

26   *Ultraminimal*
Student turns that consist of one word only or two-word speech fragments such as article plus noun, preposition plus noun etc. Ultraminimal is not used for teacher turns. This is discussed in Chapter 4.

8&27   *Minimal*
Teacher and student turns that consist of more than one or two words, long phrases, one or two main clauses or sentences. For the teacher, one-word responses or speech fragments are coded as minimal.

9&28   *Sustained*
Teacher and student turns that consist of at least three main clauses.

Reaction to Form or Message
This feature is intended to measure whether teachers and/or learners react to the form or the meaning of an utterance.

10&32   *Form*
Reaction to form; that is, to the linguistic form (e.g., grammar, vocabulary, pronunciation) of the preceding utterance/s.

11&33   *Message*
Reaction to message; that is, to the meaning/content of the preceding utterance/s.

Rationale
This feature is closely related to the Content feature in Part A. Research in L1 acquisition has shown that child-directed speech tends to focus on errors in content rather than on grammatical errors in children's language. Some advocates of communicative language teaching, particularly those who claim that first and second language acquisition are similar processes, argue that grammatical correction can interfere with the process of 'natural' development. This feature was developed to characterize the extent to which teachers and learners react to the meaning or to the form of a message.

Incorporation of Student/Teacher Utterances
This feature refers to the various ways in which teachers and students react to each others' utterances. To allow coding for a limited selection of reactions to preceding utterances, seven categories have been identified and they are outlined below.

12&34 *Correction*

Any linguistic correction of a previous utterance or indication of incorrectness (e.g., "We don't say *he go*; we say *he goes*").

13&35 *Repetition*

Full or partial repetition of previous utterance/s.

Student: I went to the movies last weekend.

Teacher: OK, to the movies. (partial repetition)

14&36 *Paraphrase*

Reformulation of previous utterance/s (including translation)

Student: I saw movie Sunday.

Teacher: Oh, you saw a movie on Sunday.

15&37 *Comment*

Positive or negative response (not correction) to previous utterance/s. Comments can either be message-related or form-related.

Message-related comment

Student: I think the rich should give money to the poor.

Teacher: That's a good idea.

Form-related comment

Teacher: Give me the past tense of 'to be'.

Student: I was.

Teacher: Very good.

16&38 *Expansion*

Extension of the content of the preceding utterance/s or the addition of information that is related to it.

Teacher: What's the capital of Canada?

Student: Ottawa.

Teacher: Right, and Ottawa is in the province of Ontario.

17&39 *Clarification request*

Requests indicating that the preceding utterance was not clearly understood, and a repetition or reformulation is required.

Student: I helped my Dad to build a ... (inaudible).

Teacher: Sorry, what did you help your Dad with?

18&40 *Elaboration request*

Requests for further information related to the subject matter of the preceding utterance/s. Included are also requests for explanations (not requests for clarification).

Student: I had a swim-meet last weekend.

Teacher: Did you do well?

Student: I did OK.

Teacher: How often do you train during the week?

Student: Five times, two hours each time.

Rationale

In the L1 acquisition literature, it has been claimed that when caretakers expand, develop, and elaborate on children's utterances this enhances their language development. Researchers in L2 language acquisition have also argued that building on the L2 learner's previous utterances can positively contribute to their development. Advocates of communicative language teaching argue for increased development of learner's utterances in classroom conversation.

19   *Discourse Initiation*

This feature measures the frequency of self-initiated turns by students. Note that this feature and the next, *Form Restriction*, refer only to student verbal interactions.

Rationale

In the classroom setting, learners rarely initiate discourse. This contrasts with natural discourse in which speakers initiate and respond in the normal course of conversational turn-taking behaviour. Restricting learners to the response mode leads to a restriction in the variety of language functions they can produce. This feature is intended to measure this type of student language use in the classroom.

Form Restriction

This feature refers to the degree of linguistic restriction imposed upon the students' utterances. Three categories have been included to examine restrictions placed on student talk: Choral work, Restricted and Unrestricted.

29   *Choral work*

The whole class repeats after a model provided by the teacher or text (audio or visual). The linguistic forms produced by the students are totally restricted.

30   *Restricted*

This category refers to the relatively restricted use of linguistic forms by individual students. That is, there is an expectation imposed by the teacher, the textbook, or the task that the students produce a particular form(s). Either all or most of the language expected to be produced is restricted.

31   *Unrestricted*

This category refers to relatively unrestricted use of linguistic forms. That is, there is no expectation by the teacher, textbook, or task for the student/s to use a particular form(s). Either all or most of the language expected to be produced is unrestricted.

Rationale

In the first language learning environment, children are constantly experimenting with language and are encouraged to do so. This is thought to aid them in the process of formulating and testing hypotheses about how the language system works, which is considered a crucial component in L1 development. In more traditional L2 classrooms, however, learners are expected to repeat, imitate, and produce language that is limited and restricted in terms of the variety of forms. Advocates of more communicative approaches to instruction argue for more creative and uncontrolled language use in the classroom. This feature is intended to measure varying degrees of restriction in terms of linguistic form so that differences along this dimension may be examined in relationship to learning outcomes.

CHAPTER 3

Part A: Coding conventions

In this chapter, the conventions for coding the Part A categories are described in the order in which they appear on the scheme beginning with the first column on the extreme left-hand side as illustrated in Figure 3.1. To demonstrate the coding conventions, typical classroom activities are described and the coding for them is provided in the figures, which feature throughout this chapter.

It is important to recall that the coding for all categories on Part A of the scheme is done in 'real time'; that is, while the observers are present in the classroom as the lesson unfolds, and/or from audio or video recordings. Audio or video recordings are necessary for later Part B coding, which is discussed in more detail in Chapter 4.

Column 1: *Time*

The starting time of each activity/episode is entered first, indicating the hour and minute as shown in Figure 3.2.

Column 2: *Activities & Episodes*

The activities and their constituent episodes are described in as much detail as possible so that the lesson can be easily reconstructed afterwards by someone who was not present during the observation. As illustrated in Figure 3.2, it may be useful to number the activities and their episodes (e.g., A1, A2, A3; E1, E2 etc.,) either during or after the observation. This makes it easier to obtain an overview of the structure of the class in terms of number and type of activities and episodes. Some teachers may maintain a quick pace of rapidly changing episodes, while others may provide time for longer activities.

Although it is difficult to precisely define *Activity*, it is relatively easy to identify.[8] The beginning or end of an activity is typically marked by a change in the overall theme or content. For example, if you look at Figure 3.2, you can see that there are four activities labelled A1, A2, A3, A4. The first activity is one in which the teacher asks students questions about the news. The second activity begins when there is a shift away from the news to the correction of grammatical errors that students produced in a previous lesson. This shift represents a change in the higher-level categories; that is, a shift from a focus on 'Other topics' to a focus on 'Language'. It is also possible for a new activity to begin if there is a major change within 'Language' and 'Other topics'. For example, the third activity is coded as separate from Activity 2 because there is a shift within 'Language' from correcting students' errors in a previous lesson to focusing on a new grammatical form (i.e., the use of conditional in hypothetical 'if' clauses).

---

8. Some researchers have expressed concern about the absence of a clearly defined 'unit of analysis' for activity and efforts have been made to provide a typology of activity types to more systematically characterize these teaching units (See Valcárcel, Chaudron, Verdú & Roca, Chapter 7).

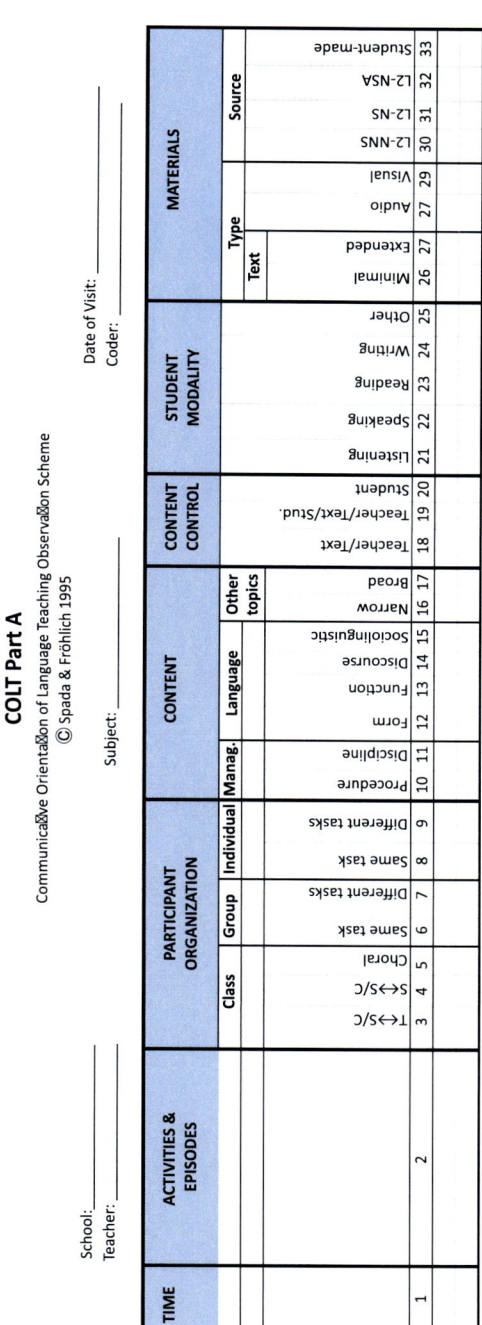

Figure 3.1 COLT (Part A)

Episodes are also relatively easy to identify. Looking at Figure 3.2 again, you see that Activity 3 consists of two episodes. As indicated, the entire activity deals with the same language point, but there are shifts within the categories which create different episodes. For example, in the first episode of Activity 3, students are given a grammatical explanation and models in a text to demonstrate how conditional 'if' clauses are formed and are asked to practise some of these model sentences. A new episode begins when students are given more linguistic freedom to produce their own sentences using the structure in question without the models or the text.

We have found it useful to consider as a separate episode any teaching/learning behaviour that is approximately a minute or longer. This, of course, is a rough estimate and an arbitrary decision. If exact timing is necessary for a specific research purpose, it may need to be done from recordings of the lesson after the observation period.

	TIME	ACTIVITIES & EPISODES	PARTICIPANT ORGANIZATION						
			Class			Group		Individual	
			T↔S/C	S↔S/C	Choral	Same task	Different tasks	Same task	Different tasks
	1	2	3	4	5	6	7	8	9
A1	9:24	Conversation – asking about the news							
A2	9:31	Grammar – Error correction of sts. production from previous class							
A3, E1	9:35	Grammar Explanation of the use of conditional in 'if' clauses							
A3, E2	9:48	Students make up own sentences using 'if - probably							
A4, E1	10.08	Question/Answer practice Expressing opinions							
A4, E2	10:10	Conversation – expressing opinions – Mt. Everest climb							

Figure 3.2 Activities and episodes

Guidelines for coding all other Part A features and categories

Coding for the remaining Part A features involves placing check marks into the appropriate columns/boxes under each of the five major features: *Participant Organization, Content, Content Control, Student Modality* and *Materials*.

During a single activity or episode, one or multiple categories may be checked off. Those cases in which only one category is checked are referred to as exclusive focus. Those instances where more than one category is checked are referred to as combinations. Combinations can be further described as primary or equal in focus. A primary focus is when most of the time is spent on a particular category. An equal focus is when approximately the same amount of time and emphasis is spent on more than one category.

To help understand how these features are coded as exclusive, primary, or equal, let's look at some examples in the category 'Class' under the major category *Participant Organization*. If the instruction is organized in a completely teacher-centred manner, with the teacher at the front of the class reacting to the students as a group for the entire activity/ episode, this would be coded as T↔S/C and a check mark would be placed in that column to indicate an exclusive focus, as illustrated in Figure 3.3.

PARTICIPANT ORGANIZATION						
Class			**Group**		**Individual**	
T↔S/C	S↔S/C	Choral	Same task	Different tasks	Same task	Different tasks
3	4	5	6	7	8	9
✓						

Figure 3.3 Coding for exclusive focus

PARTICIPANT ORGANIZATION						
Class			**Group**		**Individual**	
T↔S/C	S↔S/C	Choral	Same task	Different tasks	Same task	Different tasks
3	4	5	6	7	8	9
✓		✓				

Figure 3.4 Coding for primary focus

An example of a primary focus in the same category is given in Figure 3.4. In this case, the check marks indicate that although Choral responses also occurred in this episode, they were minor compared with the predominant feature: Teacher-to-student/class interaction. To indicate a primary focus, a circle is drawn around the predominant feature.

In those instances where equal time or emphasis is placed on two or more categories, for example, Teacher-to-class/student interaction and Choral work, two check marks are used to indicate equal emphasis (Figure 3.5).

Other variations are possible, as illustrated in Figure 3.6 where the coding indicates that equal time or emphasis was placed on Teacher-to-student/class interaction, Student-to student/class interaction and Choral work. One may wonder how it would be possible to have an equal focus on the three features of *Participant organization* in one episode. Recall that episodes are characterized by any teaching/learning behaviour that is approximately a minute or longer. Thus, if in that period, equal amounts of time were spent on multiple features then all three should be coded as equal focus. It is also possible that three or more columns are checked off and two are circled. The circles always indicate the primary feature/focus.

PARTICIPANT ORGANIZATION						
Class			Group		Individual	
T↔S/C	S↔S/C	Choral	Same task	Different tasks	Same task	Different tasks
3	4	5	6	7	8	9
√		√				

Figure 3.5 Coding for equal focus (two categories)

PARTICIPANT ORGANIZATION						
Class			Group		Individual	
T↔S/C	S↔S/C	Choral	Same task	Different tasks	Same task	Different tasks
3	4	5	6	7	8	9
√	√	√				

Figure 3.6 Coding for equal focus (three categories)

Columns 3–9: *Participant organization*

Class: T↔ S/C (3)
S ↔ S/C (4)
Choral (5)
Group: Same task (6)
Different tasks (7)
Individual: Same task (8)
Different tasks (9)

The categories for *Participant Organization* are listed above, together with the number of the appropriate column in brackets. Examples for coding the category 'Class' have already been given. To illustrate this further, Figure 3.7 shows what the coding would be for 'Class' in the activities and episodes depicted in Figure 3.2. Figure 3.8 illustrates the coding conventions for 'Group' and 'Individual'.

Class

Figure 3.7 represents the coding from an observation in an adult ESL class. Almost all *Activities/Episodes* involved Teacher-to-student/class interaction. In the last episode in activity 4, a conversation about a climbing expedition of Mt Everest, some Student-to-student/class interaction was involved; however, the primary focus was on Teacher-to-student/class interaction. In Figure 3.8 a greater variety of *Participant organizatio*n categories have been coded over a thirty-minute lesson in a French second language classroom.

	TIME	ACTIVITIES & EPISODES	PARTICIPANT ORGANIZATION						
			Class			Group		Individual	
			T↔S/C	S↔S/C	Choral	Same task	Different tasks	Same task	Different tasks
	1	2	3	4	5	6	7	8	9
A1	9:24	Conversation – asking about the news	√						
A2	9:31	Grammar – Error correction of sts. production from previous class	√						
A3, E1	9:35	Grammar Explanationof the use of conditional in 'if' clauses	√						
A3, E2	9:48	Students make up own sentences using 'if' probably	√						
A4, E1	10.08	Question/Answer practice Expressing opinions	√						
A4, E2	10:10	Conversation – expressing opinions – Mt. Everest climb	√	√					

Figure 3.7 Participant organization (ESL)

Group work

Check mark(s) are entered in the appropriate columns following the guidelines provided earlier regarding exclusive, primary and equal focus. If desirable, the number of groups and the number of members per group can be indicated in columns 6 and 7; for example, in Figure 3.9, the number 4/5 in column 6 indicates four groups with five members in each group and 3/3–6 indicates three groups with the number of participants per group varying from three to six members.

Individual work

In Figure 3.9, the last activity is an example of how Individual work is coded. The check marks indicate that while most of the students worked alone on the same task, a few did other tasks individually.

TIME	ACTIVITIES & EPISODES	PARTICIPANT ORGANIZATION						
		Class			Group		Individual	
		T↔S/C	S↔S/C	Choral	Same task	Different tasks	Same task	Different tasks
1	2	3	4	5	6	7	8	9
9:03	Warm-up exercise drill (Greeting, counting)	√		√				
9:07	Identifying objects in pictures (Vocabulary practice)	√						
9:09	Dialogue Repetition	√	√	√				
9:10	Pronunciation drill	√						
9:12	Dialogue repetition	√	√	√				
9:15	Dialogue repetition in pairs						√	
9:20	Pairs take roles and read dialogue to class	√	√					
9:26	Reading aloud isolated sentences (homework correction, judging content, T/F questions	√						
9:28	Picture identification (spelling exercise)	√						
9:31	Writing (students write a short composition on 'my favorite dinner')						√	
9:38	Class ends							

Figure 3.8 Participant organization (FSL)

ACTIVITIES & EPISODES	PARTICIPANT ORGANIZATION						
	Class			Group		Individual	
	T↔S/C	S↔S/C	Choral	Same task	Different tasks	Same task	Different tasks
2	3	4	5	6	7	8	9
Students work in groups on the same communication task.				4/5			
Students work on different tasks in groups.					3/3-6		
Students complete written exercises alone at their desks.						√	√

Figure 3.9 Group and individual

Columns 10–17: *Content*

Management: Procedure (10)
                Discipline (11)
Language: Form (12)
                Function (13)
                Discourse (14)
                Sociolinguistics (15)
Other topics: Narrow (16)
                Broad (17)

The next major feature is *Content* and the categories within it, together with the appropriate column numbers, are listed above. Although each of the above categories can form the exclusive focus of an activity/episode, more often than not, they tend to co-occur. Thus, during one activity/episode, several check marks are frequently placed in the *Content* columns. It is therefore particularly important to mark the primary/predominant focus (or foci).

Management

Procedural and disciplinary remarks are coded as a separate episode only if they last for one minute or longer. For directives, such as "Open your books", a check mark can be placed under Procedure, but do not consider this as a separate episode. The same convention applies to short disciplinary statements. That is, if the teacher sprinkles the activity with remarks like "Please keep quiet" or "Stay in your seat", put a check mark but do not consider these to be a separate episode. Also remember to draw a circle around the primary focus.

Language

In many, but certainly not all second language classes, an exclusive focus on language tends to be rare. The 'Language' categories more typically co-occur with categories in 'Other topics'. Thus, within an activity, the primary focus may shift from meaning ('Other topics') to form ('Language'), or both 'Language' and 'Other topics' may receive equal emphasis.

In general, a primary focus is coded for the 'Language' categories when it is evident from the teacher's verbal (or non-verbal) behaviour that the focus is on language This is usually the result of such features as successive metalinguistic statements, emphasis on linguistic features, frequent repetition of formal aspects or repeated form corrections.

Figures 3.10 to 3.17 illustrate the kinds of activities/episodes which would be coded for the 'Language' categories. This includes an exclusive and primary focus on different features of language as well as co-occurrence with 'Other topics'.

Form

The category Form has not been elaborated or further specified in terms of the particular aspects of Form. However, it is possible to indicate which aspects of formal language features are the focus of instruction by entering different notations in the column (e.g., 'V' for vocabulary, 'P' for pronunciation/phonology, 'G' for grammar and 'Sp' for spelling) in addition to placing a check mark under *Form*.

Exclusive focus on form

Figures 3.10a–e are examples of coding for exclusive focus on Form.

a. The teacher shows large cards with numbers on them; individual students are asked to say the number in the second language (i.e. vocabulary=V).

TIME	ACTIVITIES & EPISODES	PARTICIPANT ORGANIZATION							CONTENT					
		Class			Group		Individual		Manag.		Language			
		T↔S/C	S↔S/C	Choral	Same task	Different tasks	Same task	Different tasks	Procedure	Discipline	Form	Function	Discourse	Sociolinguistics
1	2	3	4	5	6	7	8	9	10	11	12	13	14	15
1	Teacher shows cards with numbers: Ss say numbers	√									√ V			

Figure 3.10a Form (exclusive, vocabulary)

b. Students are working in small groups. One student thinks of a number from 1 to 100. The others have to guess the number by asking questions such as "Is it... is it under/over ...?" "Is it an odd/even number?" The purpose of the activity is to practise vocabulary and yes/no questions.

TIME	ACTIVITIES & EPISOD	PARTICIPANT ORGANIZATION							CONTENT					
		Class			Group		Individual		Manag.		Language			
		T↔S/C	S↔S/C	Choral	Same task	Different tasks	Same task	Different tasks	Procedure	Discipline	Form	Function	Discourse	Sociolinguistics
1	2	3	4	5	6	7	8	9	10	11	12	13	14	15
1	Students guess numbers (is it over/under; odd/even						√				√ V G			

Figure 3.10b Form (exclusive, vocabulary and grammar)

c. Students are doing individual seat work. They are given an exercise in which they are asked to fill in the appropriate verb ending and preposition (e.g., 'tu joues au hockey; nous jouons du piano').

TIME	ACTIVITIES & EPISODE	PARTICIPANT ORGANIZATION							CONTENT					
		Class			Group		Individual		Manag.		Language			
		T↔S/C	S↔S/C	Choral	Same task	Different tasks	Same task	Different tasks	Procedure	Discipline	Form	Function	Discourse	Sociolinguistics
1	2	3	4	5	6	7	8	9	10	11	12	13	14	15
	Exerc. Jouerà/de						√				√ G			

Figure 3.10c Form (exclusive, grammar)

d. Students are working in pairs on an exercise on homonyms. They have to fill in the correct word: 'son/sont, ses/ces' (French).

TIME	ACTIVITIES & EPISODES	PARTICIPANT ORGANIZATION							CONTENT					
		Class			Group		Individual		Manag.		Language			
		T↔S/C	S↔S/C	Choral	Same task	Different tasks	Same task	Different tasks	Procedure	Discipline	Form	Function	Discourse	Sociolinguistics
1	2	3	4	5	6	7	8	9	10	11	12	13	14	15
	Exerc. Son/sont, ses/ces				√						√ Sp G			

Figure 3.10d Form (exclusive, spelling and grammar)

e. Students working in groups are asked to underline all the words in a text that have an [o] sound in French (e.g. 'beau', 'mot').

TIME	ACTIVITIES & EPISODES	PARTICIPANT ORGANIZATION							CONTENT					
		Class			Group		Individual		Manag.		Language			
		T↔S/C	S↔S/C	Choral	Same task	Different tasks	Same task	Different tasks	Procedure	Discipline	Form	Function	Discourse	Sociolinguistics
1	2	3	4	5	6	7	8	9	10	11	12	13	14	15
	Exerc. Find words with [o] in text				√						√ Sp P			

Figure 3.10e Form (exclusive, spelling and pronunciation)

Combinations of form and other topics

As already noted, in many teaching/learning situations a focus on meaning (i.e., 'Other topics') and a focus on form (i.e. 'Language') are combined. Both may receive equal emphasis or either may become the predominant feature of an episode or activity. Figures 3.11a to 3.11c illustrate this.

a.   Teacher and students are discussing international news. The teacher occasionally corrects grammar or pronunciation, or provides the missing vocabulary.

ACTIVITIES & EPISODES	PARTICIPANT ORGANIZATION								CONTENT							
	Class			Group		Individual		Manag.		Language				Other Topics	
	T↔S/C	S↔S/C	Choral	Same task	Different tasks	Same task	Different tasks	Procedure	Discipline	Form	Function	Discourse	Sociolinguistics	Narrow	Broad
2	3	4	5	6	7	8	9	10	11	12	13	14	15	16	17
Discussion on news	√									√					√

Figure 3.11a   Form and other topics (primary, broad)

b.   The students are working in small groups. They have to make a list of the items, not exceeding a certain weight, that they want to bring on a camping trip. They are encouraged to use the dictionary to develop their vocabulary (V).

ACTIVITIES & EPISODES	PARTICIPANT ORGANIZATION								CONTENT							
	Class			Group		Individual		Manag.		Language				Other Topics	
	T↔S/C	S↔S/C	Choral	Same task	Different tasks	Same task	Different tasks	Procedure	Discipline	Form	Function	Discourse	Sociolinguistics	Narrow	Broad
2	3	4	5	6	7	8	9	10	11	12	13	14	15	16	17
Students make list of items for camping trip using dictionary.				√ 6/5						√ V						√

Figure 3.11b   Form and other topics (broad)

c.   In the first episode of an activity, the teacher is explaining how to form hypothetical clauses ('If.../would...'). In the second episode, the students work in small groups asking each other hypothetical questions, with the intention of eliciting genuine responses.

ACTIVITIES & EPISODES	PARTICIPANT ORGANIZATION							CONTENT							
	Class			Group		Individual		Manag.		Language				Other Topics	
	T↔S/C	S↔S/C	Choral	Same task	Different tasks	Same task	Different tasks	Procedure	Discipline	Form	Function	Discourse	Sociolinguistics	Narrow	Broad
2	3	4	5	6	7	8	9	10	11	12	13	14	15	16	17
Explanation – use of 'if' + conditional in hypothetical clauses.	√									√					
Students ask hypothetical questions.				√ 8/4						√					√

Figure 3.11c Form and other topics (episodes 1 and 2)

Function

This category refers to communicative acts, such as introducing yourself, complaining and expressing an opinion.

Exclusive and primary focus on function

In almost all cases, a focus on Function co-occurs with other categories. However, an exclusive focus is possible, as Figure 3.12a illustrates.

a. The teacher asks the students what "I'll be back at two" could mean in the context of different situations. They discuss how this could simply function as a response to an information question or as a threat or a promise and so on.

ACTIVITIES & EPISODES	PARTICIPANT ORGANIZATION							CONTENT							
	Class			Group		Individual		Manag.		Language				Other Topics	
	T↔S/C	S↔S/C	Choral	Same task	Different tasks	Same task	Different tasks	Procedure	Discipline	Form	Function	Discourse	Sociolinguistics	Narrow	Broad
2	3	4	5	6	7	8	9	10	11	12	13	14	15	16	17
Teacher explains functions of forms.	√										√				

Figure 3.12a Function (exclusive)

b. An example of a primary focus on Function would be the following: The teacher explains to the students that there are different ways of expressing one's opinion (e.g. "I think...", "In my opinion..."). In this case, by giving students examples of the linguistic realizations of these functions the teacher is also focusing on Form. The coding of this is illustrated in Figure 3.12b.

ACTIVITIES & EPISODES	PARTICIPANT ORGANIZATION							CONTENT								
	Class			Group		Individual		Manag.		Language					Other Topics	
	T↔S/C	S↔S/C	Choral	Same task	Different tasks	Same task	Different tasks	Procedure	Discipline	Form	Function	Discourse	Sociolinguistics	Narrow	Broad
2	3	4	5	6	7	8	9	10	11	12	13	14	15	16	17
Teacher gives examples of different ways to express an opinion.	v									v	(v)				

Figure 3.12b Function (primary)

Combinations of function with other content categories

To illustrate combinations of focus on Function and other *Content* categories, a few examples are presented in Figures 3.13a–d.

a. The students have been introduced to different ways of expressing opinions and of agreeing and disagreeing with someone. They are now discussing a controversial school topic (uniforms) and have to use these functions to express themselves. The teacher occasionally corrects errors. As can be seen, check marks are placed under Form, Function and Narrow. Circles are placed around the check marks under Function and Narrow because the primary focuses are on using these functions to debate a topic related to the students' lives in school. Although Form is checked off, it does not receive as much emphasis as Function and 'Other topics' and is therefore not considered primary in this activity.

ACTIVITIES & EPISODES	PARTICIPANT ORGANIZATION							CONTENT								
	Class			Group		Individual		Manag.		Language					Other Topics	
	T↔S/C	S↔S/C	Choral	Same task	Different tasks	Same task	Different tasks	Procedure	Discipline	Form	Function	Discourse	Sociolinguistics	Narrow	Broad
2	3	4	5	6	7	8	9	10	11	12	13	14	15	16	17
Discussion of uniforms: use of expressions for opinions	v									v	(v)			(v)	

Figure 3.13a Function and narrow (primary)

b. The students are asked to complete a worksheet in which different situations are presented. At the end of each situation, they are asked to make a suggestion to someone, choosing from a list of expressions (e.g., "Why don't you...; You could..."; "Have you thought of...; How about...", etc). The teacher reminds them that some expressions require the infinitive, others an -ing form of the verb. The categories Form, Function and Narrow have been checked to indicate a combined focus. None of them has been circled because there is an equal focus on these particular aspects of form and meaning.

ACTIVITIES & EPISODES	PARTICIPANT ORGANIZATION							CONTENT							
	Class			Group		Individual		Manag.		Language				Other Topics	
	T↔S/C	S↔S/C	Choral	Same task	Different tasks	Same task	Different tasks	Procedure	Discipline	Form	Function	Discourse	Sociolinguistics	Narrow	Broad
2	3	4	5	6	7	8	9	10	11	12	13	14	15	16	17
Worksheet on 'suggesting'				√ 10/3						√	√			√	

Figure 3.13b Function, form and narrow (equal)

c. In Figure 3.13c, two episodes of an activity are illustrated to indicate a focus on Function with Form and Narrow topics. In the first episode, the students are being taught the form 'Je voudrais' to express a request (e.g., in a store: "Je voudrais acheter un livre") or a desire (e.g. "Je voudrais aller au cinéma").

In the second episode, the students are completing a worksheet on which they have to fill in the correct form of 'vouloir' and find an appropriate verb to complete the sentence (e.g., "Elle voudrait regarder la télévision", "Nous voudrions aller au cinéma"). In this episode Form was circled to indicate a primary focus because the emphasis shifted from Function to Form.

ACTIVITIES & EPISODES	PARTICIPANT ORGANIZATION							CONTENT							
	Class			Group		Individual		Manag.		Language				Other Topics	
	T↔S/C	S↔S/C	Choral	Same task	Different tasks	Same task	Different tasks	Procedure	Discipline	Form	Function	Discourse	Sociolinguistics	Narrow	Broad
2	3	4	5	6	7	8	9	10	11	12	13	14	15	16	17
Teacher explains "je voudrai" (request/wish).		√								√	√			√	
Students complete worksheet on "vouloir".						√				√	√			√	

Figure 3.13c Function (primary) and form (primary) with function and narrow topics

Discourse

This category refers to the rules and features of coherence (i.e., the logical connection between sentences) and cohesion (i.e., the grammatical links between sentences).

Primary focus on discourse

It appears to be virtually impossible to have an exclusive focus on Discourse, since the nature of discourse is extended text (spoken or written), which always has a theme and would, therefore, involve categories from 'Other topics'. However, it is possible to have a primary focus on Discourse, particularly when the emphasis is on coherence. Consider the following examples illustrated in Figures 3.14a and b.

a. The students are learning about the production of hydroelectric power. They receive a worksheet with notes on the different steps in the production of hydro-electric power. They are asked to order these notes to achieve a logical/coherent sequence. Some work alone, others with a partner.

ACTIVITIES & EPISODES	PARTICIPANT ORGANIZATION								CONTENT							
	Class			Group		Individual		Manag.			Language				Other Topics	
	T↔S/C	S↔S/C	Choral	Same task	Different tasks	Same task	Different tasks	Procedure	Discipline	Form	Function	Discourse	Sociolinguistics	Narrow	Broad	
2	3	4	5	6	7	8	9	10	11	12	13	14	15	16	17
Students order notes on hydroelectric power				√		√						√			√

Figure 3.14a Discourse (primary) and broad topics

b. The students receive a worksheet on which they find jumbled dialogue parts. The task is to reconstruct the dialogue so that it has a coherent/logical structure. They are working in pairs.

ACTIVITIES & EPISODES	PARTICIPANT ORGANIZATION								CONTENT							
	Class			Group		Individual		Manag.			Language				Other Topics	
	T↔S/C	S↔S/C	Choral	Same task	Different tasks	Same task	Different tasks	Procedure	Discipline	Form	Function	Discourse	Sociolinguistics	Narrow	Broad	
2	3	4	5	6	7	8	9	10	11	12	13	14	15	16	17
Students order dialogue parts				√ 8/12								√		√	

Figure 3.14b Discourse (primary) and narrow topics

Combinations of discourse with other content categories

As with all other categories discussed so far, different combinations may occur. In addition to combinations with 'Other topics', Discourse frequently co-occurs with Form, especially when the emphasis is on cohesion. Consider the following two episodes of an activity which are illustrated in Figure 3.15.

In the first episode, the students are drafting a story on the adventures of an imaginary person. Both Discourse and Broad (i.e., 'Other topics') are checked because students are engaged in producing extended text on a particular topic.

In the second episode, an additional feature is coded (i.e., Form) to account for the following activity: while walking around, the teacher has noticed that the students are constantly switching back and forth between the present tense and the past. She now asks the students to work in pairs and to correct each others' work, paying attention to form and tense cohesion. As a result, the categories Form and Discourse are circled to indicate a primary focus.

ACTIVITIES & EPISODES	PARTICIPANT ORGANIZATION							CONTENT							
	Class			Group		Individual		Manag.		Language				Other Topics	
	T↔S/C	S↔S/C	Choral	Same task	Different tasks	Same task	Different tasks	Procedure	Discipline	Form	Funtion	Discourse	Sociolinguistics	Narrow	Broad
2	3	4	5	6	7	8	9	10	11	12	13	14	15	16	17
Students write a story						√						√			√
Students correct story			√						√			√			√

Figure 3.15 Discourse and broad (equal) and discourse and form (primary)

Suggestions for an expanded definition of discourse

Some users of the COLT scheme have suggested that the definition of the Discourse category is too narrow with its focus on explicit attention to the rules and features of coherence and cohesion. As a result, the category fails to capture instances of exposure to, and use of, discourse when the emphasis is on meaning. It has been suggested that the Discourse category be subdivided into form and meaning and that within these, an indication of whether the focus is on oral or written discourse could be provided by placing an 'o' or a 'W' in the appropriate column.[9]

A focus on the form of written discourse would be coded if, for example, the teacher emphasizes the structure of a written composition (e.g., how to form paragraphs, different

---

9. Thanks to Roy Lyster for his suggestions regarding an expanded definition of the discourse category based on his use of COLT in French immersion classes.

parts of a letter etc.,) whereas the focus on the meaning of written discourse would be coded when the instruction emphasizes the comprehension and/or interpretation of a text. While a focus on form in oral discourse is likely to be less frequent, this would involve an emphasis on the forms required, for example, to appropriately structure a conversation (e.g., how to take the floor) or an oral exposé (e.g., how to introduce the topic). A focus on meaning in oral discourse would involve the expression of authentic messages in communicative interaction.

Although we have not included these distinctions in our operational definition of the Discourse category due to the fact that all other categories under 'Language' relate primarily to the forms of language and 'Other topics' to meanings, we recognize that the nature of discourse makes this distinction somewhat problematic. We consider these suggested revisions to the Discourse category to be useful and they could easily be incorporated into the operational definition and use of this category on the scheme. In doing so, however, it would be necessary to consider the implications of this with regard to other categories on the scheme (e.g., extended text).

Sociolinguistics

This category refers to forms or styles (spoken or written) appropriate to different contexts or genres.

Exclusive focus on sociolinguistics

Two examples are presented in Figures 3.16a and b to illustrate an exclusive focus on Sociolinguistics.

a. The French teacher explains differences in the use of 'tu' (used with friends, family, relatives etc.,) and 'vous' (used with some adults, strangers, superiors etc.,).

ACTIVITIES & EPISODES	PARTICIPANT ORGANIZATION						CONTENT							
	Class			Group		Individual		Manag.		Language				Other Topics
	T→S/C	S→S/C	Choral	Same task	Different tasks	Same task	Different tasks	Procedure	Discipline	Form	Function	Discourse	Sociolinguistics	Narrow	Broad
2	3	4	5	6	7	8	9	10	11	12	13	14	15	16	17
Teacher explains the distinction between 'tu/vous'.	✔												✔		

Figure 3.16a Sociolinguistics (exclusive)

b. In this example, adult L2 learners are working in groups and are asked to choose the sociolinguistically appropriate sentence in different situations, for example, at a business meeting said by one adult to another:

a. Would you mind closing the door?
b. Close the door.
c. Would you be so kind as to close the door please?

ACTIVITIES & EPISODES	PARTICIPANT ORGANIZATION							CONTENT								
	Class			Group		Individual		Manag.		Language				Other Topics	
	T↔S/C	S↔S/C	Choral	Same task	Different tasks	Same task	Different tasks	Procedure	Discipline	Form	Function	Discourse	Sociolinguistics	Narrow	Broad
2	3	4	5	6	7	8	9	10	11	12	13	14	15	16	17
Worksheet: Students choose the appropriate sentence in different situations.				√									√		

Figure 3.16b Sociolinguistics (exclusive)

Combinations of sociolinguistics and other content categories

Four episodes of an activity are presented in Figure 3.17 to illustrate different combinations. In the first episode, students are being taught how to write a letter of application in French. The teacher gives explanations about the style (use of 'vous'), the type of introductory phrases to use, the points that should be covered and how to finish the letter in a polite manner. The following check marks are entered: Sociolinguistics, Discourse and Broad. Since the primary focus is Sociolinguistics, this is circled.

In the second episode, the students are drafting their letter of application. In this case, the students are focusing equally on the teacher's sociolinguistic explanations, the content/ meaning of the letter and the way in which sentences combine together.

After the students have written a first draft, they read it out to their partner. The partner has to judge whether it sounds logical, provides enough information about the applicant's background, is sufficiently polite, and so on. This task is coded in Episode 3.

In the last episode, the partners work together to edit their letters of application with respect to correctness of grammar and spelling. As illustrated, check marks appear under Form, Discourse, Sociolinguistics and Broad ('Other topics'). Form is circled because the primary focus of this episode is on grammatical and orthographic accuracy.

Other topics

In Chapter 2, it was noted that a binary system is used to identify the different topics which may arise in the classroom. The topics are categorized as either Narrow or Broad and this depends on the range of reference by topics covered in class. For example, if the topics are familiar, they would be coded as Narrow. This includes personal information, school topics, everyday routines/activities, family life and so on. If, however, the topics encompass a broader range of reference – including such things as international events, subject matter instruction (e.g., geography, science) and imaginary events – they would be coded as Broad. We recognize that to characterize a particular topic as broad or narrow is not always straightforward. Because this decision is based not only on the content of a topic but also to some extent on how a topic is dealt with, it is a highly inferential category. It is therefore important to obtain high levels of inter-rater reliability for these judgments.

ACTIVITIES & EPISODES	PARTICIPANT ORGANIZATION							CONTENT							
	Class			Group		Individual		Manag.		Language					Other Topics	
	T→S/C	S→S/C	Choral	Same task	Different tasks	Same task	Different tasks	Procedure	Discipline	Form	Function	Discourse	Sociolinguistics	Narrow	Broad
2	3	4	5	6	7	8	9	10	11	12	13	14	15	16	17
Teacher explains letter of application	✔											✔	✔		✔
Students draft application						✔						✔	✔		✔
Students read draft to partner				✔								✔	✔		✔
Students edit letters				✔					✔			✔	✔		✔

Figure 3.17 (Episode 1) sociolinguistics (primary) with discourse and broad topics (Episode 2) sociolinguistics, discourse and broad topics (equal) (Episode 3) sociolinguistics, discourse and broad topics (equal) (Episode 4) sociolinguistics with form (primary), discourse and broad topics

As previously explained, 'Other topics' was originally a tripartite system with Narrow, Limited and Broad used to describe topic type. Based on our experiences with the scheme, a binary system has proved more effective in distinguishing between topic types. Clearly, if one were interested in investigating the nature and variety of topics and content in L2 classrooms and how they are used for different purposes, a considerably expanded and more detailed set of categories would be required. This may be particularly important in subject-matter L2 classrooms (e.g. French immersion, bilingual education programs, English for academic purposes etc.,). In contexts such as these one may want to distinguish, for example, between content which is used to teach comprehension skills and content which is used to teach interpretive skills. Adaptations to the 'Other topics' category have also been made in other L2 contexts (see Zotou & Mitchell, Chapter 7).

Exclusive focus on other topics
If the emphasis of an activity/episode is exclusively on meaning, and not on any of the categories under 'Language', only check marks under 'Other topics' are entered. A few examples of this are illustrated in Figures 3.18a–d.

a. The students are silently reading a story on the adventures of a child of their own age. The purpose is to understand the general meaning of the story.

ACTIVITIES & EPISODES	PARTICIPANT ORGANIZATION							CONTENT								
	Class			Group		Individual		Manag.		Language				Other Topics		
	T↔S/C	S↔S/C	Choral	Same task	Different tasks	Same task	Different tasks	Procedure	Discipline	Form	Function	Discourse	Sociolinguistics	Narrow	Broad
2	3	4	5	6	7	8	9	10	11	12	13	14	15	16	17
Students read story						✓									✓

Figure 3.18a Broad topics (exclusive)

b. Teacher and students are discussing whether the whole school or only the older grades should go to a winter camp.

ACTIVITIES & EPISODES	PARTICIPANT ORGANIZATION							CONTENT								
	Class			Group		Individual		Manag.		Language				Other Topics		
	T↔S/C	S↔S/C	Choral	Same task	Different tasks	Same task	Different tasks	Procedure	Discipline	Form	Function	Discourse	Sociolinguistics	Narrow	Broad
2	3	4	5	6	7	8	9	10	11	12	13	14	15	16	17
Discussion	✓													✓	

Figure 3.18b Narrow topics (exclusive)

c. The students are asking each other questions about biographical and other personal information, such as: "Do you have a pet?" "When's your birthday?" The purpose of the activity is to get to know each other, not to ask grammatically correct questions.

ACTIVITIES & EPISODES	PARTICIPANT ORGANIZATION							CONTENT								
	Class			Group		Individual		Manag.		Language				Other Topics		
	T↔S/C	S↔S/C	Choral	Same task	Different tasks	Same task	Different tasks	Procedure	Discipline	Form	Function	Discourse	Sociolinguistics	Narrow	Broad
2	3	4	5	6	7	8	9	10	11	12	13	14	15	16	17
Students ask each other questions				✓										✓	

Figure 3.18c Narrow topics (exclusive)

d. The students are watching a documentary film in their second language on climate change.

ACTIVITIES & EPISODES	PARTICIPANT ORGANIZATION							CONTENT							
	Class			Group		Individual		Manag.		Language					Other Topics
	T↔S/C	S↔S/C	Choral	Same task	Different tasks	Same task	Different tasks	Procedure	Discipline	Form	Function	Discourse	Sociolinguistics	Narrow	Broad
2	3	4	5	6	7	8	9	10	11	12	13	14	15	16	17
Students watch film				√											√

Figure 3.18d Broad topics (exclusive)

Combinations of other topics with other content categories

In the previous sections, several examples have already been presented which show co-occurrence of 'Other topics' with different *Content* categories. As indicated earlier, a common combination is with Form. Another example of this is illustrated in Figure 3.19. After the students have watched the documentary on World War II (Figure 3.18d), the teacher asks comprehension questions, explains important vocabulary and writes the words on the blackboard.

ACTIVITIES & EPISODES	PARTICIPANT ORGANIZATION							CONTENT							
	Class			Group		Individual		Manag.		Language					Other Topics
	T↔S/C	S↔S/C	Choral	Same task	Different tasks	Same task	Different tasks	Procedure	Discipline	Form	Function	Discourse	Sociolinguistics	Narrow	Broad
2	3	4	5	6	7	8	9	10	1	12	13	14	15	16	17
Teacher asks questions on film, explains vocabulary	√									√ √					√

Figure 3.19 Other topics (broad) with form

Columns 18–20: *Content control*

Teacher/Text (18)
Teacher/Text/Student (19)
Student (20)

The categories in *Content Control* refer both to the initial selection of a topic or task and to the control over the content of an activity/episode. Several examples of how content is controlled are provided below and the codings for these are illustrated in Figures 3.20a–c.

a.   The teacher is asking questions about a text that the students have read. Therefore, Teacher/Text is checked.
b.   The teacher asks the students to write in their diaries about their summer vacation. The teacher initially selects the task and the general topic, but the students have some choice and freedom within the task/topic. Therefore, this activity would be coded as Teacher/Text/Student.
c.   Several students ask the teacher if they can play a particular game in class that they enjoy a great deal. Since this activity was initiated by the students, it would be coded as Student.

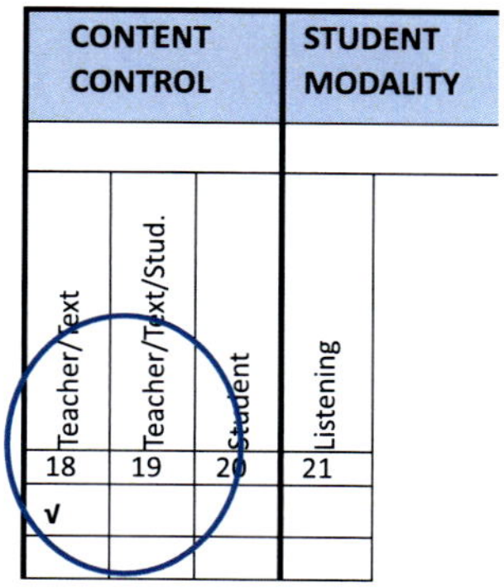

Figure 3.20a Teacher/text (exclusive)

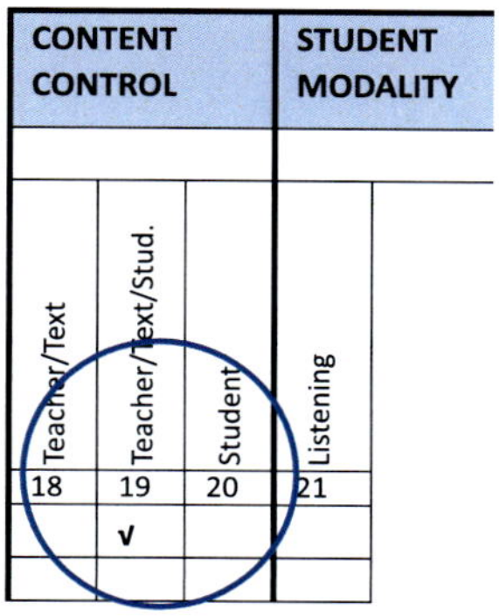

Figure 3.20b Teacher/text/student (exclusive)

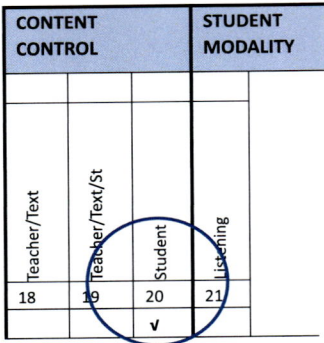

	CONTENT CONTROL			STUDENT MODALITY	
	Teacher/Text	Teacher/Text/St	Student	Listening	
18	19	20	21		
		√			

Figure 3.20c Student (exclusive)

Columns 21–25: *Student modality*

Listening (21)
Speaking (22)
Reading (23)
Writing (24)
Other (25)

The categories in *Student Modality* are checked to indicate which modality/modalities are involved for most of the students. Several examples of *Student Modality* are below, and the coding is illustrated in Figures 3.21a–c. Many other combinations are possible.

a. The teacher is asking questions and individual students answer.
b. The students are discussing a topic in group work.
c. Individual students take turns in reading aloud while the others read along silently. The predominant modalities for the majority of the students have been circled.

CONTENT CONTROL			STUDENT MODALITY					
Teacher/Text	Teacher/Text/Stud.	Student	Listening	Speaking	Reading	Writing	Other	
18	19	20	21	22	23	24	25	
			√	√				

Figure 3.21a Listening (primary) with speaking

CONTENT CONTROL		STUDENT MODALITY					
Teacher/Text	Teacher/Text/Stud.	Student	Listening	Speaking	Reading	Writing	Other
18	19	20	21	22	23	24	25
			√	√			

Figure 3.21b Listening & speaking (equal)

CONTENT CONTROL		STUDENT MODALITY					
Teacher/Text	Teacher/Text/Stud.	Student	Listening	Speaking	Reading	Writing	Other
18	19	20	21	22	23	24	25
			√	√	√		

Figure 3.21c Listening & reading (primary) with speaking

Columns 26–33: *Materials*

Type: Text (minimal/extended written) (26, 27)
        Audio (28)
        Visual (29)
Source: L2 – NNS (30)
        L2 – NS (31)
        L2 – NSA (32)
        Student-made (33)

Although the *Materials* categories are self-explanatory and relatively easy to code, a few examples are presented below along with the coding illustrated in Figures 3.22a–f.

a. A student presents his project on a geography topic to the class. During his oral presentation he also shows pictures and maps. Note that the categories under Source relate only to language and not to audio-visual material. Therefore L2-NS is not checked for the pictures and maps.

b. The students complete a worksheet on which they have to fill in the correct tenses and prepositions in isolated sentences.

STUDENT MODALITY	MATERIALS							
	Type				Source			
	Text							
	Minimal	Extended	Audio	Visual	L2-NNS	L2-NS	L2-NSA	Student-made
	26	27	28	29	30	31	32	33
				√				√

Figure 3.22a Materials: Visual and student-made (equal)

STUDENT MODALITY	MATERIALS							
	Type				Source			
	Text							
	Minimal	Extended	Audio	Visual	L2-NNS	L2-NS	L2-NSA	Student-made
	26	27	28	29	30	31	32	33
	√				√			

Figure 3.22b Materials: Text (minimal) with L2-NNS

c. The students are completing a cloze test. Both Minimal and Extended text are checked off because students need to read the whole text in order to fill in the blanks.

d. The students watch a movie in its original version (i.e., it was intended for native speakers of the target language).

STUDENT MODALITY	MATERIALS							
	Type				Source			
	Text							
	Minimal	Extended	Audio	Visual	L2-NNS	L2-NS	L2-NSA	Student-made
	26	27	28	29	30	31	32	33
	√	√			√			

Figure 3.22c Materials: Text (minimal and extended) with L2 NNS

STUDENT MODALITY	MATERIALS							
	Type				Source			
	Text							
	Minimal	Extended	Audio	Visual	L2-NNS	L2-NS	L2-NSA	Student-made
	26	27	28	29	30	31	32	33
			√	√		√		

Figure 3.22d Materials: Audio & visual with L2-NNS

e. Students read an abbreviated and annotated version of 'Macbeth', in which difficult vocabulary has been explained and partially translated into the students' L1.[10]

f. The students use notes they created from a magazine article to prepare a presentation

---

10. Many native-speaking students read simplified and annotated versions of classical literature in their L1. This type of text would be coded 'L2-NS' (i.e., for native speakers of the target language), since they were not adapted with the second language learner in mind.

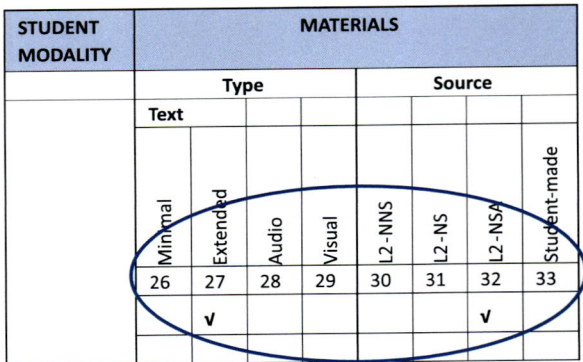

Figure 3.22e Materials: Text (extended with L2-NSA

STUDENT MODALITY	MATERIALS							
	Type				Source			
	Text							
	Minimal	Extended	Audio	Visual	L2-NNS	L2-NS	L2-NSA	Student-made
	26	27	28	29	30	31	32	33
		√					√	

STUDENT MODALITY	MATERIALS							
	Type				Source			
	Text							
	Minimal	Extended	Audio	Visual	L2-NNS	L2-NS	L2-NSA	Student-made
	26	27	28	29	30	31	32	33
						√		√

Figure 3.22f Materials: (Student-made primary) with L2-NS

In Chapter 4, the coding conventions for COLT Part B are presented, illustrated, and discussed.

CHAPTER 4

Part B: Coding conventions

In this chapter the coding conventions for Part B are presented in three parts. General aspects of the coding conventions are discussed first. This is followed by descriptions of the specific coding procedures for the main features of Part B and their categories. Finally, excerpts from classroom transcripts, together with the coding for Part B, are used to illustrate the conventions. Figure 4.1 presents the Part B spreadsheet for teacher and verbal interaction.

General overview

As discussed in Chapter 2, Part B characterizes the verbal interactions that take place between students and teachers within activities and episodes. This section of the scheme is divided into seven main communicative features. The last two features (*Discourse initiation* and *Form restriction*) are used exclusively for coding student verbal interaction.

1. *Target language*
2. *Information gap*
3. *Sustained speech*
4. *Reaction to form/message*
5. *Incorporation of student/teacher utterances*
6. *Discourse initiation*
7. *Form restriction*

Unlike the Part A coding which is done in 'real time', coding for Part B is done after the observation based on audio and/or video recordings of the instruction. This is necessary because the focus of analysis in Part B is on the linguistic output and interactions of teachers and students, and is therefore much more detailed and intensive than the Part A analysis. We strongly advise that coding for the Part B features be done from transcripts of the classroom interaction. With more experience, coding may be done directly from audio recordings, but this is difficult and not recommended.

The general coding procedure for Part B is to place check marks in the appropriate columns for any of the relevant features and categories which occur within a teacher or student turn. A turn is defined as any (and all) speech which is produced by a speaker until another person begins speaking. Therefore, a turn can include as little speech as one word or as much as several sentences in extended discourse.

Before proceeding further let's look at two excerpts from transcripts of two different ESL classes to get a general sense of how coding for Part B works. In these transcripts, the speech of the teacher (T) and students (S) is on the left-hand side, and the speech has been coded on the right-hand side. In cases where there is speech from multiple students, they are numbered (e.g., S1, S2…). The excerpts have been fully coded using the Part B categories

COLT PART B: COMMUNICATIVE FEATURES

Communicative Orientation of Language Teaching Observation Scheme

© Spada & Fröhlich 1995

School _____

Teacher _____

Subject _____

Date of visit _____

Coder _____

TEACHER VERBAL INTERACTION

Target language	Off Task	1			
	L1	2			
	L2	3			
Information gap — Giving Info.	Predict.	4			
	Unpred.	5			
Information gap — Request Info.	Pseudo requ.	6			
	Genuine requ.	7			
Sustained speech	Minimal	8			
	Sustained	9			
Restriction to form/ message	Form	10			
	Message	11			
Incorporation of student utterances	Correction	12			
	Repetition	13			
	Paraphrase	14			
	Comment	15			
	Expansion	16			
	Clarif. request	17			
	Elab. request	18			
Discourse Initiation		19			

STUDENT VERBAL INTERACTION

Target language	L1	20			
	L2	21			
Information gap — Giving Info.	Predict.	22			
	Unpredict.	23			
Information gap — Request Info.	Pseudo Requ.	24			
	Genuine Requ.	25			
Sustained speech	Ultra-minimal	26			
	Minimal	27			
	Sustained	28			
Form restriction	Choral	29			
	Restricted	30			
	Unrestricted	31			
Restriction to form/ message	Form	32			
	Message	33			
Incorporation of student /teacher utterances	Correction	34			
	Repetition	35			
	Paraphrase	36			
	Comment	37			
	Expansion	38			
	Clarif. request	39			
	Elab. request	40			

(Row labels: A, E, M)

Figure 4.1 COLT (Part B)

and a legend explaining the abbreviations for the coding categories is provided after Excerpt B. Following the excerpts, we summarize and compare some of the features coded in the two transcripts. At this point you are not expected to fully understand how and why the speech has been coded in this manner. All of this will be explained in more detail in this chapter. The purpose here is to give you an overall view of what classroom speech coded with Part B looks like.

Excerpt A[11]

Teacher and student speech	Coding
(Teacher looks at the calendar.) T: What's the date today?	L2/Pseudo Req./Min.
S1: April 15th.	L2/Pred.Info/Ultram./Restr.
T: Good	L2/Form-Comment/Min.
(Turning to another student) What day is it?	L2/Pseudo Req./Min.
S2: Monday.	L2/Pred.Info/Ultram./Restr.

Excerpt B

Teacher and student speech	Coding
T: What did you do on the weekend?	L2/Gen.Req./Min.
S: I go see a movie.	L2/Unpred.Info/Min./Unrestr.
T: Oh, that's fun.	L2/Mess.-Comment
So did I.	L2/Mess.-Exp.
What did you see?	L2/Mess.-Elab.Req./Sust.
S: Terminator 2.	L2/Unpred.Info/Unrestr.
What you see?	D.I./L2/Mess.-Elab.Req./Min.
T: Terminator 2!	L2/Unpred. Info/Sust.
My son wanted to see it. It's not my kind of a movie, but the special effects were great.	
S: Yeah, agree.	D.I./L2/Mess.- Comment/ Unrestr./Min.

As seen in both excerpts, the teachers and students use the L2 in all their turns. In Excerpt A, the teacher's speech consists primarily of Pseudo requests (questions to which she already knows the answer) and brief comments. Correspondingly, the students' speech provides Predictable information in one word or two and is therefore characterized as Ultram-

---

11. Adapted from Allen, Fröhlich, & Spada (1984).

Legend : Coding abbreviations

PseudoReq: Pseudo request	Unrestr: Unrestricted
Min: Minimal	Mess: Message
Pred.Info : Predictable information	Exp: Expansion
Ultram: Ultraminimal	Elab.Req: Elaboration request
Restr: Restricted	Sust: Sustained
Gen.Req: Genuine request	D.I.: Discourse initiation
Unpred.Info Unpredictable information	

---

minimal in nature. Furthermore, because of the drill-like nature of the task, the students' responses are coded as Restricted.

In Excerpt B the nature of the verbal interaction changes quite considerably. The teacher tends to ask Genuine questions (i.e., questions to which the answer is not known in advance). This leads the students to provide Unpredictable information. As a result, there is more latitude for the students to use a greater variety of linguistic features (i.e., Unrestricted language) to communicate their message, even though they are clearly limited by their proficiency level. It is also interesting to note that the teacher's turns, as well as the students' turns, are more extended than in the first excerpt. Thus, the teacher's turns are coded as Sustained on several occasions and the students' speech is always Minimal as opposed to Ultraminimal as it was in Excerpt A.

Figure 4.2 shows how these verbal interactions are coded on the Part B observation grid. The left-hand side of the sheet represents coding for teacher speech and the right-hand side for student speech. As you can see, the first teacher utterance "What did you do on the weekend?" is coded as L2, Genuine request and Minimal. This completes the teacher's turn, and a line is drawn underneath the coding to indicate this. The student responds with "I go see a movie" which is coded as L2, Unpredictable, Minimal and Unrestricted. This completes the student's turn, and a line is also drawn underneath it. What follows is a series of utterances on the part of the teacher. The first utterance, "Oh, that's fun" is coded as L2, Message and Comment. The teacher's next utterance, "So did I", represents a message-related expansion of the student's previous utterance and this is indicated by checking off Expansion and Message on the next line down. The teacher's final utterance in this turn is coded as a message-related Elaboration request in the L2. Notice that each time there is a change in the categories under *Incorporation of student/teacher utterances*, a check mark is also entered under *Target language and Reaction to form/message*. Also note that the category *Sustained speech* is not coded until the entire turn is completed.

Before presenting more detailed information on the coding conventions for each of the major communicative features and their categories, a few more general comments are in order.

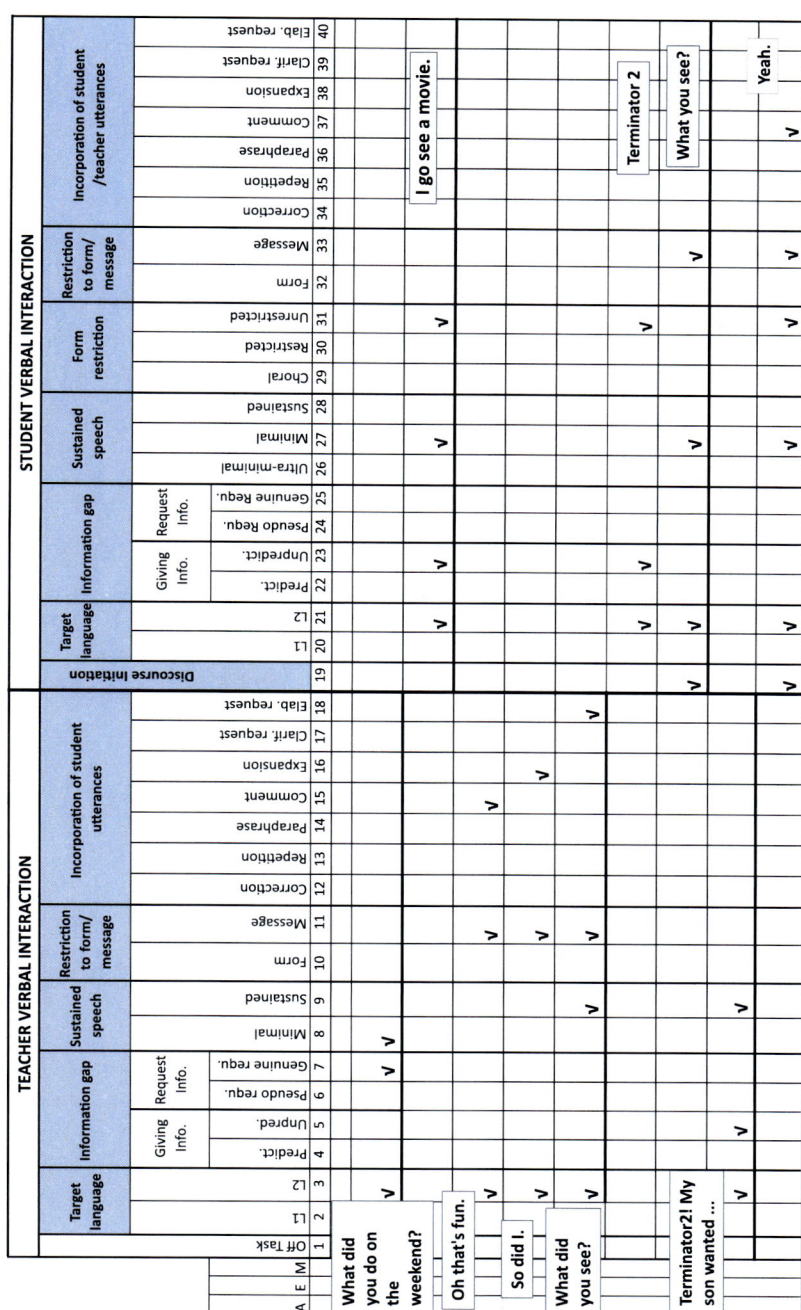

Figure 4.2 Coding for Excerpt B

Matching Part A and Part B

To facilitate matching the activities and episodes coded on Part A with the coding of teacher and student verbal interactions on Part B, enter the number of the activity (A) and episode (E) in the left margin, as shown in Figure 4.3.

Time sampling

Instead of coding the occurrence of Part B features for the entire observation period, a time sampling procedure may be preferred. For example, the researcher may decide to code for one minute, stop for two and code for the next minute and so on; thus, coding for one third of the observed time.

A	E	M	Off Task	Target language		Information gap			
						Giving Info.		Request Info.	
				L1	L2	Predict.	Unpred.	Pseudo requ.	Genuine request
			1	2	3	4	5	6	7
1	01								
1	02								
2	01								
3	01								
3	02								

TEACHER VERBAL INTERACTION

Figure 4.3 Matching Part A and Part B

Another possibility is to follow a time-sampling procedure within activities. In this case, coding would start at the beginning of each activity for one minute and would resume after a two-minute interval. During the one-minute coding periods, the frequency of occurrence of each category of the communicative features would be recorded. If a within-activity time-sampling procedure is followed, the coding minute should be entered in the left margin in addition to the number of the activity and episode. The counting of the coding minute (M) starts with 01 when an activity changes. When the coding minute is incomplete because a new activity started, write 'inc.' beside the minute count as shown in Figure 4.4.

Detailed guidelines for coding Teacher/Student verbal interaction

In this section details regarding the coding conventions for each major feature and their categories are described. Since most of the categories are common to both teacher and student interaction, coding conventions for these are provided first. The two categories which deal exclusively with student speech (*Discourse initiation* and *Form restriction*) are discussed last.

Off task

This category is reserved for verbal interaction, which is unrelated to the activity, episode, or overall lesson. For example, if there is an announcement on the school's public address system, which leads to discussion in the classroom, this would be coded as *Off task*. Coding for this feature is optional. However, it may be of interest to note whether off-task talk is carried out differently from on-task talk, for example, in terms of the language used (i.e., L1 or L2).

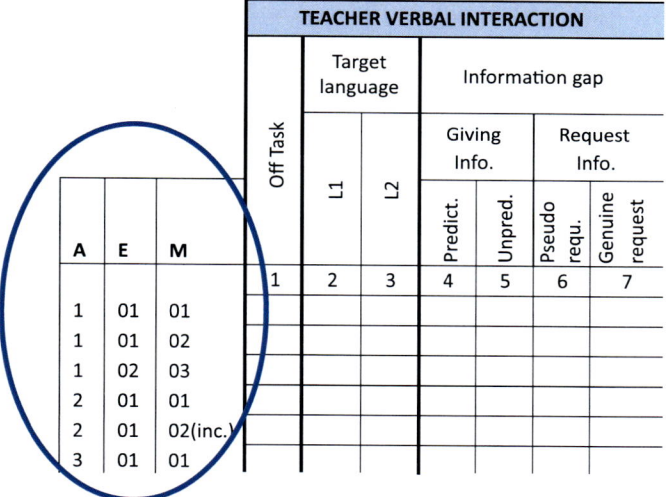

Figure 4.4 Time sampling

Target language

All verbal utterances produced by the teacher or student are coded as L1 or L2. In general, we do not code for any further categories in the L1. However, if the L1 is consistently used for specific purposes, such as giving managerial directives or explanations, the observer may wish to code for these categories by using some other symbols, such as *M* for managerial or *D* for discipline.

Information gap: Giving and Requesting Information

As indicated in the definition of categories in Chapter 2, the two categories under *Information gap* are designed to capture the extent to which the information requested or provided is unpredictable. Below are some examples of how speech would be coded under each of these categories, beginning with 'Giving information'.

Giving information

Both teachers and students can provide predictable and unpredictable information during classroom interaction. Recall that Predictable information is defined as that which is easily anticipated and known in advance to the questioner. On the other hand, Unpredictable information is not easily anticipated in that there is a wide range of information that can be provided. A straightforward example of the teacher providing Predictable information would be if he/she said in an activity describing what everyone is wearing, "I'm wearing pants and a sweater". Unpredictable information would include telling the students something they didn't know in advance – either about language (e.g., "The past tense of hang is hung") or other topics (e.g., "My birthday is next week"). Most managerial and disciplinary directives are also coded under Unpredictable information (e.g., "I don't want you to open your books yet"; "You are disturbing the whole class.").

Students can also provide Predictable and Unpredictable information and it can be elicited or non-elicited. Giving predictable information on the part of students tends to follow a pseudo request. For example, in more traditional classrooms where teachers ask a lot of questions to which they (and often the students) already know the answers in advance, students provide a great deal of predictable information. We saw this illustrated in Excerpt A of the classroom transcripts. Students were asked to say the date and day of the week when it was known in advance by everyone. However, in Excerpt B there were examples of a student providing information that was not easily anticipated (e.g., reporting on what the student did over the weekend).

Although the giving of Predictable and Unpredictable information can be provided separately, in isolated turns, it is also possible that they occur within the same turn. For example, if the teacher asks for the date and the student not only tells her the date thus giving predictable information, but also adds that it's a classmate's birthday, the student is providing unpredictable information as well.

Reading aloud constitutes a special case of giving information. When students are reading aloud an unknown text (i.e., not read before), it is coded as giving Unpredictable information. This is also the case when individual students read a text to the class which they have written themselves. In contrast, when a text is already known and is familiar to the students, reading aloud is coded as giving Predictable information.

A special mention is necessary about coding student answers such as "I don't know" or "I can't remember" and incorrect responses. If a student responds to a request for information by indicating that she/he does not know the answer, this answer is coded as giving Unpredictable information irrespective of whether the preceding request was a genuine or pseudo request for information. In contrast, the decision on whether to code an incorrect response as either giving predictable or unpredictable information is based upon the type of request that preceded the response. In other words, if the teacher (or another student) requests predictable information (i.e., a pseudo request) the student's answer would be coded as giving Predictable information, albeit incorrect. If, however, the incorrect response follows a genuine request for information, it is coded as giving Unpredictable information. Look at the following two examples for further clarification. More information about pseudo and genuine requests for information follows in the next section.

Example 1

Teacher and student speech	Coding
T: What's the past tense of 'I go'?	Pseudo request
S: I goed.	Giving Predictable information (although info, is incorrect)

Example 2

Teacher and student speech	Coding
T: Does anyone know when José's birthday is?	Genuine request
S1: I think it's the 24th.	Giving Unpredictable info. (although info, is incorrect)
S2: No, it's the 25th; 1 know because it was my birthday on the 26th and hers is the day before mine.	Giving Unpredictable info.

Practice 1

Look at the excerpts of classroom speech below and decide whether each turn should be coded as the giving of Predictable or Unpredictable information. Code only the student turns that are underlined. The answers are provided in the Answer Key at the end of the book.

1 Situation: The students are being assigned class jobs for the day. To assign the jobs, the teacher is drawing students' names from a hat and asking them each a question. The students must answer one question correctly to get a class job.

Teacher and student speech	Coding
T: Uh, David, give me the name of two stores in Chambly (the name of the town in which the students live).	
S: Uh, Continental. _____	_____
T: Continental is one store.	
S: Canadian Tire. _____	_____
T: Boy, David is wide awake this morning!	

2 Situation: The teacher is talking with the students about having papers signed by their parents.

Teacher and student speech	
T: I want your paper here at one o'clock this afternoon absolutely.	
S: I can't by then.	
T: Why?	
S: My, my father's working.	
T: Did you check with your parents yesterday?	
S: He's a teacher.	

3 Situation: Teacher reviews the book-borrowing procedure in class.

Teacher and student speech	Coding
T: No. Just. No. I want the procedure. If you want a book, what do you do?	
S: Uh, I take uh, a piece of uh paper and uh mark the date, the name of the book and uh my name.	
T: Mmhm.	
S: And after [ben][12] aft – I [ben] book and I put the, the piece of paper, the book's ticket out. After my [ben] it's finished [la] I take my paper and uh...	

4 Situation: Teacher asks a student to organize meals at lunchtime.

Teacher and student speech	Coding
T: Danny, would you take care of the paper before I forget again?	
S: Who wants a hot meal?	
T: What is the hot meal on uh, Tuesday?	
S: Spaghetti or fish & chips.	

Requesting information

It is relatively easy to differentiate between pseudo and genuine requests for information. Generally, pseudo requests are those to which the speaker already knows the answer. In genuine requests, on the other hand, the information requested is not known in advance by the questioner.

For example, when a teacher asks the question "What colour is my suit?" she not only knows the answer to the question, but the students do as well. As a result, a check mark is

---

12. The word [ben] is a transcription of the francophone students' pronunciation of 'bien'.

placed under the category Pseudo request. Similarly, when the teacher asks a question like "What is the date today?" (when it is written on the board), this is also coded as a Pseudo request. However, if the teacher asks, "What's the date today?" in a context where it is clear she doesn't know or has forgotten, a check mark would be placed under Genuine request.

Genuine requests are often elicitations of opinions or interpretative questions. Note that they are not always explicitly formulated as opinion questions; for example, compare "Was the hero of this story a happy character?" (Genuine request) with "Do you think that the hero was a happy character?" (Genuine request).

In most cases, Genuine requests are also considered to be questions where the questioner may have some idea about possible answers. For example, a teacher might ask what the reasons were for the large number of immigrants after World War II. The teacher will probably know some reasons when asking this question. But unless it is evident that the question is a review of previous classroom discussion on immigration, it would be coded as a Genuine request for information. When directives function as requests for information and a verbal response is expected (e.g., "Give me the past tense of this verb") they are coded under requests. Consider the following examples.

Teacher and student speech	Coding
T: Give me the opposite to dark.	Pseudo request
T: Tell me what this means in French	Genuine request or Pseudo request

The first example would be coded as a Pseudo request because the teacher knows the answer in advance. The second example would be coded as a Genuine request, if it is evident that the teacher does not know the meaning of the word in French; however, if the teacher does know what it means in French and just wants the student to display knowledge, it is coded as a Pseudo request.

A student's response to a teacher's request for information is usually coded under 'Giving information'. However, sometimes the teacher may ask a student to request information from another student. In cases like this, the student's response is coded under 'Requesting information'. Consider the following example:

Teacher and student speech	Coding
T: Ask your neighbour about his weekend.	Giving Unpredictable information (managerial)
S1: How was your weekend?	Genuine request[13]
S2: Boring.	Giving Unpredictable information

Questions which are repeated several times, even if slightly different in form, are coded only once, unless there is a pause indicating that a response was expected, but not given. When

---

13. This is coded as a genuine request because the answer is not known in advance. We recognize that the student may not be genuinely interested in asking it, but having done so, she/he is requesting unpredictable information.

the question is repeated or reformulated after this pause, it is coded again as shown in the next two examples.

Example 1

Teacher and student speech	Coding
T: What day is it? What day is it?	Pseudo request (coded only once)

Example 2

Teacher and student speech	Coding
T: What day is it?	Pseudo request
(Pause no answer is given)	
T: What day is it? The day of the week, Monday, Tuesday?	Pseudo request (coded again)

Similarly, if an incorrect answer has been given and the teacher asks the question again, the repetition of the question is coded as another request for information. For example:

Teacher and student speech	Coding
T: What day is it?	Pseudo request
S: Sunday	Giving Predictable information (although answer is incorrect)
T: What day is it today?	Pseudo request (coded again)

Practice 2

Look at the examples of classroom speech below and code only the teacher turns that are underlined according to whether they represent a genuine or a pseudo request. The answers are provided in the Answer Key at the end of the book.

1 Situation: The teacher is asking students what they watched on TV the previous evening.

Teacher and student speech	Coding
T: I would like to know what you watched on TV last night? Anything special? Steve, what did you watch?	
S: Friends.	
T: Friends at 7:30??	

S: Yes, Channel 6.

2 Situation: The teacher is asking the students in the English class what they did yesterday when she was absent, and about the games they play in class.

Teacher and student speech	Coding
T: Did it go well, uh, yesterday when I was absent?	
S: Yes	
T: Yes? Jesse?	
S: She spoke in French all morning.	
T: Oh well.	

Teacher and student speech	Coding
T: Did you play the games?	
S: Yes. 99. *(class talks at once)*	
T: Everybody played 99?	
S: Or uh, other games.	

Teacher and student speech	Coding
T: Annick. Please give me uh, the name of two games we play in class.	
S1: Uh...	
T: Uh...let's go, Annick.	
S1: The bank.	
T: Thank you, Annick.	

T: The bank, do we play the bank?

_____

S2: No.

S1: Stock Market.

T: Stock Market, is that the game?

_____

S1: Yes.

T: Yep, give me the name of another game, Annick.

Sustained speech

As already stated, what is important to remember when coding for this category is that decisions about whether the teacher's or student's speech is Ultraminimal, Minimal or Sustained, are made based on turns not utterances. Therefore, if a student says "Yes, I like it too. It is more good than Terminator 2… the effects are more good," this is coded as Sustained, not as three Minimal turns. Recall from Chapter 2 the definitions of the categories: Ultraminimal (i.e., student turns which consist of one or two words; e.g., an article plus a noun or just a noun), Minimal (i.e., teacher and student turns which consist of more than two words, long phrases and one or two main clauses or sentences; for the teacher, one-word turns are coded as Minimal), Sustained (i.e., teacher and student turns which consist of at least three main clauses). You will note that we do not code teacher's speech as Ultraminimal since most teacher talk is either minimal or sustained.

When students are reading aloud in different roles or presenting a role-play, their speech is coded as Ultraminimal, Minimal or Sustained with respect to their turns. You may wish to identify the students and their respective turns by S1, S2 etc. Each new turn should be coded on a new line.

Reaction to form/message

The feature _Reaction to form/message_ is intended to differentiate between a reaction to the linguistic form of an utterance (form) and to the content of an utterance (message). As the label of the category indicates, this feature describes _reactions_. This means that the category is coded only when the teacher and/or students react to something that was previously said. Because of this, _Reaction to form/message_ is coded in combination with the categories under _Incorporation of student/teacher utterances_. Before we provide examples of how these categories are coded together, let us first look at some examples of _Reaction to form/message_.

> T: Quel temps fait-il?
>
> S: Il font beau
>
> T: Il **font** beau? (spoken with rising intonation stressing 'font').

In this exchange the teacher makes a pseudo request since everyone can see that the weather is wonderful, and the student responds with a predictable although grammatically incorrect response. The teacher reacts to this by indicating (through emphasis and rising intonation) that the student has made an error. Therefore, Form would be checked off under *Reaction to form/message*. If, however, the teacher had responded differently and said:

> T: Oui, c'est vrai, mais on dit il fait beau.

"Oui, c'est vrai" would be coded as *Message* and "mais on dit il fait beau" would be coded as *Form*. Following are two examples which would be coded only as message related. As can be seen, the students make errors, but the teacher responds only to the message or content of their utterances.

Example I

> T: What did you do on the weekend?
>
> S: I go to ski.
>
> T: Oh, that's fun!

Example 2

> T: Why are you late for class?
>
> S: Uh, the bus, uh, not come at the time.
>
> T: That's the second time this week your bus was late, right?

Incorporation of student/teacher utterances

As indicated above, the categories Form and Message are always coded in combination with other categories under *Incorporation of student/teacher utterances* because they represent reactions to what was previously said. Before illustrating how this works, some general comments on the category are in order.

Recall that these categories have been developed to provide more detailed information on the type of interactions that take place between student/teacher and student/student. They are Correction, Repetition, Paraphrase, Comment, Expansion, Clarification request, and Elaboration request. The first category, Correction, will often co-occur with other categories under *Incorporation of student/teacher utterances*, particularly with Repetition, Comment, and Paraphrase.

As described earlier, Correction refers to an attempt to provide the speaker with the information that they have provided a linguistically incorrect utterance. Therefore, if the teacher corrects a student's utterance by repeating it with stress or rising intonation, check marks are placed under Correction and Repetition. If the teacher responds by commenting "No, that's not quite right", check marks are placed under Correction and Comment. If the teacher responds to a student's error by paraphrasing the sentence in a way which provides the correct form, check marks are placed under the categories Correction and Paraphrase. The only time the category Correction is checked on its own is when correction comes in the form of metalinguistic information (e.g., "Where's your auxiliary?") It is important to note that the Correction category is only used to code errors in form, not errors in content or meaning. If desired, this could be incorporated into the scheme and might be particularly useful in content-based and subject-matter L2 instruction.

Practice 3
Look at the examples of teacher Correction below and decide whether they would also be coded as Repetition, Comment or Paraphrase. The answers are provided in the Answer Key at the end of the book.

Teacher and student speech	Coding
1. S: Uh ... she goed her friend last night.	
T: Denise goed with her friend last night?	Correction + _____
2. S: He have sixteen years old.	
T: No, I don't think so... try again.	Correction + _____
3. S: We look at the people.	
T: What's the ending we put on verbs to talk about action in the past?	Correction + _____
4. S: Is he.... is reading a book?	
T: Is he is reading a book?	Correction + _____
5. S: They go in Monday.	
T: Should we use the preposition in or on here?	Correction + _____
6. S: The bee string me.	
T: Oh... the bee stingS me.	Correction + _____
7. S: There are two book on the desk.	
T: Think about what you just said.	Correction + _____

Correction and Repetition in combination with Reaction to form/message

As indicated above, while multiple categories are coded under *Incorporation of student/ teacher utterances,* the categories *Message* and/or *Form* are also checked off under the category *Reaction to form/message.* Although this may create some redundancy in the coding (as some of the examples below will illustrate), we have found this information to be useful when analyzing classroom data in different ways for different purposes. For example, while one user of the scheme may be interested only in whether teachers and/or students react to form or meaning, others may be interested in the ways in which teachers respond to form. Coding the relevant categories under each major feature will more easily permit both types of analyses. Let's recall an earlier example to illustrate how this works.

> T: Quel temps fait-il?
>
> S: Il font beau.
>
> T: Il **font** beau? (*spoken with rising intonation stressing 'font'*)

The above example was given previously, in the section *Reaction to form/message*, to illustrate when Form is checked off under *Reaction to form/message*. However, because the teacher said this in response to the student's previous (incorrect) utterance, it would also be coded under the feature *Incorporation of student/teacher utterances*. Because she responded to the student's linguistically incorrect utterance, Correction would be checked; because she chose to respond by repeating the student's utterance, Repetition would also be checked. The coding of this example is illustrated in Figure 4.5.

Correction and Paraphrase in combination with Reaction to Form/Message

At times it can be difficult to decide on *Reaction to Form/Message* when Repetition and Paraphrase are involved. Recall that in a Repetition there is no change of linguistic form; however, an utterance may be repeated to confirm the content (i.e., Message) of the preceding utterance or the linguistic form (i.e., Form). In a paraphrase, there is always some change. If the change appears to be an attempt to provide linguistic correction, then a check mark is placed under Form. Look at the following example and the coding for it in Figure 4.6.

> T: What did you do yesterday?
>
> St: I go see my mother. She in l'hôpital.
>
> T: Oh, you went to see your mother in the hospital (with slight emphasis on 'went'). I didn't know she was sick. I hope she's going to be better soon.

As seen in Figure 4.6, the teacher's response to the student's utterance is coded under several categories. If we break down the teacher's utterance, the coding decisions become clearer. The first utterance "Oh, you went to see your mother in the hospital" is coded as Correction and Paraphrase under *Incorporation of students' utterances*. This is because of the emphasis on the past participle 'went' and the provision of the English word for hospital. As you can see, this also constitutes a check mark under Form in *Reaction to form/message*. The utterances "I didn't know she was sick" and "I hope she's going to be better soon" are coded as one Expansion. Both are also coded as Message under *Reaction to form/message*, and the entire turn is coded as Sustained.

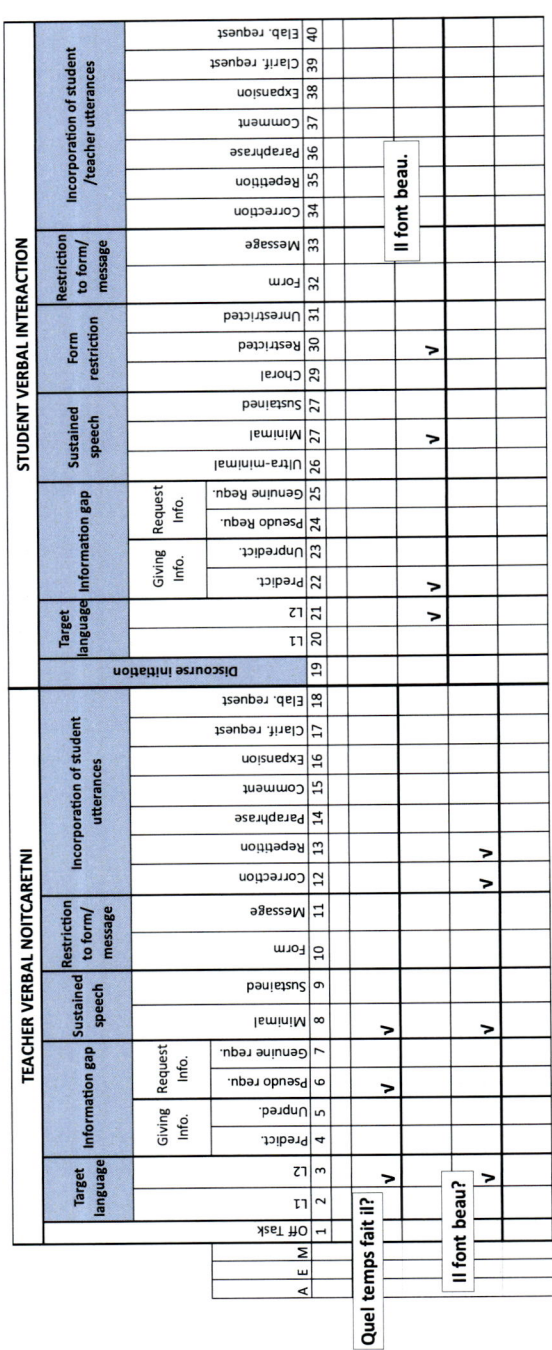

Figure 4.5 Correction (Repetition) with Reaction to form/message

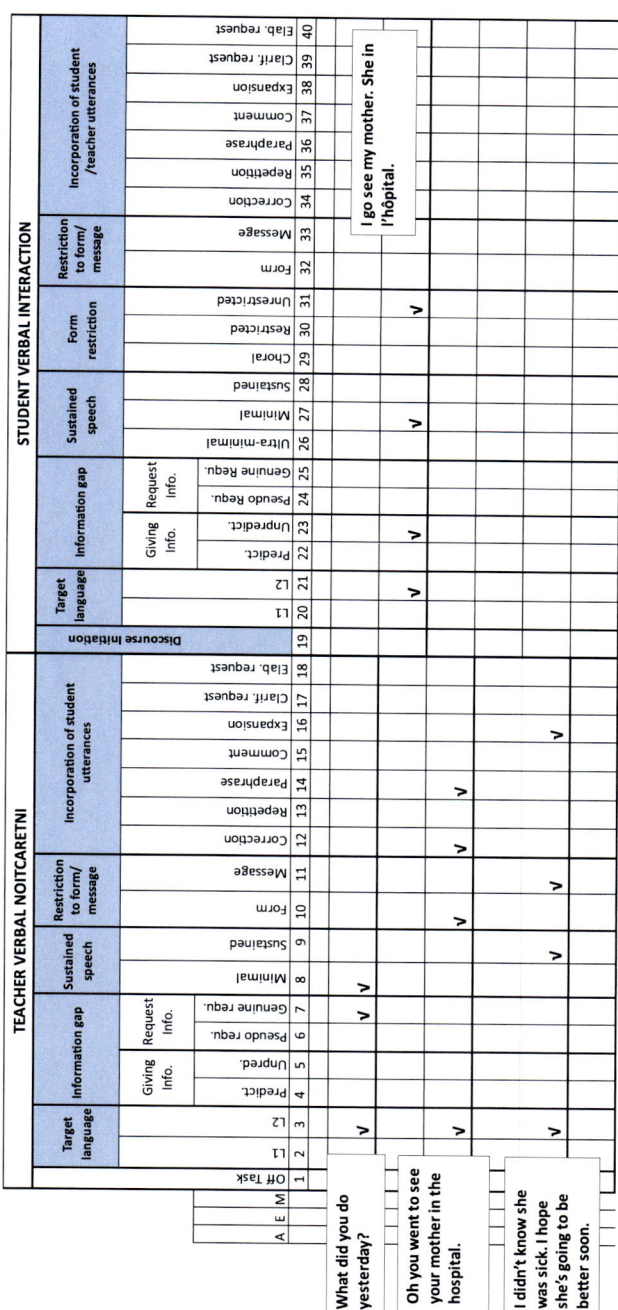

Figure 4.6 Correction (Paraphrase) with Reaction to form/message

When a student repeats a linguistic correction, Repetition and Form are checked off. Cues provided by the teacher to assist a student in giving a response, such as providing a missing vocabulary item while the student is speaking, are ignored. Consequently, repetition of such cues is not coded as illustrated in the next example.[14]

Situation: The students are describing a picture.

Teacher and student speech	Coding
T: What is the girl wearing?	
S: The girl is wearing a blue, blue	
T: Sweater	(not coded)
S: A blue sweater.	Predictable information
	(Repetition not coded)

Comment in combination with Reaction to form/message

In the next four sections, the focus is on the remaining categories under *Incorporation of student/teacher utterances* – Comment, Expansion, Clarification request, and Elaboration request. These categories also co-occur with those in *Reaction to form/message*. We describe how the categories combine and provide examples and practice activities.

As discussed in Chapter 2, comments are any positive or negative responses, but not corrections to previous utterances. They can be evaluative in nature and respond to either form or meaning as the following two examples illustrate. In the first example, the teacher responds to the message of the student's utterance by making the comment that his opinion is not shared by his classmates. In the second, the teacher indicates that the student provided the correct lexical item, and this is therefore a comment on form.

Example 1

Teacher and student speech	Coding
S: I think school should start at 7:00 am.	
T: You're the only student who wants to start school earlier than later!	Message-Comment

Example 2

Teacher and student speech	Coding
T: What's the word in English?	
St: Trailer.	
T: Yes, that's right.	Form-Comment

---

14. If there is a need to code for these cues an additional category can be added.

Expansion in combination with Reaction to form/message

Recall that Expansions are defined as any extensions of the information provided in a preceding utterance or the addition of information which is related to it. Expansions can also be characterized as either form or message related. Look at the following two examples.

Example 1

Teacher and student speech	Coding
S: My father work at Bell....	
T: Veronique's mother does too – at the Bell Telephone Company.	Message- Expansion

Example 2

Teacher and student speech	Coding
S: J'ai arrivée.	
T: Je suis arrivée.	Form-Correction + Paraphrase
Remember 'arriver' is one of the verbs that takes 'être'.	Form-Expansion

In the first example, the teacher expands on the message of the student's previous utterance by extending it and providing additional information related to it. In the second example, the teacher first corrects the student's form through paraphrase. But she also expands on the student's utterance by providing additional information which is form related. It is important to note that when an incomplete utterance is completed by another student or the teacher, these completions are not considered as expansions. Look at the examples below. The first one contrasts with the second where S2 expands on the utterance.

Teacher and student speech	Coding
T: What movie did you see?	
S1: We saw...	Unpredictable information
S2: Avatar.	Unpredictable information

Teacher and student speech	Coding
T: What movie did you see?	
S1: We saw Avatar.	Unpredictable information
S2: Yeah, we saw it twice.	Message-Expansion

Clarification requests in combination with Reaction to form/message

Recall that Clarification requests are defined as requests indicating that the preceding utterance was not clearly understood, and a repetition or reformulation is required. They are most often coded as Message because they indicate that the preceding utterance was not heard or that something was missing (e.g., "Sorry, what did you say you wore to the party?"). In some cases, however, Clarification requests may also be form-related as in the example below.

Teacher and student speech	Coding
S: She gave her a fruit.	
T: What ...what did she give her? (pointing to a picture of a basket of fruit)	Form-Clarification request
S: Ah, she gave her a basket of fruit.	

Elaboration requests in combination with Reaction to form/message

Any requests for further information related to the subject matter of the preceding utterance are coded as Elaboration requests. Also, any requests for explanation (not for clarification) are coded under this category. They are coded as Message virtually all the time because they are defined as additional information related to the content of the preceding utterance. It is important to note that Elaboration requests are not coded as Pseudo or Genuine requests since they are considered requests that build on the shared discourse between speakers. If, however, there is a reason to distinguish between pseudo-elaboration requests and genuine-elaboration requests, a 'P' or a 'G' can be placed in the grid where a check mark would go. In the following excerpt, full coding has

Teacher and student speech	Coding
T: What did you do on the weekend?	L2/Genuine Req./Min.
S: I went to the ... (inaudible)	L2/Unpred.Info/Min./Unrestr.
T: Sorry, where did you go?	L2/Mess.-Clarif.Req./Min.
S: I went to see a movie.	L2/Unpred.Info/Min.Unrestr.
T: OK. What did you see?	L2/Mess.-Comment/L2/Mess.-Elab.Req./Min.
S: A movie with Julia Roberts. I can't remember the name.	L2/Unpred.Info/Unrestr./Min.

been provided for all relevant features on Part B. The teacher did not hear the last part of the student's initial response, therefore, the utterance "Sorry, where did you go?" is coded as a Clarification request. Subsequently, the teacher involved the student in further interaction by asking a related question and this has been coded as an Elaboration request (i.e., "What did you see?"). Note that a student's response following an elaboration request is coded under Predictable or Unpredictable information, and not under *Incorporation of student/teacher utterances.*

It is also worth noting that Elaboration requests can only follow a complete response; that is, the requested information has been provided. If a student gives an incomplete response or part of it was in the L1, and the teacher asks the same or a rephrased question, this would be coded as a Clarification request. The example below illustrates this.

Teacher and student speech	Coding
T: What did you do on the weekend?	
S: I went to a … (inaudible)	
T: Sorry, what did you do on the weekend?	Clarification request
S: I went to a party.	
T: Oh, you went to a party.	

Further requests for information are coded as Elaboration requests only if they are asked of the same student. Questions addressed to a new student or the whole class which may be thematically related would be coded as a Pseudo or Genuine request for information. Look at the following example.

Teacher and student speech	Coding
T: Which program did you watch last night?	
S: Star Trek.	
T: Did anyone else see Star Trek last night?	Genuine request

Practice 4

Look at the excerpts of classroom speech below and code the teacher turns that are under-lined according to whether they are Expansions, Clarification, or Elaboration requests. The answers are provided in the Answer Key at the end of the book.

1 Situation: The teacher is discussing a classroom procedure with a student.

Teacher and student speech	Coding
T: You return your paper	
S: Yes, and uh, I give at librarian.	
T: Give to the librarian?	
S: No, to the teacher	

2 Situation: The student is telling the teacher some songs that they have sung.

Teacher and student speech	Coding
T: What's another one that we have sung?	
S: Up, up, up.	

T: Up, up, up?

S: Yeah

3 Situation: The teacher is reading out loud to the whole class a story one of the students wrote.

Teacher and student speech	Coding
T: Exactly. So he said, "This is your friend and she is burned." When I said this story to my mother, she said, "Your friend is in hell." What's hell? Beatrice, can you explain hell?	
S1: Ah ha ha.	
S2: It's uh, opposite place of … it's uh where she the god is… the god.	
T: It's the opposite of where God is. Where is God?	
S1: In the sky.	

4 Situation: The teacher is asking the students about the television programs they watched.

Teacher and student speech	Coding
T: Yes. He was his clever self as usual? He was eh? What else? Anything else? Sebastien?	
S: Alf.	
T: You watched Alf. Do you watch it regularly? Every week or just sometimes?	
S: Every week.	
T: Every week. Is it a good program. Do you like it? Is it good every week?	
S: Yes.	

5 Situation: A student is describing an episode of a TV show called 'Head of the Class'.

Teacher and student speech	Coding
T: A TV program	
S: Yeah.	
T: Oh, OK.	
S: Yeah. He think he's like in that. And because I need the other in the class, um, the girl had hair like that.	
T: Spiky hair.	

S: Yeah, [ben], no, he uh, spiky ear.

T: Ears.

5: Like uh

T: Oh, like Mr. Spock. Thank you.

OK So... 'Head of the Class' it's about a group of   Code for utterances after this point only
students. There are not many students. I think
maybe six or seven students. And they are smart,
very intelligent and they are all in the same class.
And it's always with these students and their
teacher.

S: Have you...

T: I just watched it once.

Limitations of Incorporation of student/teacher utterances

Although the categories under *Incorporation of student/teacher utterances* allow for some distinction between the kinds of interactions which take place between teachers and students, it is important to emphasize that they are not sufficient to describe every feature of an utterance that occurs in the discourse. For example, the categories allow for distinctions in the way in which teachers correct (through paraphrase, repetition etc.), but they are not further broken down into categories such as repetition with or without emphasis or partial/complete paraphrase. The categories also do not permit distinctions in the kinds of clarification requests one might observe (i.e., confirmation requests versus comprehension checks).

Our intention in developing the categories under *Incorporation of student/teacher utterances* was to describe some features of the interactions between students and teachers, particularly those which are thought to represent important distinctions between form-based and meaning-based instruction. Depending on the observer's purpose, other categories can be added. For example, some users of COLT have expanded the categories for form-focused instruction and error correction. Examples of this are reported in Chapter 7. Alternatively, and as discussed in the introduction, more detailed analyses of classroom speech are probably best obtained through a discourse analysis approach to classroom observation.

Discourse initiation

Recall that the two remaining categories, *Discourse initiation and Form restriction*, are coded only for the student. While teachers initiate discourse virtually all the time in classrooms, there is considerable variation in the extent to which students are at liberty to do so. This is dependent on several factors including the teacher's style, the methodology and the size of the class.

As indicated in the category definitions in Chapter 2, *Discourse initiation* is measured in terms of the frequency of self-initiated turns by students. A check mark is placed in the column for any self-initiated requests for information or unsolicited responses to teacher or student utterances. Non-elicited incorporations of preceding utterances are also coded as *Discourse initiation*.

Some examples of *Discourse initiation* are given in Excerpt B at the beginning of this chapter in Figure 4.2. When the student made an unelicited comment on the special effects in the film 'Terminator 2' ("Yeah, that's true.") and asked the teacher about the movie she had seen ("What you see?"), this was coded as *Discourse initiation*. It is important to note that self-allocations, such as calling out an answer in response to a question, are not considered to be *Discourse initiation*.

Form restriction

The category *Form restriction* characterizes the extent to which the language students produce is limited in terms of linguistic form. The decision whether to code student speech as Restricted or Unrestricted is based upon the relative limitations on language use that are imposed by teacher, textbook, or type of activity and/or task. Note that the content of a student's utterance may be quite restricted while the form remains unrestricted. Look at the following example.

> T: What tense did we work on yesterday?
>
> St: Past

The content of the student's utterance is restricted since the student is expected to provide the answer "the past tense". However, the linguistic form the student uses to express the idea that it was the past tense is unrestricted since the teacher is not expecting the student to use specific language to express the idea. Typical examples of restricted use of form are:

- transformation and substitution drills
- reading aloud by individual students
- identification of vocabulary items (e.g., translations, giving synonyms, opposites etc.)
- singing (note that singing would be coded under *Choral* if the whole class is singing)
- rewriting a paragraph by changing present tense into past.

In exercises and activities like these, the language the students produce is restricted. Also coded as Restricted are student utterances/turns in which some linguistic freedom is permitted, but it is clear that the expectation of the teacher, text, or task is that the student produces a particular form(s). Consider the following example in which the teacher questions individual students in turn during an exercise on hypothetical clauses.

Teacher and student speech	Coding
T: What would you do if you had a million dollars?	Genuine request for information
S: I would buy a car.	Unpredictable/restricted form (the students were expected to use 'I would ...' in an isolated sentence)

Just as the students' language can be restricted and yet leave some room for linguistic variation, their language can also be largely unrestricted but include some restriction of linguistic forms. For example, the teacher may ask the students to write a composition about what they would do if they had a million dollars, but she reminds them to use the conditional form 'would'. This written activity contrasts with the oral drill-like example because most of the language produced would be unrestricted in a task that requires extended production through writing.

When coding for Restricted and Unrestricted it is important to keep in mind that several contextual factors (e.g., goals of a task or nature of interaction) contribute to these decisions. It is, therefore, important to verify levels of inter-rater reliability with this category as well as with other high inference categories.

Practice 5

Below are some excerpts from classroom transcripts. Code the student utterances that are underlined in terms of *Restricted/Unrestricted*. The answers are provided in the Answer Key at the end of the book.

1 Situation: The teacher is asking the students what they ate for lunch. Each student is expected to respond using the past tense.

Teacher and student speech	Coding
T: What did you eat? ... What did you eat? Andrée.	
S1: I ate egg rolls with chicken soo guy and rice.	_____
T: Oh, you're very lucky. Martin, what did you eat?	
S2: I ate a yammy and I drink 7up.	_____
T: You drank 7up. France?	
S3: I ate French fries and ... chips an a....	_____

2 Situation: The teacher is asking the students to answer a question correctly to be assigned a class job.

Teacher and student speech	Coding
T: Mélanie ... What is uh the word I want. What am I doing?	
S: Door knob. Door knob.	
T: OK. So if I say What am I doing? What do you answer?	
S: You are doing. you are turning off the light.	
T: Yeah. Good. Turning off the lights. And right now?	
S: Turning. you are turning on the lights.	

3 Situation: The students are describing foods they didn't want to try but later learned to like.

Teacher and student speech	Coding
T: What? What was it?	
S1: It was ah. ah chop suey.	
T: Chop suey.	
S1: I don't like but when I ate and ah. ah.	
T: Then you liked it? Somebody else? Yes, Pascal.	
S2: Fish.	
T: Fish? OK, so now you like it?	
S2: Yes.. ... mushroom.	

4 Situation: The students are describing weird things to eat.

Teacher and student speech	Coding
T: ... that's weird, do you know something weird?	
S: On the morning I take all the foo...... the food of all the jam of the Maple-Spread butter, caramel and I put all all what I found on my toast.	

Classroom transcripts

In this section, four excerpts of classroom transcripts are presented and coded for the Part B categories. The first two are from intensive ESL primary school classes in Quebec, Canada. These are classes in which young francophone learners at the grades 5 or 6 level receive approximately five hours of daily English instruction for five months of the school year. The ESL instruction is communicatively oriented and focuses on topics and themes relevant to the students' ages and interests. In the remaining 5 months of the school year, the students receive instruction in the regular school curriculum (i.e., mathematics, language arts) in French, the first language of most learners. Thus, these programs are not the same as Canadian French immersion programs in which the regular school curriculum is taught through the medium of the second language, French (see Lightbown & Spada, 1994 for more information about intensive ESL programs). The third transcript is an excerpt from a French junior secondary class in Australia (see the McKay summary in Chapter 7 for more discussion of these data). Transcript 4 is an excerpt from another intensive ESL class[15] and is included in Practice 6 as a coding activity.

Before we present the transcripts, a few general remarks on how they are organized, presented, and coded. For each transcript and as with previous examples in this chapter, the teacher (T) and student (S) speech are presented on the left-hand side of the page. The students' turns are marked by a number (S1, S2, etc.,) to indicate whether the same or a new student is speaking. On the right side of the page, the coding for the Part B communicative features is presented. At this point, it may be useful to review a few important coding conventions.

– The basic unit for coding is the teacher and student turn. Within each turn check marks are placed in the appropriate columns under each of the communicative features.
– Each time a check mark is placed in any of the categories under *Giving information* and *Requesting information* as well as under *Incorporation of student or student/teacher utterances*, a check mark is also entered for *Use of L1 or L2*. In addition, the categories under *Incorporation of student or student/teacher utterances* are also coded under *Reaction to Form/Message*.
– When coding for Predictable/Unpredictable, Pseudo request/Genuine request and the different *Incorporation of student or student/teacher utterances* categories, a new check mark is entered only when there is a change of category (e.g., when a pseudo request is followed by a genuine request) and not when, for example, three pseudo requests follow each other.

---

15. The first two transcripts, from intensive ESL classes, are unpublished data from Spada & Lightbown. Transcript 3 is unpublished data from McKay. Transcript 4 is adapted from Lightbown & Spada (1993).

- It is not until the end of each turn when decisions are made regarding whether the teacher turn was Minimal or Sustained and whether the student turn was Ultraminimal, Minimal or Sustained.

The coding categories for the Part B features have been separated by slashes (/). Sometimes there are two slashes (//) in the transcript and in the coding categories. This has been done to make it easier for the reader to see how utterances are coded in relation to changes in the categories. This is particularly helpful when a turn is long, and several categories follow each other. Note also that all turns are separated by ruled lines. Below is the key for the abbreviations used in the Part B coding. Some of them have already been explained and others are being used for the first time in the transcripts that follow.

Key abbreviations	Communicative features categories
L1	L1
L2	L2
Pred.Info	Giving predictable information
Unpred.Info	Giving unpredictable information
Pseudo Req.	Pseudo request
Gen.Req.	Genuine request
Ultram.	Ultraminimal (turn)
Min.	Minimal (turn)
Sust.	Sustained (turn)
Form	Form (reaction)
Mess.	Message (reaction)
Corr.	Correction
Rep.	Repetition
Para. (Para.(TR))	Paraphrase (Paraphrase – Translation)
Comment	Comment
Exp.	Expansion
Clarif.Req.	Clarification request
Elab.Req.	Elaboration request
D.I.	Discourse initiation
Chor.	Choral
Restr.	Restricted (form)
Unrestr.	Unrestricted (form)

Additional symbols

A hyphen is used between *Reaction to form/message* and the *Incorporation of student or student/teacher utterances* categories to indicate double coding, for example:

Mess.-Para.	a message-related paraphrase
Form -Clarif.Req.	a form-related clarification request

To indicate the type of correction, a + symbol is used, for example: correction + paraphrase. This means that the teacher corrected the student's utterance through paraphrasing.

Transcripts: Part A and B coding

Transcript 1: Intensive ESL

Figure 4.7 illustrates the Part A coding for three activities in an intensive ESL class for grade 6 learners. An excerpt of the transcript of the verbal interactions between the teacher and students in Activity 2 is also provided and this speech has been coded with the Part B categories. First, examine the activity descriptions and the coding on Part A. Then read the accompanying transcript for Activity 2 and look at how it has been coded according to the categories on Part B.

TIME	ACTIVITIES & EPISODES	PARTICIPANT ORGANIZATION							Manag.		CONTENT						CONTENT CONTROL			STUDENT MODALITY					MATERIALS							
		Class			Group		Individual				Language				Other topics										Type				Source			
																									Text							
		T↔S/C	S↔S/C	Choral	Same task	Different tasks	Same task	Different tasks	Procedure	Discipline	Form	Function	Discourse	Sociolinguistics	Narrow	Broad	Teacher/Text	Teacher/Text/Stud.	Student	Listening	Speaking	Reading	Writing	Other	Minimal	Extended	Audio	Visual	L2-NNS	L2-NS	L2-NSA	Student-made
1		3	4	5	6	7	8	9	10	11	12	13	14	15	16	17	18	19	20	21	22	23	24	25	26	27	28	29	30	31	32	33
A1 8:26	Greetings & Discussion of substitute teaching	✓							✓						✓		✓			✓	✓											
A2 8:30	Discussion of TV programs	✓													✓		✓			✓	✓				An excerpt of A2 has been coded for Part B.							
A3 8:38	Discussion of plans for next activity (skits)	✓							✓								✓			✓	✓											

Figure 4.7 Part A coding (transcript 1)

As illustrated in Figure 4.7, in Activity 2 the teacher is asking about what English TV programs the students watched. This activity has been coded as teacher-centred under the feature *Participant organization* on Part A. It has also been coded as Narrow under 'Other topics' in the main feature *Content*. Under the category *Content control*, it has been coded as Teacher/text, and Listening and Speaking have been coded under *Student modality*. Now let's look at the language produced in this activity and see how the teacher and student verbal interactions were coded with Part B.

Teacher & student speech	Coding
T: Did anyone watch a TV program last night?	L2/Gen.Req./Min.
S1: No.[16]	L2/Unpred.Info/Unrestr./Ultram.
T: Lyna? Watched it in English?	L2/Gen.Req./Min.
S2: The (inaudible)	L2 (uncodable)
T: I want, I don't want to know if you watched French TV programs, I want to know if you watched English. Remi?	L2/Mess.-Comment/Min.
S3: Yes.	L2/Unpredinfo/Unrestr./Ultram.
T: What?	L2/Mess.-Clarif.Req./Min.
S3: 'Highway to Heaven', that's a good program.	L2/Unpredinfo/Unrestr./Min.
S4: On, uh, Tuesday, uh, what going to do on Tuesday, I uh.	D.I./L2/Gen.Req./Unrestr./Min.
T: Watch 'Who's the Boss'. That's good, this is one of my favourites. It's very good. Yes?	L2/Unpred.Info/Sust.

---

16. All student turns have been numbered to indicate whether a new student is speaking or whether the teacher is involved in more extended discourse with one student. We cannot always tell from the audio-recordings or transcripts whether the same student may have had another turn later, i.e., S1 and S5 may be the same student. To maintain more precision and to examine individual students, video recording of the classroom interaction is recommended.

S5: Have you, have you seen the TV program// because yesterday I have uh … how do you say a [rendezvous]?	D.I./L2/Gen.Req.//[17] L2/Unpred.Info// L2/Gen.Req./Min. L2/Unpred.Info/Min.
T: Uh, uh, a meeting.	
S5: Meeting// for my teeth.	L2/Form-Rep.// L2/Mess.-Exp./Unrestr./Min.
T: Ah.	L2/Mess.-Comment/Min.
S5: At the dentist. And the dentist don't like a wait.	L2/Mess.-Exp/Unrestr./Min.
T: OK// Someone else? José?	L2/Mess.Comment//L2/ Gen.Req./Min.
S6: I, uh, watch 'Head of the Class' –	L2/Unpred.Info/Unrestr./Min.
T: 'Head of the Class'!! Was it the first time you watched it?	L2/Mess.Rep.//L2/Elab.Req./Min.
S6: Yes.	L2/Unpred.Info/Unrestr./Ultram.
T: Did you like it?	L2/Mess.-Elab.Req./Min.
S6: Yes	L2/Unpred.Info/Unrestr.f Ultram.
T: 'Head of the Class'. Could you tell the class, uh, … 'Head of the Class'. Could you tell the class what it's about?	L2/Mess.-Elab.Req/Min.
S6:[benl uh, a boy with, uh, the test dream all the time the the test and when the he come back after and test is finished and uh was was the first question in the …	(Ll ignored)[18]/L2/Unpred.Info/Sust.

---

17. Here is an example of a double slash which indicates that the category has changed and the coding for the next category should be on a separate line on the coding sheet for Part B.

18. We have decided to ignore expletives or fillers in the LI.

T: He was only at the first question.	L2/Mess.-Para/Min.
S6: Because, um, [ben] dreaming all the time.	L2/Mess.-Exp./Min.
T: OK	L2/Mess.-Comment/Min.
S6: Because of, he uh he at the girl. for the girl.	L2/Mess.-Exp./Unrestr./Min.
T: Ah, he was thinking of his girlfriend.	L2/Mess.-Para./Min.
S6: No, //but not a girl [ben] ...	L2/Mess.-Comment// L2/Mess.-Exp./Unrestr./Min.
T: Girls in general.	L2/Mess.-Para/Min.
S6: Yes.// All the, the like uh a cosmos, he dreaming of uh cosmos named (inaudible)	L2/Mess.-Comment/L2/Mess-Exp./Unrest./Min.
T: What's that?	L2/Mess.-Clarif.Req./Min.
S6: Program TV.	L2/Unpred.Info/Unrestr./Ultram.
T: A TV program?	L2/Mess.-Clarif.Req.[19]/Min.
S6: Yeah.	L2/Unpred.Info/Unrestr./Ultram.
T: Oh. OK	L2/Mess.-Comment/Min.
S6: Yeah. He think he's like in that. And because I need the other in the class, um, the girl had hair like that.	L2/Mess.-Exp./Unrestr./Sust.
T: Spiky hair.	L2/Mess.-Exp./Min.
S6: Yeah, [ben], no, he uh, spiky ear.	L2/Mess.-Comment/L2/Mess.-Para./Unrestr./Min.

19. One could argue that the teacher's utterance 'A TV program?' could also be coded as a Form-related Correction + Paraphrase. We decided to code it as a Message-related Clarification request, since the teacher seems to be focusing on what (rather than how) the student is saying it. In cases like these it may help to listen to the audio-recording again, if, for example, the teacher had emphasized 'A' to indicate that an article is needed or stressed the position of 'TV' in the sentence, it would more likely be a form-related reaction.

T: Ears.	L2/Form-Corr.+Para./Min.
S6: Like uh...	L2/Mess.-Exp./Unrestr./Ultram.
T: Oh, like Mr. Spock. Thank you. OK So... 'Head of the Class' it's about a group of students. There are not many students. I think there are maybe six or seven students. And they are smart, very intelligent and they are all in the same class. And it's always with these students and their teacher. Something like that.	L2/Mess.-Exp.// L2/Gen.Req.// L2/Mess.-Exp./Sust.
S6: Have you...?	D.I./L2/Gen.Req./Unrestr./Ultram.
T: I just watched it once. Someone else watch a TV program? [20]	L2/Unpred.Info// L2/Gen.Req./Sust.

Transcript 2: Intensive ESL

Below is another example of Part A and B coding for an excerpt from a grade 5 intensive ESL class. Look at the description and the coding for the Part A activity level analysis first (Figure 4.8) and then examine how the speech within the activities has been coded for Part B. For this example, the Part B coding begins in Activity 2, Episode 2. In this episode, the teacher asks students to correct errors in compositions written by the students on the topic 'A mysterious waiter'. The Part B coding extends into Episode 3 in which the teacher continues to read the students' compositions but with more focus on meaning than form.

---

20. In this excerpt the teacher has a long interaction with the same student (S6), even though the student's turns are principally Ultraminimal or Minimal. As a way of indicating such sustained interactions on your coding sheet for Part B, brackets {...} could be placed around the section coded for the student's verbal interaction.

TIME	ACTIVITIES & EPISODES	PARTICIPANT ORGANIZATION							CONTENT								CONTENT CONTROL			STUDENT MODALITY					MATERIALS							
		Class			Group		Individual		Manag.		Language				Other topics										Type				Source			
																									Text							
		T↔S/C	S↔S/C	Choral	Same task	Different tasks	Same task	Different tasks	Procedure	Discipline	Form	Function	Discourse	Sociolinguistics	Narrow	Broad	Teacher/Text	Teacher/Text/Stud.	Student	Listening	Speaking	Reading	Writing	Other	Minimal	Extended	Audio	Visual	L2-NNS	L2-NS	L2-NSA	Student-made
1	2	3	4	5	6	7	8	9	10	11	12	13	14	15	16	17	18	19	20	21	22	23	24	25	26	27	28	29	30	31	32	33
A2,E1 9:20	T reads Sts compositions about a mysterious waiter	√														√		√		√	√					√						√
A2,E2 9:23	Tdiscusses Sts errors; asks students to correct	√									√					√		√		√	√											
A2,E3 9:38	Teacher continues reading Sts compositions	√									√					√		√		√	√					√						√

Part B coding starts with A2, E2 and extends into Episode 3.

Figure 4.8 Part A coding (transcript 2)

Teacher & student speech	Coding
T: Now we have another disgusting story.//Now here, can someone tell me the mistake?// Listen to the first sentence that the person wrote. 'There are two days ago.'	L2/Unpred.Info// L2/Pseudo Req.// L2/Unpred.Info/Sust.
S1: Is.[21]	L2/Pred.Info/Unrestr./Ultram.
S2: Are. Are.	L2/Pred.Info/Unrestr./Ultram.
S3: It's 'it'.	L2/Pred.Info/Unrestr./Min.
S4: There are?	L2/Pred. Info/Restr./Min.
S5: Il y a deux jours – en français.	LI (Para.(TR))[22]
T: There are two days ago. What's the problem here? S6: Two day ago.	L2/Pseudo Req./Min. L2/Pred.Info/Restr./Min.
T: Well, what's the, what should it be, Caroline? … Can someone tell me the correct answer?	L2/Pseudo Req./Min.
S7: The…	L2/Ultram.Rest uncodable
T: I might have a ticket here for for the correct answer. Sylvia? (This refers to some kind of reward system the teacher has introduced.)	L2/Unpred.Info/Min.
S8: Uh, two days ago.	L2/Pred.Info/Restr./Min.
T: Correct.// OK. So you get a ticket.	L2/Mess.-Comment//Unpred.lnfo/Min.
S: 9: I know, I know it too.	D.l./L2/Unpred.Info/Unrestr/Min.
S10: Hey!	D.1. (uncodable)

21. Student turns are again numbered to indicate that a new student is speaking; in other words, to indicate that the teacher is not involved in prolonged discourse with the same student.

22. Depending on the user's purpose it may be useful to code L1 utterances in more detail.

S11: I had my hand before uh, her.	D.I.1L2/Unpred.Info/Unrestr./Min.
S12: Na, na, na ..	Uncodable)
T: Remember, when we're talking you, this person mixed up the French. In French you would say [Il y a …] the, we say two days ago'. So that was the little problem at the beginning.// (Time: 9:24 – compare Part A) OK. Are you ready for this disgusting story?// (Reads) Two days ago I said to my mother: 'Can I go to, can I go with my friend to the restaurant please?' And she didn't want. But I went to hide with Jenny. Later, I went to the restaurant and! saw a strange waiter. The waiter was mysterious because he had a hole in his stomach.	L2/Unpred.Info// L2/Gen.Req.// L2/Unpred.Info[23]/Sust.
S13: A what?	D.I./L2/Mess.-Clarif.Req./Unrestr./Ultram.
T: A hole in his stomach.	L2/Mess.-Rep./Min.
S13: What's a hole?	D.I./L2/Form-Clarif.Req./Unrestr./Min.
T: What's a hole?// In English!	L2/Pseudo Req.// L2/Unpred.Info(managerial)/Min.
S14: I know.	L2/Unpred.Info/Unrestr./Min.
S15: It's a, a big uh, no, uh …	L2/Unpred.Info/Unrestr./Min.
T: OK. There is nothing. Yeah. OK. Nothing. OK. There's a hole there.// On your paper you have three holes.	L2/Mess.-Para.// L2/Mess.-Exp/Sust.
S16: Oh, It's a [trou].	D.1./L2/L1/Form-Para(TR)/Unrestr./ Min.
T: Who said it's a [trou]?	L2/L1/Gen.Req./Min.

---

23. Since the text is being read for the first time, it is coded as Unpredictable information. Note that if a text is known to the class and is not read for the first time, it is coded as Predictable information.

S16: Me.	L2/Unpred.lnfo/Unrestr./Ultram.
T: I said specifically no French!! OK, then. So anyway. The waiter was mysterious because he had a big hole in his stomach. He said, 'How many people?'. I said, 'Two people and in the No Smoking section.' But he gave my friend one table for one person and one big table for me. Later, he went next to me and said, 'What would you like?' And I said, 'Poutine and one coke.' Very later, waiter came with a very, very big plate. And he opened the plate and said, 'This is your friend, and she is burnt.'// Burnt, what's burnt?	L2/Mess.-Comment// L2/Unpred.Info// L2/Pseudo Req./Sust.
S17: Burn. Burned. Burned.	L2/ (uncodable)
S18: Like a sunburn. Like a sunburn.	L2/Unpred.Info/Unrestr./Mm.
T: Sun burn.// We had sunburn. Yes. If I take some matches and put it here, you'd burn yourself.	L2/Mess.-Rep.// L2/Mess.-Exp./Sust.

Transcripts: Part B coding

The next two excerpts from classroom transcripts are not accompanied by the Part A activity level analysis. Transcript 3 is from a French junior secondary class in Australia and Transcript 4 is from another communicative intensive ESL class. The first transcript has been fully coded with the Part B categories. Transcript 4 has not been coded. Instead, it is presented in Practice 6 for the reader to code and then to check it with the Answer Key at the end of the book.

Transcript 3: French junior secondary class

In this transcript you will notice the frequent use of translation in the L1 (i.e., English). Although it was indicated earlier that we do not code for any further categories of Part B when the L1 is used, because there is so much use of the L1 in this transcript, we have coded the Part B categories which occur in the L1.

Teacher & student speech	Coding
T: ... bon ... (reading) chez le médecin ... Monsieur Laurent est malade ... Monsieur	L2/Pred.lnfo// L1/Gen.Req./Sust.

Laurent est malade ...,// er did you understand about the articles?.., for homework you did ... 286 A and B?	
S1: A and B	L1/Unpred.Info/Unrestr./Ultram.
S2: What page?	D.I./L1/Gen.Req./Unrestr./Ultram.
T: Page two hundred and eighty-six// Chez le médecin ...// Lisez, s'il vous plait ...// qui veut etre medecin?// Who wants to be the doctor?	Ll/Unpred.Info// L2/Pred.Info// L2/Unpred.Info (managerial)// L2/Gen.Req.// Ll/Gen.Req. (TR)[24]/Sust.
S3: Ooh...	(Uncodable)
S4: Doctors and nurses	D.I./Ll/Unpred.Info/Unrestr./Ultram.
S5: Moi.	L2/Unpred.Info/Unrestr./Ultram.
T:- Maria ... le médecin ...// Monsieur Laurent? ... qui veut être Monsieur Laurent? ... Paul// Allez Lisa ... allez vite ...// (reading) Monsieur Laurent est malade il va chez le médecin...// Allez le médecin	L2/Unpred.Info (managerial)// L2/Gen.Req.// L2/Unpred.Info (managerial)// L2/Pred.Info// L2/Unpred.Info (managerial)[25]/Sust.
S5: OK[26]... (reading) Comment allez-vous aujourd'hui?	L2/Pred.Info/Restr//Min.
S6: (Reading) Pas trop bien ...j'ai mal ... partout	L2/Pred. Info/Restr./Min

---

24. Note that translation is generally coded under Paraphrase when the translation is an incorporation of a previous speaker's utterance. In this transcript, however, the teacher frequently translates his/her own utterances. This does not constitute an incorporation. In the context of this transcript, the symbol TR therefore indicates that this Part B category (i.e., Genuine Request) is a translation of the previous one. This symbol will be used throughout the coding of this transcript.

25. This segment of the teacher's speech was interpreted as a command for the student to start reading his/ her part and therefore coded it as a managerial directive.

26. Filler words, such as 'OK', are ignored in this coding.

S5: (*Reading*) Vous avez de la [fever]?	L2/LI/Pred.Info/Restr./Min.
Non //.. de la fièvre.	L2/Form-Comment// L2/Form-Corr.+Para./Min.
OK... de la fièvre.	L2/Form-Rep/Restr./Min.
T: Fever is English//... de la fièvre hn?	L1/Form-Exp.// L2/Form-Rep./Min.
S5: Well ... you know	L1/uncodable[27]/Unrestr./Min.
T: OK.. (*reading*) oui un peu...	L2/Pred.Info/Min.
S6: (*Reading*) Oui ... un peu... j'ai trente..... trente huit... le matin et trente neuf le soir	L2/Pred.Info/Restr./Min.
S5: (*Reading*) Est-ce que vous prenez des médicaments?	L2/Pred.Info/Restr./Min.
(*Reading*) Oui .. de l'aspirine parce que j'ai trés mal... très mal à la tête... c'est grave docteur?	L2/Pred.Info/Restr./Min.
(*Reading*) Mais non.... vous avez un bon rhume ...//isn't that right, Miss?	L2/Pred.Info/Restr.// L1/Gen.Req./Unrestr./Min.
T: Qui//un bon rhume	L2/Unpred.Info// L2/Form-Rep.[28]/Min.
S5: OK... (*reading*) C'est tout?	L2/Pred.lnfo/Restr./Min.
S6: (*Reading*) Qu'est-ce que je peux faire, docteur?	L2/Pred.Info/Restr./Min.
S5: (*Reading*) Pas grand-chose restez à la maison et continuez à prendre de l'aspirine.	L2/Pred.Info/Restr./Min.

27. It is not clear what the student intends to say, but it could possibly be coded as a Message-Comment.
28. It was assumed that the student wanted to check his/her pronunciation of 'un bon rhume' and that the teacher subsequently confirmed the correctness and repeated the student's utterance.

T: De l'aspirine// ... bon alors[29] (*reading very fast*) Monsieur Laurent est malade, il va chez le médecin ... Comment allez-vous aujourd'hui?//Vous comprenez la première question?//You understand?// Comment allez-vous aujourd'hui, hn? Pas trop bien ... pas trop bien// Not...?	L2/Mess.-Rep.[30]// L2/Pred.Info// L2/Gen.Req.// L1/Gen.Req. (TR)// L2/Pred.Info// L1/Pseudo Req.[31]/Sust.
S5: Not very well.	Ll/Pred.Info (TR)/Restr./Min.
T: Very... too ...... not very well.// J'ai mal partout ... ehn? //I'm...	L1/Form-Rep.// L2/Pred.Info// Ll/Pseudo Req./Min.
S5: I've got a...	L1/Pred.Info (TR)/Restr./Min.
S7: sore everywhere.	L1/Pred.lnfo./Restr./Ultram.
T: ... aching everywhere .... I'm aching everywhere// (*reading*) Vous avez de la fièvre...// alors	L1/Form-Para.// L2/Pred.Info// L2/Pseudo.Req./Min.
S8: You've got a fever.	Ll/Pred.Info (TR)/Restr./Min.
T: (*Reading*) Oui un peu...// What does it mean 'un peu'?	L2/Pred.Info// L1/L2/Pseudo Req./Min.

---

29. 'Bon alors' is considered a filler and is therefore ignored.

30. From the transcript alone it is impossible to judge whether this repetition is message-or form-related. In a case like this it would be necessary to check the audio-recording. If, for example, the teacher corrected the student's pronunciation of 'de l'aspirine' by repeating it, Form would be checked off. If, on the other hand, the teacher repeated the last few words the student has read, perhaps to indicate the end of the reading passage, the repetition would most likely be Message related.

31. Here the teacher is eliciting a translation, which is a pseudo request for information. We do not have a specific category for eliciting translation. If a teacher uses this strategy consistently to check comprehension, it might be useful to make a special note of it.

S8: Yes...ah, yes	L1(uncodable)
T: Un peu?//... opposite of ?// A little bit...... not too well// (reading) er .. un peu J'ai trente huit le matin et trente neuf le soir, hn?// le soir, what's 'le soir'...Tran?//... le matin ... le soir...... vous savez le matin...	L2/Pseudo Req.// L1/Pseudo Req// LI /Pred.Info// L2 /Pred.Info// L1/L2Pseudo Req.// L2/Unpred.Info/Sust.

Practice 6

Code Transcript 4 with the Part B features and check your decisions with the coding provided in the Answer Key.

Transcript 4: Intensive ESL

Situation: Students tell class what 'bugs' them. They have written 'What bugs me' on a card or piece of paper which they hold up while speaking.

Teacher & student speech	Coding
St: It bugs me when a bee string me.	
T: Oh, when a bee stings me.	
S1: Stings me.	
T: Do you get stung often? Does that happen often? The stinging many times?	
S1: Yeah	
T: Often?// (T turns to students who aren't paying attention) OK Chantal Luc, you may begin working on a research project, hey? (T turns her attention back to 'What bugs me')	
S2: It bugs me (inaudible) and my sister put on my clothes	
T: Ah! She ... borrows your clothes?//	

When you're older, you may appreciate it because you can switch clothes, maybe.//	
Monique ... this is yours, I will check ... OK. It's good.	
S3: It bugs me when I'm sick and my brother doesn't help me my, my brother, cause he ... me...	
T: OK. You know, when ...(*inaudible*) sick, you're sick at home in bed and you say, oh, to your brother your sister: Would you please get me a drink of water?' ... Ah! Drop dead!',you know, 'Go play in the traffic!' You know, it's not very nice. Jean!	
S4: It bug me to have ...	
T: It bugs me. It bugzz me.	
S4; It bugs me// when my brother takes my bicycle. Every day.	
T: Every day?// Ah! Doesn't your bro.. (inaudible) his bicycle? Could his brother lend his bicycle? Uh, your. brother doesn't have a bicycle?	
S4: Yeah.! A new bicycle (*inaudible*) bicycle.	
T: Ah, well. Talk to your morn and dad about it. Maybe negotiate a new bicycle for your brother.	
S5: (inaudible)	
T: He has a new bicycle.// But his brother needs a new one too?	
S5: Yes.	

T: Hey, whoa, just a minute!

S6: Frédérique's brother has...

T: Frédérique, who has a new bicycle?
You or your brother?

S4: My brother.

T: And you have an old one?

S4 (inaudible)

T: And your brother takes your old one?

S4: ... clutch ... (inaudible) bicycle.

T: His bicycle!//
Ah! How old is your brother?

S4: March 23.

T: His birthday?

S4: Yeah!

T: And how old was he?

S4: Fourteen.

T: Fourteen!!
Well, why don't you tell your brother that when
he takes your bike you will take his bike. And he
may have more scratches than he figures for.
OK?

CHAPTER 5

Analyzing the data

The last few chapters have presented detailed information about the coding conventions for COLT Part A and Part B. This chapter provides guidelines for the analysis and synthesis of the coded data. It also includes additional information about data collection, which was briefly referred to in Chapters 3 and 4. It is important to emphasize that the methods of data analysis and synthesis described here are best viewed as suggestions. There are many ways in which the instructional data can be treated, and this will necessarily depend on the purposes for using the COLT scheme.

There are three sections in this chapter: the first describes the collection, analysis, and synthesis of data coded with Part A and the second focuses on Part B. Both sections are based on the original procedures carried out by hand using the COLT spreadsheets (i.e., paper and pencil). In the third section, information about how to use a new computer-based numerical approach for the coding, analysis, and synthesis of Part B data is provided. In the next chapter descriptions of how to use the recently developed digital systems for the analysis and synthesis of data collected with COLT Part A are outlined.

COLT Part A

Data collection

At the beginning of Chapter 3, we pointed out that the categories in Part A are coded in 'real time', that is, while the observer is present in the classroom or via audio and/or video recordings. While coding for the Part A categories, it may also be useful to take additional notes about other aspects of the instruction that might not be adequately covered by the categories to obtain as complete a picture as possible of the overall period of observation. These notes can either be written on the back of the COLT Part A spreadsheet or on separate sheets of paper.

Collecting the Part A data in 'real time' in a classroom setting requires that the observer is present in as unobtrusive a manner as possible. Our experience has been that students and teachers adjust quickly to an observer and after a short period of time proceed as usual. During the observation period, brief activity/episode descriptions are recorded in the blank space on the spreadsheet and check marks are placed in all the relevant categories of Part A. If recordings (audio and/or video) of the classroom interaction are made, these can be used for subsequent Part B analysis and verification, if necessary, of the Part A coding. Ideally, video recordings capture the most information; however, video equipment is also more obtrusive, and it usually takes teachers and students much longer to feel comfortable and to proceed normally. Furthermore, for the purposes of transcription, it is usually easier to work from audio than from video recordings.

When the observation period is over and all the coding has been completed, the observer may want to verify some of the coding decisions with the teacher. It is also important to determine, in those cases where two observers are present, that they are making the same coding decisions by investigating inter-rater reliability.

Recall that the basic unit of analysis is the episode or the activity if the latter does not consist of any episodes. It is important to ensure that the activities and their constituent episodes have been timed and numbered during the observation period to determine the percentage of time spent on the various categories both within individual activities/episodes and across the entire lesson.

Analysis and synthesis of the coded data

To illustrate the coding procedures, we will use the data in Figure 5.1, where the observed lesson lasted thirty minutes. First, calculate the duration of each episode or activity, by subtracting the starting time of an episode/activity from the starting time of the following episode/activity. In this lesson, there were three activities. The first two activities had two episodes each and the last activity stood on its own. Activity 1, Episode 1 lasted three minutes (from 9:00 to 9:03), the second episode in this activity lasted two minutes. Activity 2, Episode 1 was five minutes long, while the second episode of Activity 2 lasted fifteen minutes. The third and final activity of this class lasted five minutes.

The next step is to calculate the percentage of time spent on each of the categories under the major features (*Participant organization, Content, Content control, Student modality* and *Materials*). For example, included within the category *Participant organization*, will be the percentage of class time the teacher worked with the whole class (T↔S/C) or did choral work, what percentage of time the students worked in groups, doing the same or different tasks, and so on. To determine this, the first step is to select those episodes which have only one check mark or one circled check mark. Recall that one check mark means an exclusive focus on that category during the activity/episode and a circled check mark indicates a primary focus. These are illustrated in Figure 5.1 for *Participation organization* and the calculations for them are described.

Calculations for exclusive focus

Column 3 (T↔S/C) was checked off as an exclusive focus in Activity 1, Episode 1. The same occurred in Activity 3. These two instructional units lasted a total of eight minutes A1, E1 = 3 minutes; A2 = 5 minutes), yielding a percentage value of 26.67. In other words, the teacher spent 26.67% of the thirty-minute class interacting exclusively with the whole class or individual students.

The categories under Group work received two check marks in column 6, indicating that the students worked in groups on the same task. In Activity 2, Episode 2, this is the only check mark for the section *Participant organization*, thus indicating an exclusive focus. However, in Activity 2, Episode 1, column 8 is also checked off, which means that during that episode, there was an equal focus on Group work and Individual seat work. Let us first deal with the exclusive check mark in Activity 2, Episode 2. This indicates that students were involved in group work, focusing on the same task for fifteen minutes which represents 50% of the entire class time.

Calculations for primary focus

In Activity 1, Episode 2, there is a circled check mark in column 4 (S↔S/C). This means that a student was interacting with the whole class or individual students, while one central activity was going on. There was also some teacher-centred interaction (as indicated by a check mark in column 3), but this was not the primary *Participant organization* during that episode. This episode lasted two minutes or 6.67% of the total lesson time. Note that the check mark in column 3 (T↔S/C) is not taken into consideration in this calculation. This is discussed in more detail below. All the percentages for the categories under *Participant organization* which received an exclusive or primary focus have now been calculated and this accounts for 83.34% of the class time (i.e., 26.67% T↔S/C; 6.67% S↔S/C; 50% Group/Same task).

	TIME	ACTIVITIES & EPISODES	PARTICIPANT ORGANIZATION						
			Class			Group		Individual	
			T↔S/C	S↔S/C	Choral	Same task	Different tasks	Same task	Different tasks
	1	2	3	4	5	6	7	8	9
	9:00	A1, E1	√						
3 min.	9:03	A1, E2	√	(√)					
2 min.	9:05	A2, E1				√		√	
5 min.	9:10	A2, E2				√			
15 min.	9:25	A3	√						
5 min.	9:30	Class Ends							

Figure 5.1 Timing activities/episodes and calculating *Participant organization*

Calculations for combinations

Activity 2, Episode 1, which lasted for five minutes, has not yet been calculated. This episode provides an example of a combination of features in which two received equal focus. Combinations should be calculated separately from an exclusive or primary focus and must be reported separately. In this case, during 16.66% of the class time, some students worked in groups, while others worked alone, all involved in the same task.

Grouping the data within features

Once the data have been analyzed in this manner, it may be useful to represent them by summarizing all percentage values under the categories Class, Group, and Individual. For example, in the data described above, a summary would indicate that 33.34% of the lesson time was spent involving the whole Class in a central activity, 50% on Group work, and 16.66% on a combination of Group and Individual seat work.

It is important to note once again that the secondary foci (i.e., check marks which do not indicate either a primary/exclusive focus or combinations with equal focus) were ignored in our calculations above. We have not included these because in our work with COLT we have been more interested in those categories which are most prominent in different classroom settings. Depending on the goals of the research, it may be important to take note of these secondary emphases.

So far, we have demonstrated the procedure for the first main feature; that is *Participant organization*. The same procedure is followed for all other main features (*Content, Content control, Student modality* and *Materials*). Below is an activity to practise these calculations with the *Content* category.

Practice 7

Using the coding for the *Content* categories in Figure 5.2, calculate the percentage of time spent on exclusive/primary and combined features. The solutions can be found in the Answer Key at the end of the book. Remember that it is important to calculate and report a combined focus of features together and not to divide them by the number of features. For example, if one check mark appears under 'Language' and another under 'Other topics' for the same activity/episode without circles to indicate a primary focus, these check marks should be calculated and reported together. That is, the activity/episode should be described as a combination of form and meaning ('Language' and 'Other topics') for 100% of the time, not as 50% form and 50% meaning.

TIME	ACTIVITIES & EPISODES	PARTICIPANT ORGANIZATION							CONTENT							
		Class			Group		Individual		Manag.		Language				Other topics	
		T↔S/C	S↔S/C	Choral	Same task	Different tasks	Same task	Different tasks	Procedure	Discipline	Form	Function	Discourse	Sociolinguistics	Narrow	Broad
1	2	3	4	5	6	7	8	9	10	11	12	13	14	15	16	17
3 min	A1, E1								✓	✓					✓	
2 min	A1, E2										✓				✓	
5 min	A2, E1										✓	✓			✓	
15 min	A2, E2											✓	✓		✓	
5 min	A3															✓
30 min	Class ends															

Figure 5.2 Calculating content categories

Grouping the data by visit, class, and program

The calculations discussed up to this point are those which are carried out separately for individual class visits. The classroom data can also be summarised by class and program. This is illustrated in Tables 5.1, 5.2 and 5.3.[32]

Table 5.1 represents two visits each to Class 1 and Class 2 in Program X. Both classes were thirty minutes in length. During the first visit in Class 1, the teacher interacted with individual students or the whole class for fifteen minutes (i.e., 50%). The remaining fifteen minutes were spent in group work (i.e., 50%). During the second visit, Class 1 spent 10 minutes in whole class interaction (i.e., 33.33%) and 20 minutes in group work (i.e., 66.67%). In Class 2, the teacher spent 100% of the time during both visits in whole class interaction.

Table 5.1 Percentage of *Participant organization* by visit

	Whole class T↔S/C		Group	
Program X				
	Visit 1	Visit 2	Visit 1	Visit 2
Class 1	50.00	33.33	50.00	66.67
Class 2	100.00	100.00	0.00	0.00

---

32. Tables 5.1, 5.2 and 5.3 are adapted from Fröhlich, Spada, & Allen (1985).

Table 5.2 shows the percentage of *Participant Organization* by class. For example, look-ing at Class 1, you can see that the teacher spent 41.66% of the time in whole class inter-action. This represents the sum of the percentages of the two visits described in Table 5.1 divided by 2. Similarly, 58.34% of the time was spent in group work interaction.

Table 5.2 Percentage of *Participant organization* by class

	Whole class T-S/C	Group
Class 1	41.66	58.34
Class 2	100.00	0.00

Table 5.3 represents the percentage of *Participant Organization* by program. For exam-ple, in Program X, 70.83% of the total observed time was spent on whole class interaction and 29.17% of the time on group work.

Table 5.3 Percentage of *Participant organization* by program

	Whole class T-S/C	Group
Program X	70.83	29.17

The observational data collected with Part A of COLT and quantified in the manner described above can provide information regarding instructional differences between classes, methods, and programs. Quantifying the data in this way also permits statistical analyses to examine relationships between a variety of classroom variables and learning out-comes. Some examples of this type of research are presented in Chapter 7.

The descriptions of class activities and their constituent episodes can also be used for a qualitative analysis of instructional variables. For example, it may be of interest to develop a typology of classroom activities to determine which activities lend themselves to differ-ent patterns of *Participant organization*, which activities are characterized by a differential focus on Language features, such as Form or Sociolinguistics etc. These questions may be of particular interest to teachers and teacher educators. A typology of activities would also provide a more clearly defined unit of analysis for research purposes (see Valcárcel et al. in Chapter 7).

Below is a description of how the data can be analyzed and synthesized using the Part B coding procedures described in Chapter 4. This is followed by a description of the recently developed numerical computer-assisted approach to coding and analyzing Part B data.

COLT Part B

Data collection

The Part B categories provide a detailed description of the verbal interactions that take place between teacher/students and students/students; therefore, it is not possible to code for these features during an observation period. Instead, audio and/or video recordings must be made for later transcription, coding, and analysis. Audio/video recordings are also useful for verifying the coding for Part A, which is especially important when a less experienced observer is using the scheme.

Depending on the size of the classroom and the type and quality of recording equipment, it is recommended to use two recorders and place them at opposite ends of the classroom. The second recorder also provides a backup in case of equipment (or human) failure. It is also advised to place a wireless microphone on the teacher. Where possible, consultation with a recording expert is useful to ensure proper placement of microphones, particularly in those cases where considerable group work interaction takes place.

Coding the data

Once the transcript is prepared,[33] coding is preferably done by two coders. If the coders differ in their coding decisions, this is usually an indication that the categories are not sufficiently clear and/or that the coders have interpreted them differently. Problems such as these must be addressed before any further coding is done. When the coding is completed, it is important to investigate inter-rater reliability.

In Chapter 3 it was suggested that the coders can choose to code the entire observation period or adopt a time-sampling procedure (e.g., code one out of every three minutes of classroom interaction). The latter choice means that a portion of the data is not accounted for and decisions about which option to select will depend on the research purpose. For example, if the focus of attention is on how conversations are structured in terms of topic initiation, expansion and continuation, a time-sampling procedure would fragment the data in ways which would make it inappropriate for coding in this manner. If, however, the goal is to determine the proportion of message reactions to form reactions, a time-sampling procedure would be able to provide this information. Again, depending on the research purpose, decisions about how many categories to code for might also vary. In some situations, a decision to code for all seven features will be made. It may be appropriate in other circumstances to select only one or two features. For example, a researcher may be interested only in whether teachers ask genuine or pseudo questions or whether their corrections provide any metalinguistic information.

---

33. Although it is possible for the coding to be done from audio/video tape, only highly experienced users of the scheme should do so. It is strongly recommended that Part B coding be done from transcripts.

It will be recalled that the basic unit for coding and for later analysis is the teacher and student turn. Within each turn, the coder places check marks in the appropriate columns whenever any of the categories occur. New check marks are entered only when there is a change in one of the categories, and not when several uninterrupted instances of the same category occur. For example, if the teacher (or student) asks three genuine questions in a sequence, only one check mark is placed under genuine requests for the *Information Gap* feature. However, if the teacher makes two genuine requests for information, followed by a pseudo request, followed by another genuine request, three check marks would be entered – one for the first two genuine requests, one for the pseudo-request and one for the last genuine request.[34]

Analysis by communicative feature

Each Part B category is calculated as a proportion of its main feature. Some of the communicative features involve binary distinctions while others have three or more categories. To calculate a proportion, the usual procedure is to count the number of check marks in a category and divide by the total number of check marks under that feature. For example, if we consider *Target language*, the first step is to count all the check marks under this feature in the two categories LI and L2. For the purposes of illustration, let's assume there are 100 check marks under this feature. The next step is to count the number of check marks for the use of L1 and L2. Let's assume there are 25 check marks under LI. To calculate the proportion of L1 use, simply divide 25 by 100. This means that the L1 was used 25% of the time. It also means that the remaining 75 check marks represent L2 use, indicating that 75% of the class time was spent using the target language.

The procedure is similar for all other categories on Part B for both teacher and student verbal interaction. This results in proportions for minimal versus sustained turns for teachers and ultraminimal, minimal or sustained for students under *Sustained Speech* as well as student and teacher *Reactions to Form/Message* and so on. Special cases, such as those where double coding is involved, will be discussed later in this section.

It is important to note that for the feature *Information gap*, each category within it is calculated as a proportion of the next higher-level category. That is, the categories Predictable and Unpredictable are calculated as proportions of *Giving information*. Similarly, the categories Pseudo request and Genuine request are calculated as proportions of *Requesting information*.

---

34. It was decided to use this coding procedure because it is often difficult to determine the boundaries between utterances (e.g., the end of one request and the beginning of another). We know such a procedure may affect the frequency counts. In our previous research using change of category as the signal for a new check mark, we have not found that this has misrepresented the data. Nonetheless, we realize the potential problems inherent in such a procedure.

There is only one feature which stands on its own without any further subdivisions -*Discourse initiation*. This feature is coded only for the student and a proportion is obtained by dividing the number of self-initiated turns by the total number of student turns. For example, if there were a total of sixty-five student turns in a particular data set and, of those, ten were self initiations, this would mean that 15% of the student turns were discourse initiations.

Calculating class averages

After the calculations are complete for each observation visit, you may want to calculate an average for a particular class. This is relatively straightforward. For example, referring to the feature *Target language*, let us assume that there were four visits to a class and that during the first visit the L1 was used 25% of the time, in the second, 45%, in the third, 10% and in the fourth visit, 30% of the time. The average use of the L1 in this class would be 28%. Of course, this calculation can be done with all other features to summarise the data by class or by program.

Average proportions by class or program can be easily presented in bar graphs. Figure 5.3 shows proportions of the use of Genuine requests within the feature *Information gap* and the use of *Sustained Speech* by several teachers in four different programs (i.e., core French, extended French, French immersion, and ESL). The bar graphs illustrate differences and similarities among the programs. In this case, the core French program shows the lowest proportion of sustained turns and genuine requests for information on the part of the teacher while the other programs are more similar with respect to these features.

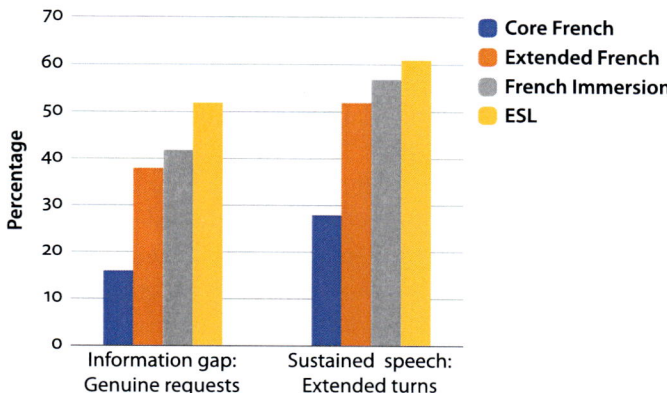

Figure 5.3 *Information gap* (genuine requests) and *Sustained Speech* (extended turns) for teacher talk in 4 L2 programs[35]

---

35. Adapted from Fröhlich, Spada, & Allen (1985).

Analysis of combinations of features (double coding)

While some of the main features on Part B have simple binary distinctions (e.g., L1/L2 under *Target Language*), others have multiple categories within them (e.g., *Incorporation of student/teacher utterances*). Some of them also require double coding (e.g., *Reaction to form/message* together with the *Incorporation of student/teacher utterances* categories). The analysis of proportions for the categories which are double coded requires special attention.

As indicated in the coding conventions for Part B, every time a category under *Incorporation of student/teacher utterances* is checked, a decision is also made as to whether it is form or message related. Although one may want to calculate the proportions of *Reaction to form/message* separately, that is, irrespective of their relationship to the categories under *Incorporation of student/teacher utterances*, this analysis will not include information about how the *Reaction to form/message* was provided. That is, it will not indicate whether the teacher (or student) responded to form by correcting, paraphrasing, commenting, etc. Similarly, if there were message reactions, this calculation will not reveal whether they were expansions, elaboration requests etc.

When calculating for these features in combination, the procedure becomes slightly more complicated. For example, in the hypothetical case illustrated in Figure 5.4, three teacher turns have been double coded under the categories in *Reaction to form/message* and *Incorporation of student/teacher utterances*. The first turn contains only message-related incorporations through repetition, expansion, and paraphrase.

The second turn is coded as a form-related paraphrase which is also a correction. Note that there is some redundancy in coding for correction as well as form because a correction is necessarily form-related (see Part B definitions in Chapter 2). It is also important to remember that correction + paraphrase belong together when referring to the same utterance and therefore are counted as one unit (see Chapter 4). The other two incorporation categories in this turn (i.e., comment and elaboration request) are both message related.

The third turn indicates a check mark for correction by itself, which means that the teacher has provided some metalinguistic information to point out the problem in the student's utterance. As indicated above, correction by its very definition is form related. Also indicated in this turn is a message-related repetition and elaboration request.

To calculate the proportions for such turns with multiple codings, count the total number of check marks under *Incorporation of student utterances* first. In this case, there are nine (not ten because correction + paraphrase is counted as one). Next, count all instances of form and message-related categories. For the example in Figure 5.4, the proportions would be calculated as follows:

TEACHER VERBAL INTERACTION										
Sustained speech		Reaction to form/ message		Incorporation of student utterances						
Minimal	Sustained	Form	Message	Correction	Repetition	Paraphrase	Comment	Expansion	Clarif. request	Elab. request
8	9	10	11	12	13	14	15	16	17	18
First teacher turn			√		√					
			√					√		
			√			√				
Second teacher turn		√		√		√				
			√				√			
			√							√
Third teacher turn		√		√						
			√		√					
			√							√

Figure 5.4 Calculating Part B features in combination

Form-related incorporations

Form-Correction + Paraphrase   1/9 = 0.11 = 11%

Form-Correction   1/9 = 0.11 = 11%

Message-related incorporations

Message-Repetition   2/9 = 0.22 = 22%

Message-Paraphrase   1/9 = 0.11 = 11%

Message-Comment   1/9 = 0.11 = 11%

Message-Expansion   1/9 = 0.11 = 11%

Message-Elaboration request   2/9 = 0.22 = 22%

Since none of the other combinations between form and message-related incorporation types occurred, they are not coded. This procedure, although somewhat complicated, is the best way we have determined to calculate categories which are doubled coded.

Global scoring

The methods described above for the analysis and synthesis of the COLT coded data represent a detailed category-by-category profile of the data collected with Part A and Part B. Below, another method of synthesizing the data is described, which is more global in nature and is intended to provide a general profile of classroom instruction. This method is referred to as 'global scoring' and to date, it has been used only with data collected with Part A of the scheme.

In Fröhlich, Spada, & Allen (1985), we tentatively proposed a global score to indicate the degree of communicative orientation of different L2 programs. To do this, we selected some of the features on Part A of the scheme often considered to be representative of a more communicatively oriented classroom. This included Group work under *Participant organization*, 'Other topics' and 'Management' under *Content*, and any combination of Language and 'Other topics'. Included under *Content control* was Teacher/text/student and Student), under *Materials* Type – Extended text, and under *Materials* Source – Use of Semi and Non-pedagogic L2 materials.[36]

For each of the features a numerical value from 1–5 was assigned based on the percentage of class time spent on that feature: 0–19% of class time equalled a value of 1; 20–39% a value of 2 etc. For example, a class which spent 10% of class time on group work, 30% on other topics combined with language, 5% on activities controlled by teacher/text/student, 80% on extended text and 20% on materials originally designed for native speakers of the target language, would be assigned the individual values of $1+2+1+5+2$, yielding a global score of 11. This score could then be compared with a score from another class to determine differences in the degree of communicative orientation. It is important to note that a higher communicative score does not necessarily represent a better learning environment, which is dependent on many other factors.

The global scoring procedure is not without its challenges and several critical issues need to be resolved before going any further with it. First, it has been argued that the percentage intervals may be too great and thus the system may fail to adequately discriminate among important differences between classes and programs. Smaller intervals may help to alleviate this problem. Another issue, one which we consider to be particularly problematic, is whether all features included in the global scoring can be considered of equal theoretical or empirical importance and if not, whether they should be weighted differently. For example, is a focus on 'Other topics' (i.e. meaning/content) a stronger indicator of communicative orientation than *Content control*? Related to this is the fact that definitions of communicative language teaching vary. This is evident when considering the role of form-focused instruction. For example, while an exclusive focus on form in L2 instruction was considered by many to be a weak indicator of communicative orientation in the 1980s, and an exclusive focus on meaning was thought to be a critical feature of communicative language teaching, today, a focus on language form that is provided within primarily meaning-based instruction is also considered to be a strong indicator of communicative orientation. Indeed, since the first edition of this book, considerable research has shown that a combination of form and meaning and the integration of language and content is the most effective L2 instruction (see discussion and references in Chapter 1). These are crucial issues that would need to be addressed by anyone wishing to adopt a global scoring

---

36. See Fröhlich, Spada, & Allen (1985) for definitions of these categories, which were subsequently changed in Spada & Fröhlich (1995).

procedure with the COLT data. Nonetheless, the concept of a global score seems to have potential and perhaps other users of the scheme will contribute to its refinement.

In the final section of this chapter, the development of a computer-based numerical system for coding and analysis using COLT Part B is described. As indicated in Chapter 1, a group of researchers in Japan have taken COLT into the 21st century by developing digital versions of the observation scheme. Below is a description of numeric COLT Part B that facilitates the coding, analysis, and synthesis of teacher and learner verbal interaction data. The digital versions of COLT Part A are described in Chapter 6.

Numeric COLT (Part B): Coding & analysis

In the early 2000's, Noriaki Katagiri and his colleagues began to develop a numerical system for coding the COLT Part B features. They have used this system to describe the characteristics of language provided by preservice teachers of English in Japan (Katagiri & Kawai, 2015; Katagiri & Ohashi, 2018). Using the same main features and categories in the original COLT Part B scheme, they have replaced the check marks with numbers and developed a coding system in which the numbers from 1–7 are used to code teacher and student utterances.

Table 5.4 illustrates how the numerical coding system works for teachers' utterances. The top row includes the 6 main features (i.e., *Off task, Target language, Information gap, Sustained speech, Reaction to form/message, Incorporation of learner utterances*). Each feature, except *Off task* has categories listed below them. The coding numbers (1–7) that are used to describe each category are indicated in the far-left column. So, for example, the feature *Target language* is divided into two categories, and they are coded as 1 for L1 and 2 for L2. The feature *Information gap* has 4 -categories, and they are coded as 1 for 'Giving information' (Predictable), 2 for 'Giving information' (Unpredictable), 3 for 'Requesting information' (Pseudo req.) and 4 for "Requesting information' (Genuine req.) The feature *Incorporation of learners' utterances* has 7 categories – the first is Correction (#1) and last Elaboration request (#7).

Table 5.5 illustrates how the coding works for students' verbal interactions. The top row includes the 7 main features that apply to their utterances (i.e., *Discourse initiation, Target language, Information gap, Sustained speech, Form restriction, Reaction to form/message, Incorporation of learner/teacher utterances*) and the categories are listed underneath. Again, the numbers 1–7 are used to code the utterances.

Recall that the procedure for calculating the proportion of teacher and student utterances for each communicative feature using the original COLT Part B included: (1) counting the number of check marks in each category and (2) dividing that number by the total number of utterances. Go back and look at Excerpt B and Figure 4.2 in Chapter 4. They present a segment of a transcript and how it was coded by hand with checkmarks, using the original COLT Part B procedures and spreadsheet.

Table 5.4 Numerical COLT (Part B) teacher verbal interaction

Coding numeral	Off task	Target language	Information gap	Sustained speech	Reaction to form/message	Incorporation of learner utterances
1	Off task	L1	Giving Info Predictable	Minimal	Form	Correction
2		L2	Giving Info Unpredictable	Sustained	Message	Repetition
3			Request Info Pseudo req.			Paraphrase
4			Request Info Genuine req.			Comment
5						Explanation
6						Clarif. request
7						Elab. request

Note. This table is adapted from Table 3 in Katagiri & Kawai (2015, p. 28). The empty cells represent non-existent categories for the main features.

Table 5.5 Numerical COLT (Part B) student verbal interaction

Coding numeral	Discourse initiation	Target language	Information gap	Sustained speech	Form restriction	Reaction to form/ message	Incorporation of learner/ teacher utterances
1	Discourse Initiation	L1	Giving Info Predictable	Minimal	Choral	Form	Correction
2		L2	Giving Info Unpredictable	Sustained	Restricted	Message	Repetition
3			Request Info Pseudo req.		Unrestricted		Paraphrase
4			Request Info Genuine req.				Comment
5							Expansion
6							Clarif. request
7							Elab. request

Note. This table is adapted from Table 4 in Katagari & Kawai (2015, p. 28). The empty cells represent non-existent sub-categories for the main features.

Now look at Table 5.6, which includes the same transcript and illustrates how the teacher's utterances have been coded using the numerical system. The 6 teacher verbal interaction features are displayed across the top of the table with their respective categories below. The coding numbers (1–7) appear in the first column on the left and mid-way down on the far-left side of the table is the transcript. Each teacher utterance has been coded using the numbers associated with each category. For example, the first utterance "What did you do on the weekend?" is coded as 2 representing L2; 4 representing a Genuine request for information, and 1 representing Minimal speech. One digit is used to describe each category except for *Incorporation of teacher and learner utterances*. This is because the category Correction sometimes co-occurs with Repetition, Paraphrase, and Comment (see Chapter 4). Thus, an additional digit is needed to indicate this when the numbers are combined into numerical strings. This procedure is described in more detail below.

The obvious advantage to the numerical coding system is that the numbers can be quickly and easily calculated using a computer application (e.g., Microsoft Excel) to determine the frequency of occurrence of the Part B categories, how they compare across activities, classes, programs, teachers, and learners. Another advantage is that the numbers can be combined (i.e., concatenated) into numerical strings to describe teacher and learner utterances. These strings of numbers can then be examined to explore whether different sets of communicative features co-occur more or less frequently than others. Again, such a procedure can be easily done using a computer application such as Microsoft Excel.

Table 5.7 presents the same transcript excerpt with the numerical coding strings that describe the teacher and student verbal interactions. On the left are the student and teacher utterances. Directly beneath them are the abbreviated Part B category descriptors. On the right are the numerical strings that correspond to the descriptors. The zeros indicate features that do not occur in the utterances. As indicated above, 2 digits are used for the last category *Incorporation of learner utterances* for teacher verbal interaction and *Incorporation of teacher/learner utterances* for student verbal interaction. This is because the subcategory Correction sometimes co-occurs with Repetition, Paraphrase, and Comment. The digit to represent Correction appears as the 2nd to the right in the numeric string. So, for example, the teacher's utterance "What did you do on the weekend" is coded as 2 (L2); 4 (Genuine request); 1 (Minimal); 0 (Reaction to form/message); 0 (Correction); 0 (other *Incorporation of learner utterances* categories). The student's utterance "What you see" is coded as 1 (*Discourse Initiation*), 2 (L2); 0 (Information Gap); 2 (Sustained); 3 (Form restriction) 2 (Message); 0 (Correction); 7 (Elaboration request). Note that the category *Off task* for teacher utterances is not coded here because the interaction is on task. When *Off task* speech occurs, it is coded as 1 and appears as the first digit on the left.

Table 5.6 Part B numerical coding for teacher verbal interaction

	Coding numeral	Off Task	Target language	Information gap	Sustained speech	Reaction to form/ message	Incorporation of learner utterances
				Teacher verbal interaction			
	1	Off task	L1	Giving Info Predictable	Minimal	Form	Correction
	2		L2	Giving Info Unpredictable	Sustained	Message	Repetition
	3			Request Info Pseudo req.			Paraphrase
	4			Request Info Genuine req.			Comment
	5						Explanation
	6						Clarif. request
T/S Teacher and learner speech	7						Elab. request
T: <u>What did you do on the weekend?</u>			2	4	1		
S: I go see a movie.							
T: Oh, that's fun. So did I. What did you see?			2			2	4
			2			2	5
			2	4	2	2	7
S: Terminator 2. What you see?							
T: 'Terminator II'! My son wanted to see it. It's not my kind of a movie, but the special effects were great.			2	2	2		
S: Yeah, agree.							

Note. This table is adapted from Table 6 in Katagiri & Kawai (2015). The teacher utterances are shaded. The second teacher turn contains three utterances and is therefore coded only once as Sustained speech.

Table 5.7 Numerical coding strings for teacher and student utterances

Teacher and student speech	Teacher numeric coding (concatenated)	Student numeric coding (concatenated)
T: What did you do on the weekend? [L2/Gen.Req./Min.]	241000	
S: I go see a movie. [L2/Unpred.Info/Min./Unrestr.]		2223000
T: Oh, that's fun. [L2/Mess.-Comment] So did I. [L2/Mess.-Exp.] What did you see? [L2/Mess.-Elab.Req./Sust.]	200204 200205 241207	
S: 'Terminator II'. [L2/Unpred.Info/Unrestr.] What you see? [D.1/L2/Mess.-Elab.Req./Min.]		2203000 12023207
T: 'Terminator II'! My son wanted to see it. It's not my kind of a movie, but the special effects were great. [L2/Unpred. Info/Sust.]	222000	
S: Yeah, agree. [D.I./L2/Mess.-Comment/Unrestr./Min]		12013204

Note. This table is adapted from Table 8 in Katagari & Kawai (2015).

Practice 8

The teacher and learner utterances below are from Transcript 4 (Chapter 4, p. 104 in COLT, 1995). Code them into numerical strings. See the Answer Key for the correct coding.

S1 It bugs me when a bee string me.   _____

T: Oh, when a bee stings me.   _____

S1: Stings me.   _____

T: Do you get stung often? Does that happen often?   _____

S1: Yeah.   _____

Figure 5.5 illustrates how the numerical system facilitates the calculation of individual features and combinations. For more information and details on the Part B numerical coding system including the preparation and uploading of transcripts into the Excel files see Katagiri & Kawai (2015), Katagiri & Ohashi (2018). A summary of Katagiri & Ohashi (2018) is presented in Chapter 7. Also in Chapter 7 is a brief description of work in progress using A.I. to assist in the coding of Part B data (Katagiri, in progress).

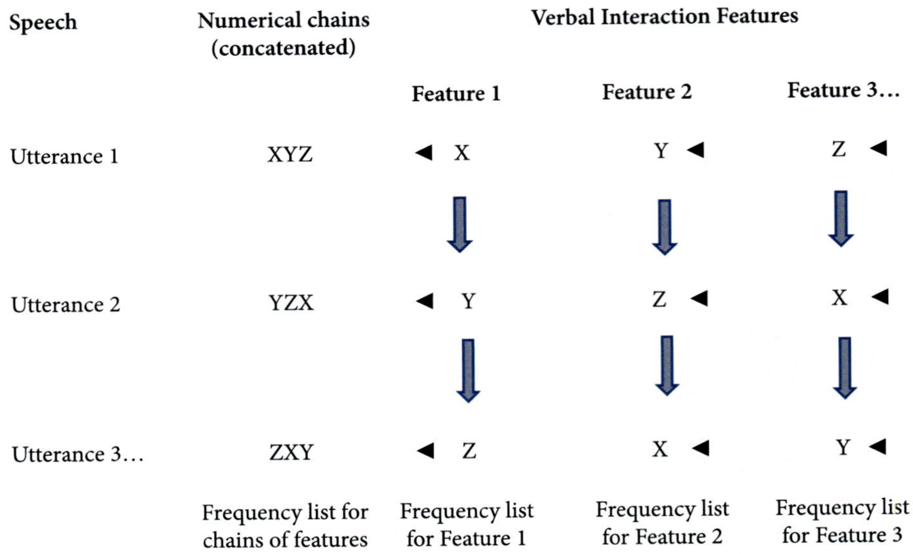

Speech	Numerical chains (concatenated)	Verbal Interaction Features		
		Feature 1	Feature 2	Feature 3...
Utterance 1	XYZ	◀ X	Y ◀	Z ◀
		⬇	⬇	⬇
Utterance 2	YZX	◀ Y	Z ◀	X ◀
		⬇	⬇	⬇
Utterance 3...	ZXY	◀ Z	X ◀	Y ◀
	Frequency list for chains of features	Frequency list for Feature 1	Frequency list for Feature 2	Frequency list for Feature 3

Figure 5.5 Flow chart for coding individual and combined Part B features

CHAPTER 6

Digital COLT (Part A)

Hiroki Ishizuka

In this chapter a description of how Part A of the COLT scheme has been transformed into different digital applications is presented. This includes 3 formats. The first section describes the video-on-demand online platform (CollaVOD) and its two primary functions: collaborative learning and COLT Part A coding. This includes information about how to access CollaVOD and navigate the online system to upload classroom videos, code for COLT Part A, and generate immediate results. The next section describes Mobile COLT, which was developed to code and analyze classroom teaching in real time. The use of this system is described along with changes that were made to some of the original Part A categories. The final section focuses on the most recent version of digital COLT referred to as Automatic COLT. This is a web-based system and includes a variety of functions for coding with Part A. It also features A.I. capabilities for automatic coding.

CollaVOD

CollaVOD (Collaborative Video on Demand) is a platform developed to analyze video-recorded language classrooms semi-automatically using Part A of the COLT observation scheme. The advent of Web 2.0 technology in the 21st century has enabled users to interact with web pages, making it possible to provide online distance learning classes in the interactive mode. Using this technology, a group of Japanese L2 educational researchers wanted to provide researchers and teachers with an innovative and convenient system for assessing and reflecting on the teaching and learning processes in English language classes in Japan. In 2012 work on the development of a new video-on-demand (VOD) platform equipped with language class analysis functions including COLT Part A began. It was completed in the spring of 2014 and finely tuned over the next two years. The development of CollaVOD was financed by the HATO Project, a collaboration of four Japanese universities with the goal of improving the teaching skills of pre-service English teachers at teacher training universities in Japan.

Two major functions were installed in a Learning Management System (LMS) called Glexa: (1) a collaborative learning VOD function and (2) the COLT Part A analysis system to code video-taped classes. When the classroom analysis function is selected, a COLT table is automatically prepared and displayed with the uploaded video of the class targeted for analysis. The coding is conducted manually as in the conventional COLT Part A coding, however, there are several advantages of using this platform. The duration of each episode of a class is automatically calculated and displayed immediately after the coding is completed.

All the coding results are stored and thus can be accessed and reviewed later. The results can also be made available to other permitted users, which enables them to compare their observations and analyses of the language classes with those of other users. The details regarding access to and use of these functions are explained later in this section.

The VOD collaborative learning function is equipped with a video authoring tool to set up tasks in which users can write their comments and reflections while watching the video and discuss them with each other. This function was originally intended to be utilized for educating teacher trainees on how to view second language classes from a broad-based qualitative perspective. The VOD tool looks like YouTube in that users can share the film, but it has distinctive features that can make the class observations more elaborate and interactive. For example, instructors can upload videos and freely insert subtitles for any scene in a video; the inserted subtitles are then displayed as a list in the columns below the screen. If a teacher-in-training clicks one of these subtitles in the list, s/he can watch its corresponding scene in the video, view questions prepared by the teacher, and submit answers to the question. At the same time the teachers-in-training can share their answers with other learners and discuss the same scenes collaboratively (Figure 6.1).

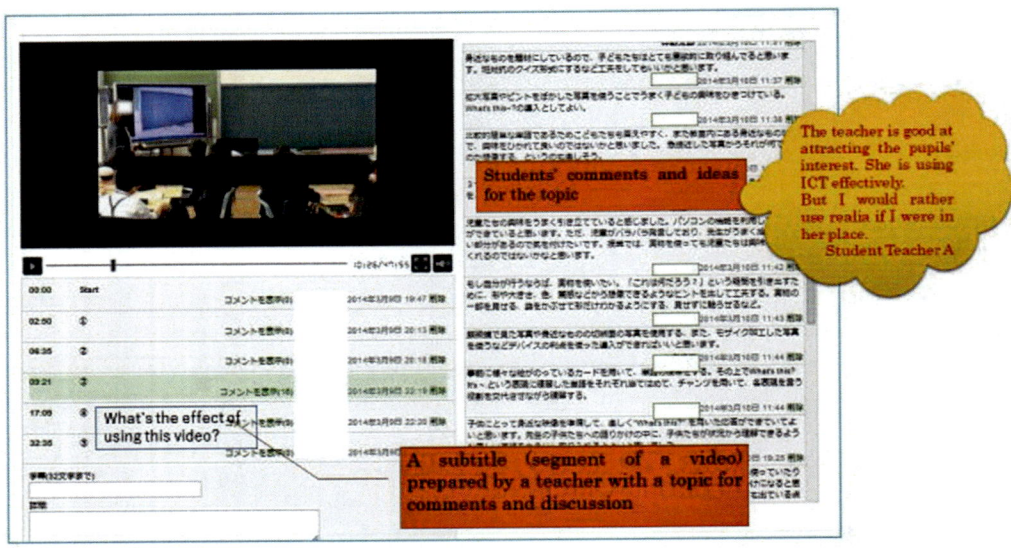

Figure 6.1 VOD collaborative learning function

COLT Coding on CollaVOD

This section focuses on the functions relevant to COLT coding using CollaVOD. Once users are registered on the platform, they can create virtual classes and use the COLT coding functions by themselves or with other users. For example, users can upload a classroom video to the server for analysis and when the COLT coding table is set up in the virtual class, all the other users, (i.e., usually other teachers-in-training belonging to the same class), can also access the same COLT coding page (Figure 6.2) and start to use their own coding sheets to code the same video-recorded class.

Instead of using check marks for coding, the digits 11 and 1 are used for the features (i.e., 11 means "✓✓" and 1 means "✓"). This numerical system is required for the automatic calculation to be done after the coding. As indicated above, the duration of each teaching episode is automatically calculated and displayed in the digital COLT Part A spreadsheet on the screen after the coding is completed. This time calculation is a key mechanism of this system because users do not need to record the amount of time spent on individual categories manually. Furthermore, the calculation of distributional rates within and across the COLT categories is also processed automatically. Thus, while the coding procedure itself is similar to the conventional Part A coding using pencil and paper, there are several advantages of using this system:

1. Coding work can be done collaboratively from distant locations either asynchronously or synchronously. The users in the same class can compare the results of their coding, which enhances their awareness of different perspectives in observing and analyzing teaching and learning behaviors in language classes (Figure 6.3). The coding results are automatically displayed using graphic images after the coding is completed.
2. The Global Communicative Orientation Scores (i.e., Global Scores) indicating the degree of the communicative orientation of a particular class/program (see Chapter 5) are automatically displayed after the coding is completed.
3. It is possible to modify the coding of a class even after the calculated result has been displayed, and the modification is quickly reflected in the new results.

Accessing COLT Part A on COLAV-E

To make CollaVOD available to a broader audience, a new platform has been created in English and named "COLAV-E". Below step-by-step instructions are provided to gain access to COLAV-E in preparation for using COLT.

– Step 1: Request an ID and a password by signing up at https://colavo.glexa.jp/ (Figure 6.4).
– Step 2: Select either "jp=Japanese" or "en"= English and log on to the server (Figure 6.4).
– Step 3: Click "Create new class," (Figure 6.5) and then on the next page, input a name for the class, and click "Submit", which appears at the bottom right corner of the online page.

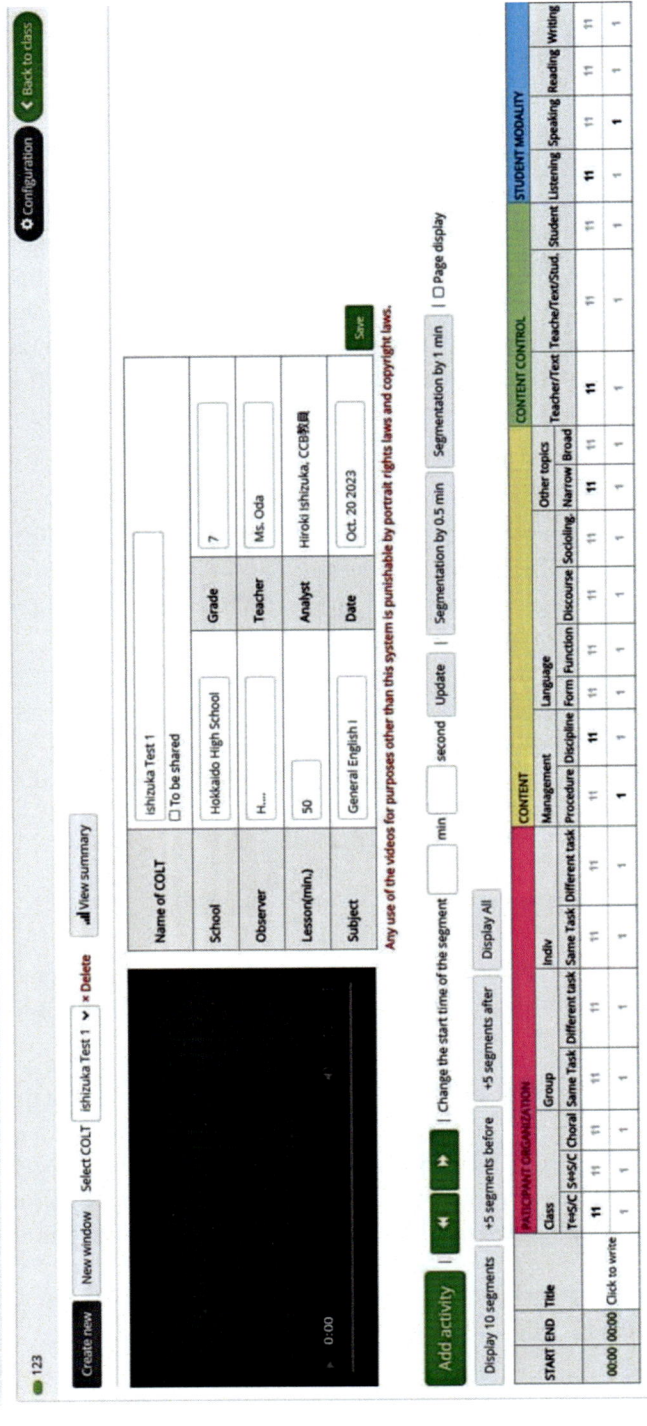

Figure 6.2 COLT coding function

Global Scoring: 10

group		min.	rate	score
PATICIPANT ORGANIZATION	Group	10»41»	25%	2
CONTENT	Management, Other Topics	34»40»	83%	5
CONTENT CONTROL	Teache/Text/Stud.,Student	04»15»	10%	1
MATERIALS Type	Extended Text	00»00»	0%	1
MATERIALS Source	L2NS,L2-NSA	00»00»	0%	1

Global Scoring: 8

group		min.	rate	score
PATICIPANT ORGANIZATION	Group	07»23»	17%	1
CONTENT	Management, Other Topics	28»14»	67%	4
CONTENT CONTROL	Teache/Text/Stud.,Student	06»54»	16%	1
MATERIALS Type	Extended Text	01»34»	3%	1
MATERIALS Source	L2NS,L2-NSA	00»00»	0%	1

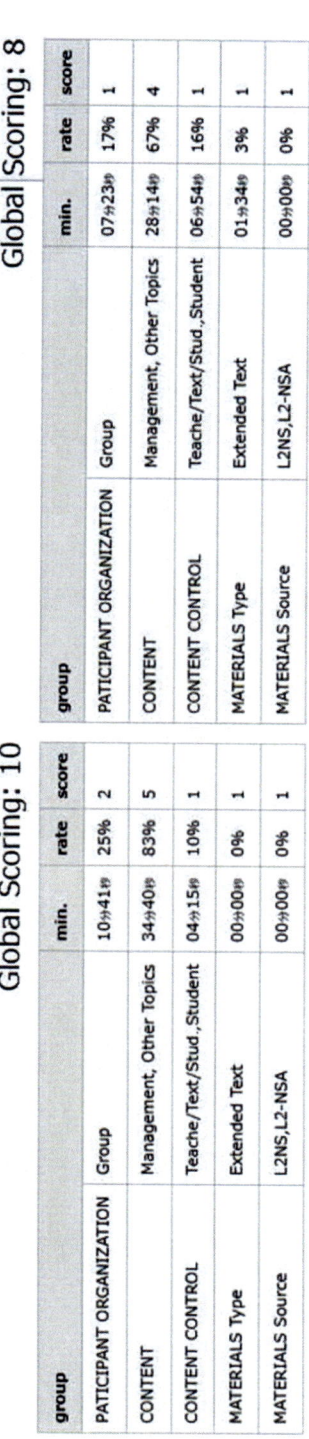
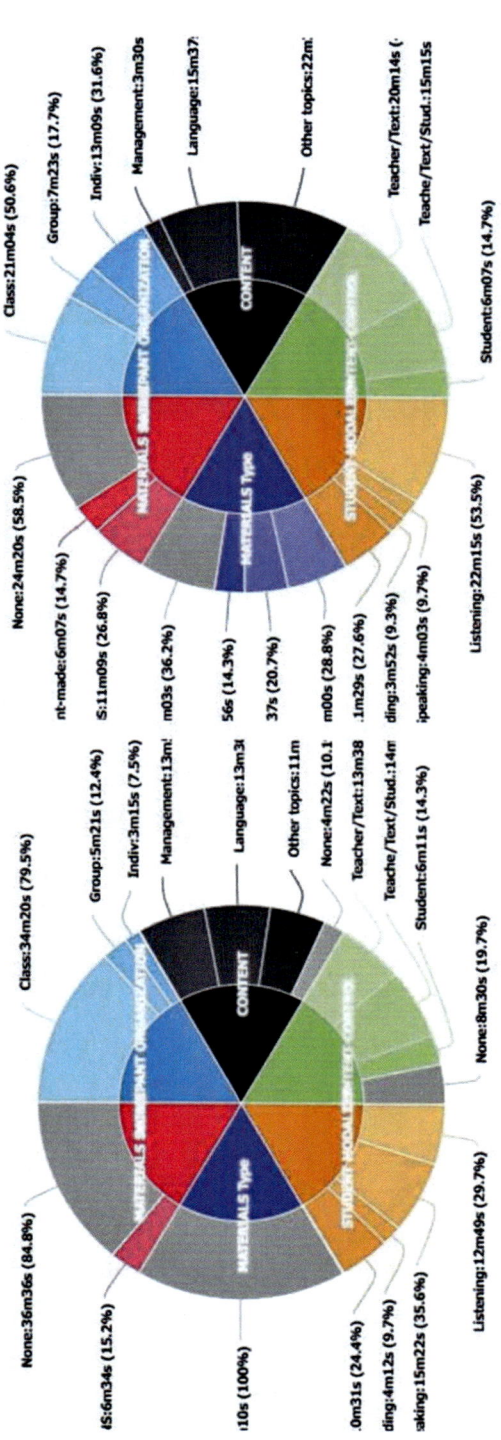

Figure 6.3 Comparison of coding results of the same class by two coders

Figure 6.4 Log-on page of COLAV-E

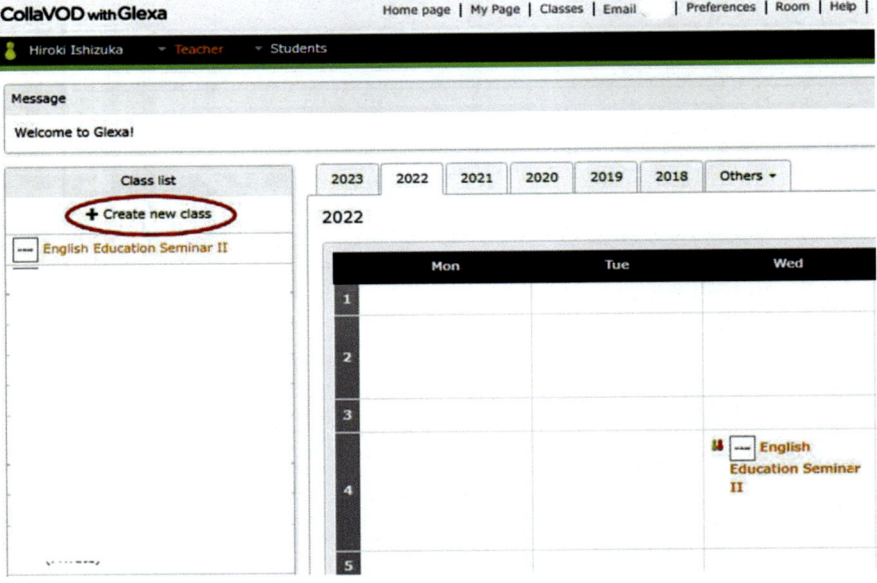

Figure 6.5 Create a new class

–   Step 4: In the class click "Create courseware" (Figure 6.6), and on the next page, make sure that "Vod" is selected as the courseware type. Input a title for "Subject" (Figure 6.7) and then click "Submit" in the bottom right corner of the online page.

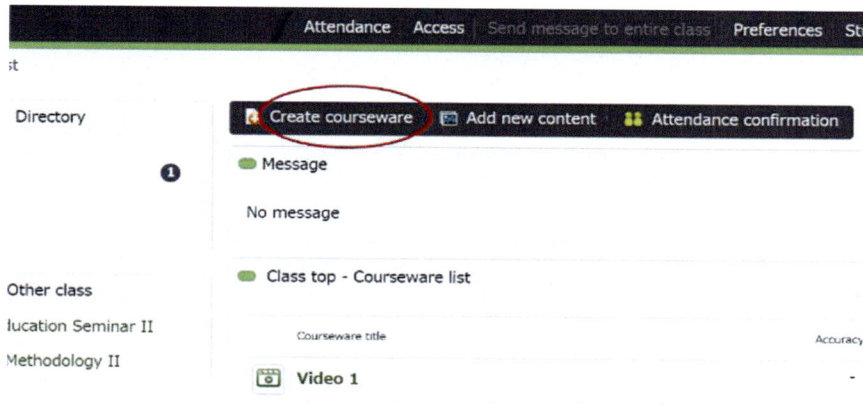

Figure 6.6 Create courseware

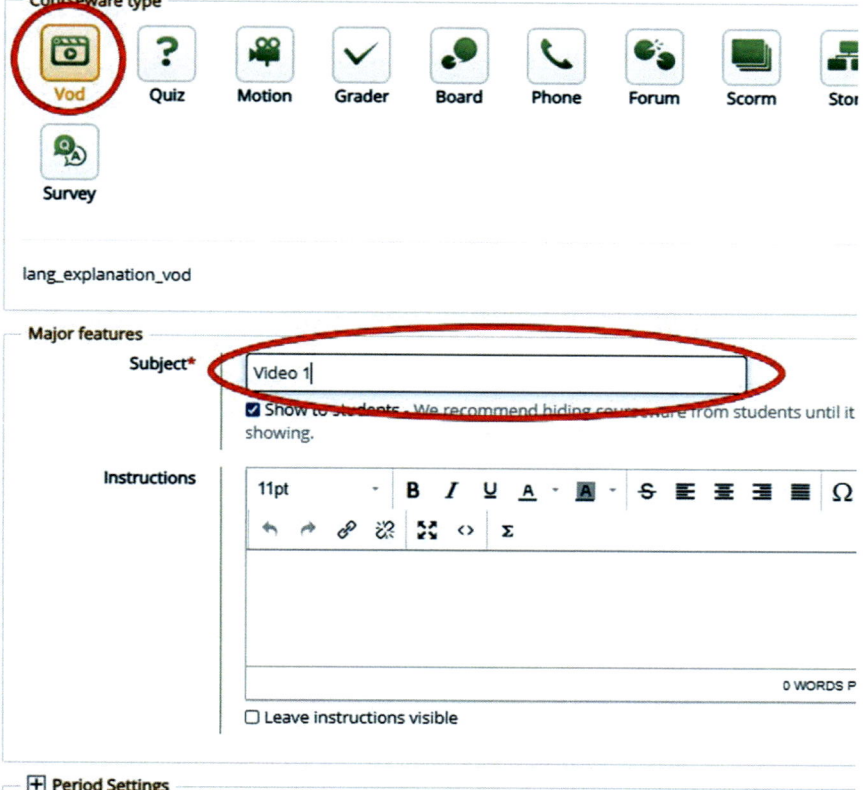

Figure 6.7 Edit the courseware

– Step 5: On the next page, check "Use COLT" (Figure 6.8) and then click "Save" in the bottom right corner of the online page.

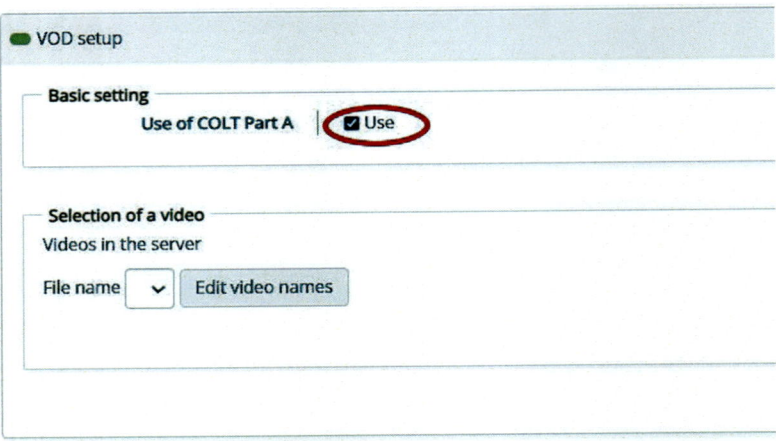

Figure 6.8 Setting up COLT in VOD setup

– Step 6: When the video file setting page opens, click "Select file" and "Upload a file" from your desktop (Figure 6.9).

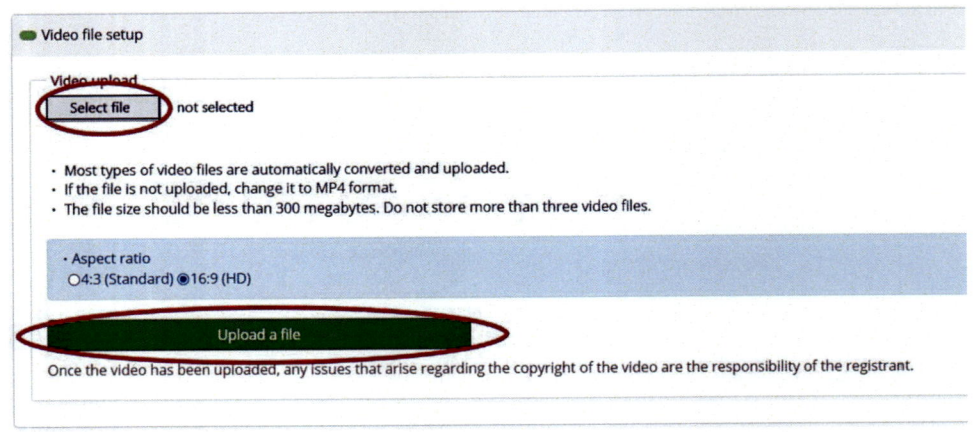

Figure 6.9 Uploading a file

– Step 7: When a new COLT setting page with the uploaded video appears, click Create new" and select "Part A" (Figure 6.10). Input the name of your COLT table and click "Create" (Figure 6.11). Now you are ready to start coding.

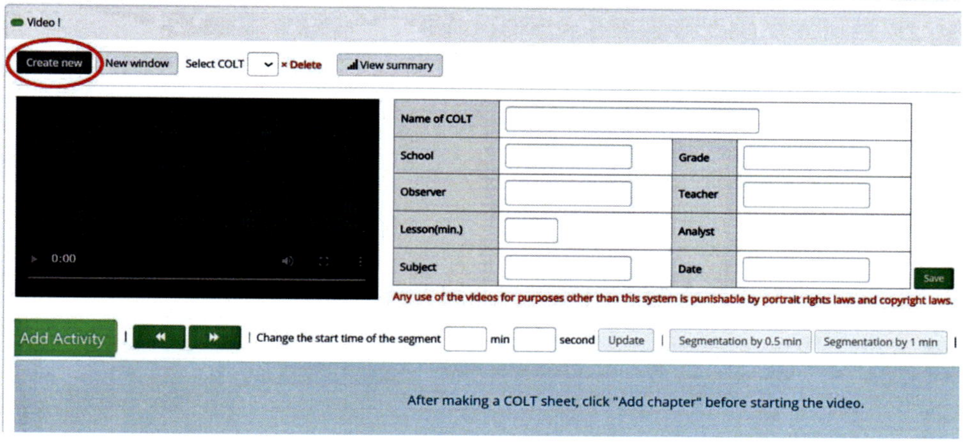

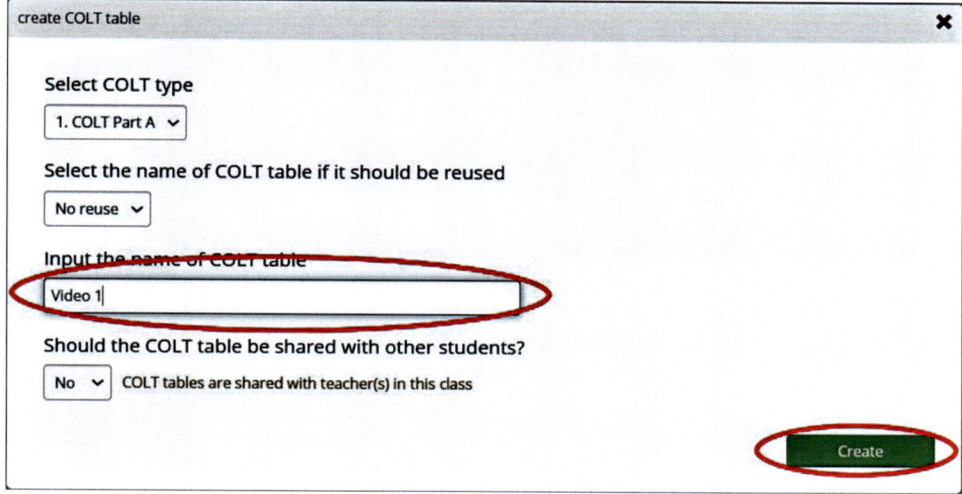

Figure 6.10 Creating COLT table

Figure 6.11 Setting up COLT table

COLT Part A coding on COLAV-E

Below are step-by-step instructions detailing how to use COLT Part A on COLAV-E.

–   Step 1: Fill the class information in the table next to the video and click save (Figure 6.12).
–   Step 2: Click "Add Activity" at the start of the class to make a new segment and start coding by choosing "11" (primary focus or equal focus) or "1" (secondary focus) while watching the video (Figure 6.13).

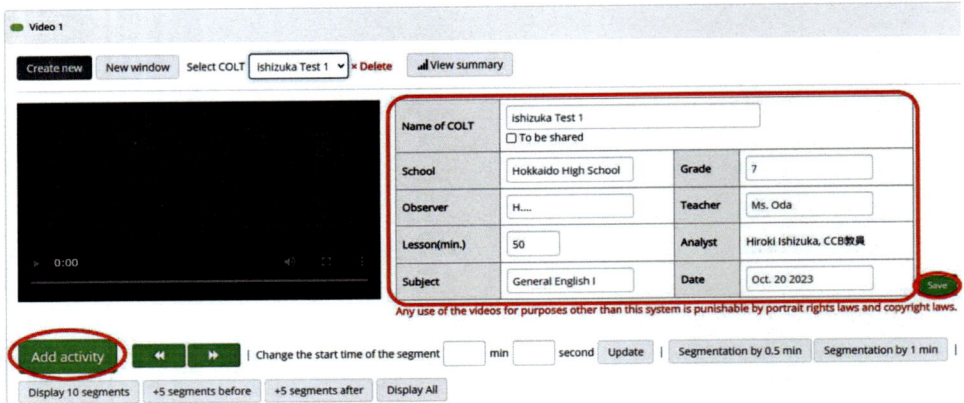

Figure 6.12 Class information and creating a new segment

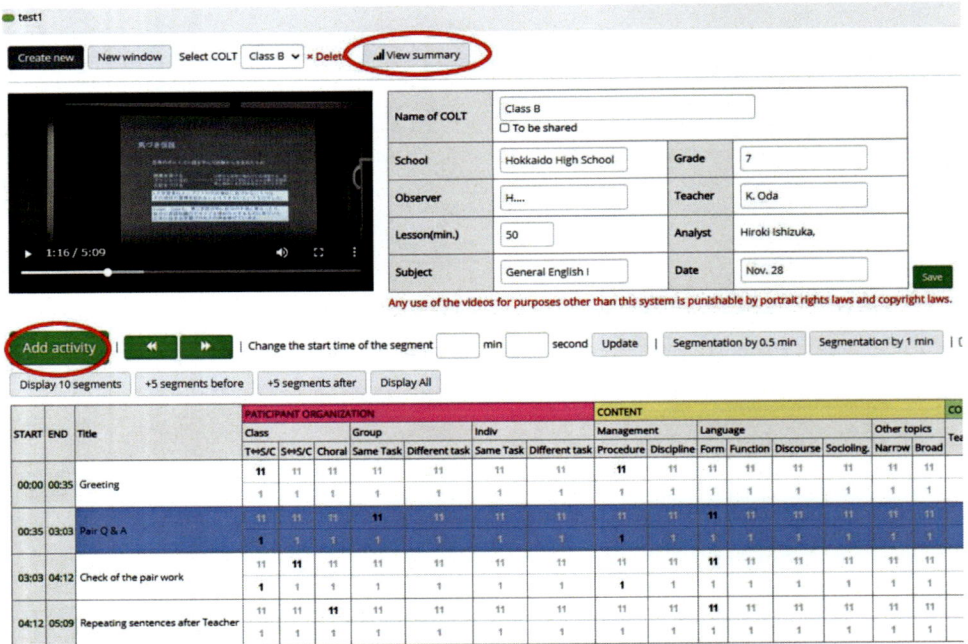

START	END	Title	PARTICIPANT ORGANIZATION							CONTENT								CO
			Class			Group		Indiv		Management		Language				Other topics		Tea
			T↔S/C	S↔S/C	Choral	Same Task	Different task	Same Task	Different task	Procedure	Discipline	Form	Function	Discourse	Socioling.	Narrow	Broad	
00:00	00:35	Greeting	11	11	11	11	11	11	11	11	11	11	11	11	11	11	11	
			1	1	1	1	1	1	1	1	1	1	1	1	1	1	1	
00:35	03:03	Pair Q & A	11	11	11	11	11	11	11	11	11	11	11	11	11	11	11	
			1	1	1	1	1	1	1	1	1	1	1	1	1	1	1	
03:03	04:12	Check of the pair work	11	11	11	11	11	11	11	11	11	11	11	11	11	11	11	
			1	1	1	1	1	1	1	1	1	1	1	1	1	1	1	
04:12	05:09	Repeating sentences after Teacher	11	11	11	11	11	11	11	11	11	11	11	11	11	11	11	
			1	1	1	1	1	1	1	1	1	1	1	1	1	1	1	

Figure 6.13 Coding and viewing results

- Step 3: At the end of one episode, pause the video, add another activity, and code the episode. Continue this process until the end of the class.
- Step 4: After finishing coding, click "View summary," and on the next page, select your own and any other coding results that are displayed when there is more than one coder.

(Figures 6.13 & 6.14). The Global Score and the times and the rates of the COLT categories composing the Global Score are displayed with their graphic images.

- Step 5: If the coding requires editing after checking the results, go back to the coding page and modify the coding. The revised modifications are reflected in the summary.
- Step 6: To save the coding results, click "Export as an excel file" on the summary page (Figure 6.14).

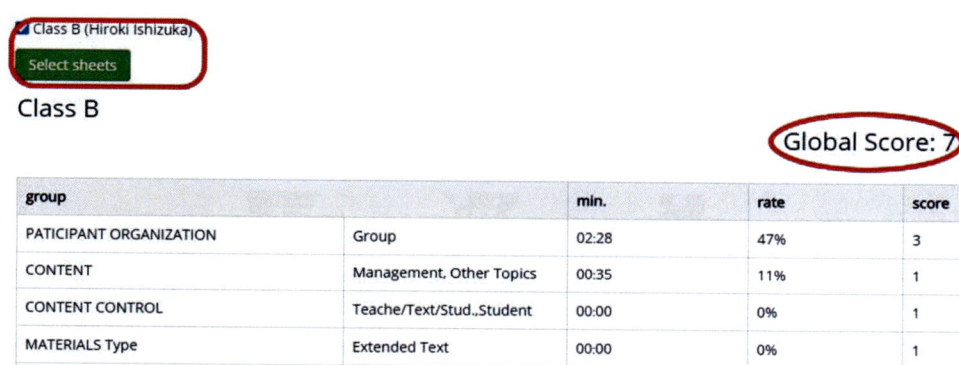

Class B

Global Score: 7

group		min.	rate	score
PATICIPANT ORGANIZATION	Group	02:28	47%	3
CONTENT	Management, Other Topics	00:35	11%	1
CONTENT CONTROL	Teache/Text/Stud.,Student	00:00	0%	1
MATERIALS Type	Extended Text	00:00	0%	1
MATERIALS Source	L2NS,L2-NSA	00:00	0%	1

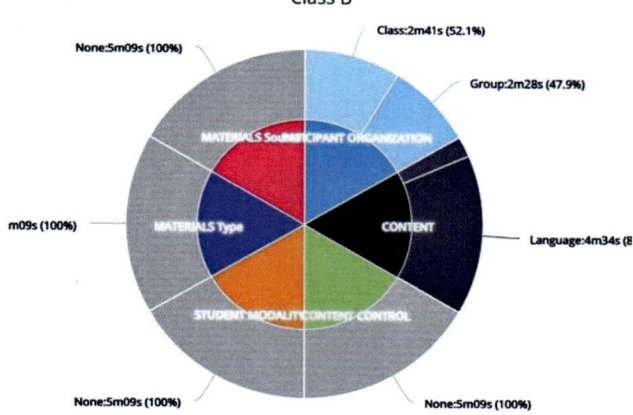

Class B

Figure 6.14 Summary of the class

Practice 9

Using the COLT A function of COLAV-E code the videoed class linked to the address: https://colavo.glexa.jp. Remember that you need to get an account to use COLAV-E by signing up to register and then to log on before following the link above. If prompted for a password, enter "colt2525" in the box that will appear and click "Attend". Then go to the home page, select the tab "COLT Activity", and click "Chapter 6 COLT Activity".

In the linked virtual classroom, first click "COLT Activity 1". Then make a new COLT A table, and code the recorded class. After completing coding, click "View summary" and check the results. Then look at the files of "The result of coding" and "Global score and graphs" below on the same page for comparison.

Notice that the number of activities (segments) is eight and the starting times for the activities are as follows: Activity (1) 0:00, Activity (2) 1:24, Activity (3) 3:40, Activity (4) 5:17, Activity (5) 9:19, Activity (6) 10:16, Activity (7) 11:27, Activity (8) 12:55.

The coding results can be viewed in the COLAV-E virtual class: Chapter 6 COLT Activity.

Mobile COLT

The Mobile COLT system was developed to record and analyze teaching and learning in second language classes in real time. It was designed for use as a portable COLT coding system and implemented as an application for a Windows tablet. The basic features of this system are the same as those used with the COLT Part A coding functions of CollaVOD/COLAV-E. Mobile COLT also automatically processes time calculations after coding and displays the results in tables and graphs (Figure 6.15).

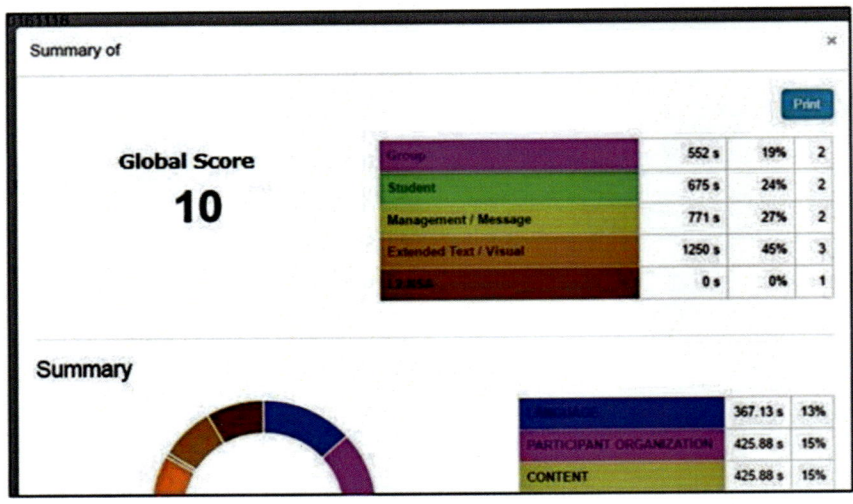

Figure 6.15 Sample results of coding with Mobile COLT

Mobile COLT uses a simplified set of Part A categories that were intended to make it easier for beginner observers to use the scheme. This simplified system was developed based on the observation results of 10 English classes in Japan that were coded with both the original COLT Part A scheme and the simplified version. First, the categories that were never or rarely used when coding with the original COLT Part A scheme were excluded or integrated into different categories. For example, Different Task in *Participant Organization* and Other in *Student Modality* were excluded, Discipline was integrated into 'Management', and Function, Discourse, and Sociolinguistics in *Content* were integrated into Form. In Source under *Materials*, L2-NS was merged with L2-NSA. Second, other original COLT Part A categories were re-arranged or integrated into the simplified version. For example, Choral was integrated into 'Class' under *Participant Organization* and in *Content Control*, Teacher/Text/ Student was excluded. A final change was the addition of the categories L1 and L2 under *Language*. Figure 16 illustrates the simplified version of Part A used in Mobile COLT.

To determine whether the simplified COLT Part A categories captured the same information as the original COLT scheme, the categories used to calculate the Global Score for both were compared. The results were virtually identical for all features except for *Content Control*. Overall, the findings from this validation study have inspired confidence in the use of the simplified Part A categories.[37]

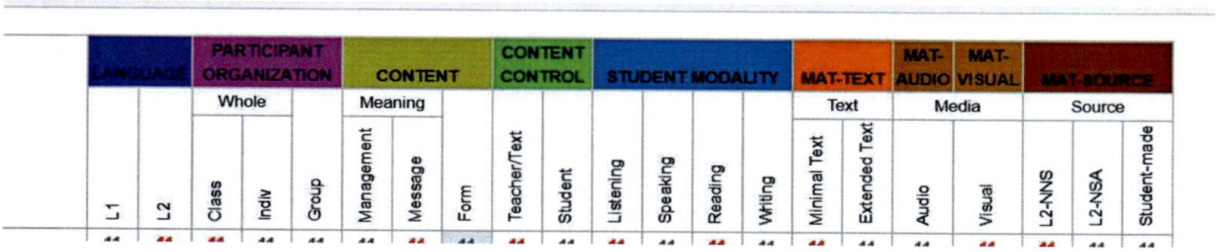

Figure 6.16 Simplified COLT Part A categories for Mobile COLT

Automatic COLT

The most recent version of digital COLT is referred to as Automatic COLT. Unlike Mobile COLT which was designed for use as an application on a Windows tablet, Automatic COLT is web based and requires an internet connection. Automatic COLT includes a variety of functions including A.I. capabilities for automatic coding.

Development of Automatic COLT

As described earlier in this chapter, when Mobile COLT is used in a classroom, a coder, who has expertise in language teaching and is trained to use the COLT scheme needs to be

---

37. There are no publications reporting the validation of the simplified Part A categories. However, readers who are interested in learning more about this aspect of the research are welcome to contact Hiroki Ishizuka, who can provide more information about the validation study at ishizuka0040@gmail.com

present in the classroom. The coders' responsibilities include coding, helping the teachers understand their teaching, and guiding lesson activities and episodes. This work can only be done by trained coders, and it has been one of the barriers to the uptake of Mobile COLT among language teachers. Given that one of the primary goals for using the COLT scheme was to provide a tool for English language teachers in Japan to reflect on their own instructional practices, the need for specialized knowledge to use it was problematic.

Therefore, in 2018, a new version of Mobile COLT was developed, initially referred to as AI Mobile COLT (Ishizuka & Pellerin, 2020), to code a language class automatically using the mechanisms of speech recognition, pattern matching of teacher utterances with reference to a collection of coding rules, and a list of keywords used to match the teacher utterances. It also has a database to adjust the coding results (Figure 6.17). The construction of the system was completed in 2021 and the validation and adaptation work were finalized in 2023. This newly developed function is referred to as AI coding and is described below with the other features and functions of Automatic COLT.

Features and functions of Automatic COLT

Automatic COLT can be used for both real-time analysis in the classroom and subsequent video analysis. It has the same manual coding functions that are used with Mobile COLT and the coding results can also be automatically calculated. Automatic COLT has the following four functions.

AI coding is the main function of this system. It can record the video and audio of a class being observed and automatically code the class at the same time. More information about how this function has been designed and works follows the description of the other functions below.

Recording and coding is the same function that was built into Mobile COLT. A coder needs to manually code the lesson while it is being recorded.

Uploading and coding is the function that can be used to code a video-taped lesson either manually or automatically (as of 2024, the adaptation of automatic coding for different browsers has not been completed, and therefore this operation doesn't always work smoothly).

Coding without recording is the function used to manually code a lesson without recording the video and audio.

Below is a description of how AI coding has been designed for use with COLT Part A. This includes a description of the key data entered for coding and a step-by-step description of the coding process. This is also illustrated in Figure 6.17.

AI coding: Data and coding process

For AI coding, two types of data are used. One is information used for pattern-matching and the other is for keyword matching. The data for pattern-matching consists of a collection of hierarchical combinations of frequently used teacher talk, such as "Open your textbook to page" followed by "Read aloud" and then followed by "Individually", and their specific coding patterns, which are Individual+Form+Teacher/Text Control+Reading+Speaking+ExtendedText+NNS). The data for keyword matching consists of words and phrases indicating the start or end of episodes, or segments, such as "Stop reading....", "OK, then....", etc.

Automatic coding process

1. Transcribing the teacher's utterances in the classroom using the latest speech-to-text technology.
2. From these transcribed utterances, extracting key words and phrases such as those referred to above (e.g., "Open your textbook to page ....", "Read aloud"), which are the cues used for coding. These phrases are matched with the coding pattern information already entered in the server.
3. Adopting the coding pattern corresponding to the hierarchical combination of these phrases and indicating its features by entering 11 or 1 (i.e., primary, or secondary focus).
4. Adjusting the coding results based on pre-entered big data information and the specific utterances used by the teacher.

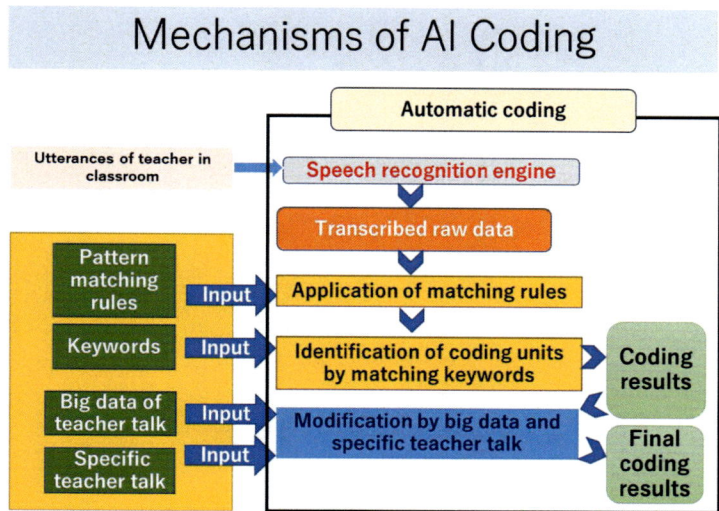

Figure 6.17 Mechanisms of AI coding

As with Mobile COLT, once the automatic coding is complete, Automatic COLT displays the coding results to indicate the percentage of classroom time spent on the main features and categories of COLT Part A and the Global Score, accompanied by graphic images (Figure 6.18). It also displays comments based on interpretations of the coding results, which can be used in future lesson planning. It should be noted that the rate of L1 use is not reflected in the summary when using AI coding.

Summary of 2023

by

Global score

9

Total time: 39:21

LANGUAGE				
1. L1	0 sec	0:00	0%	
2. L2	2361 sec	39:21	100%	Almost all is done in the second language
PARTICIPANT ORGANIZATION				
3. Class	2047 sec	34:07	86%	Most of activities in whole class mode
4. Indiv	0 sec	0:00	0%	No individual activities
5. Group	314 sec	5:14	13%	A little group work
CONTENT				
6. Management	175 sec	2:55	7%	A little content related to classroom management
7. Message	964.5 sec	16:04	40%	Some meaning focus

1. Group	314 sec	5:14	13%	1	A little group work is used. Use a little more.
2. Management / Message	1139 sec	18:59	48%	2	A great amount of learner free speech and writing it intermediate learners and above.
3. Student	224 sec	3:44	9%	1	A little meaning focus. Use less form focus and mor
4. Extended Text / Visual	1055 sec	17:35	44%	2	A lot of discourse and visual information are used. 1 lesson. Use more for reading lessons.
5. L1+L2	1307 sec	21:47	55%	3	Materials for native speakers are used at a high rat of high school students and university students.

Figure 6.18 Summary results of automatic coding

Accessing COLT Part A on Automatic COLT

Below step-by-step instructions are provided to gain access to Automatic COLT.

– Step 1: Request an ID and a password by signing up at https://mobilecolt.glexa.jp/ (Figure 6.19).

Figure 6.19 Request ID

– Step 2: Once logged on, enter the title of the COLT analysis, and click "Start" (Figure 6.20). The COLT coding menu page will then appear (Figure 6.21).

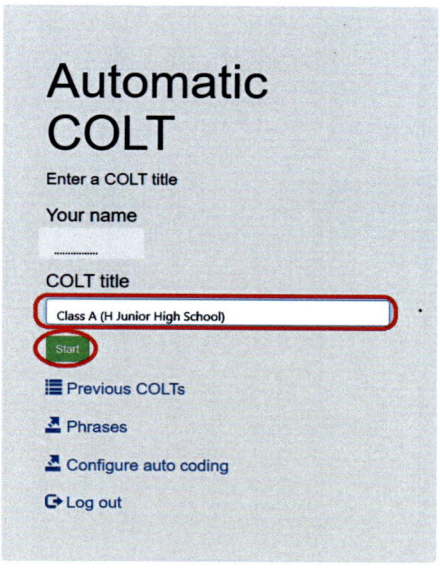

Figure 6.20 Enter title

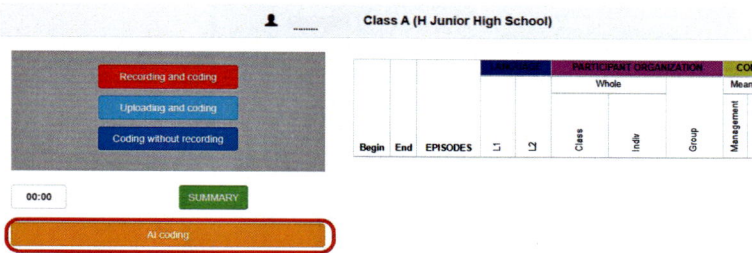

Figure 6.21 Four functions of mobile COLT

- Step 3: On the menu page, first select one of the four functions: AI coding, Recording and coding, Uploading and coding, or Coding without recording (Figure 6.21). The following is a guide to using these four functions.

AI coding

When using AI coding, first set up a PC or a tablet on the pod at the back of the classroom. Use a wireless microphone or a neck speaker for the teacher to wear and connect it to the PC. Click AI coding and allow your PC's microphone and camera to be used. Adjust the volume by checking the waves in the indicator. When you are ready to start the lesson, click "START" (Figure 6.22) and then Automatic COLT will start coding the class. Leave the PC as it is. When the lesson is finished, stop the coding by clicking "STOP STT" (Figure 6.23).

After some computation time, the message "Succeeded uploading" appears, and the coding process is complete. Press "Summary" to view the summary of the class features.

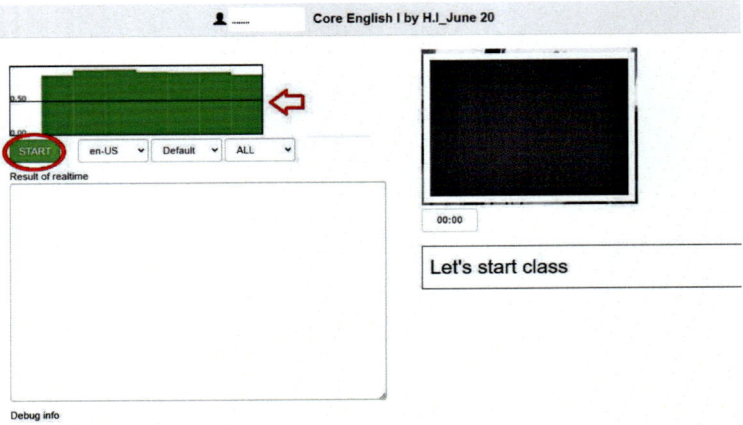

Figure 6.22 Auto coding start

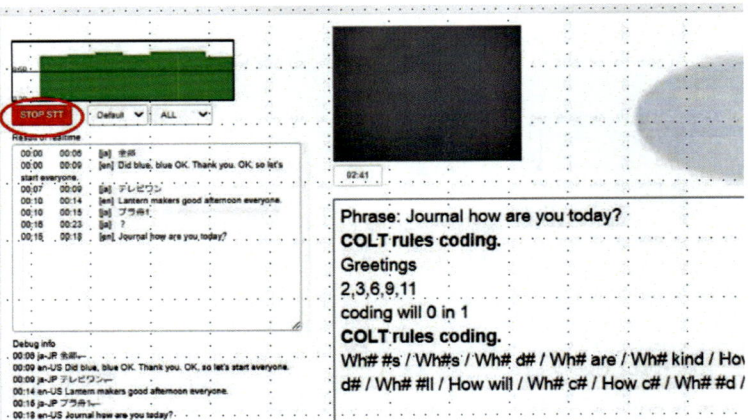

Figure 6.23 Auto coding stop

To make the automatic coding more precise and to elaborate on the information contained in the AI system, there are two different functions for correcting the coding that can be used. One is "Phrases" and the other is "Configure auto coding" (Figure 6.24). "Phrases" permits the user to change the database referred to above that contains the list of pre-entered key phrases teachers generally use to signal activities with certain patterns of COLT features.

The information in this database is prioritized when the AI system codes segments. For example, if a teacher usually says, "Read it aloud individually" to indicate the start of an activity, which is text-controlled and form- and message-focused (i.e., equal focus), this

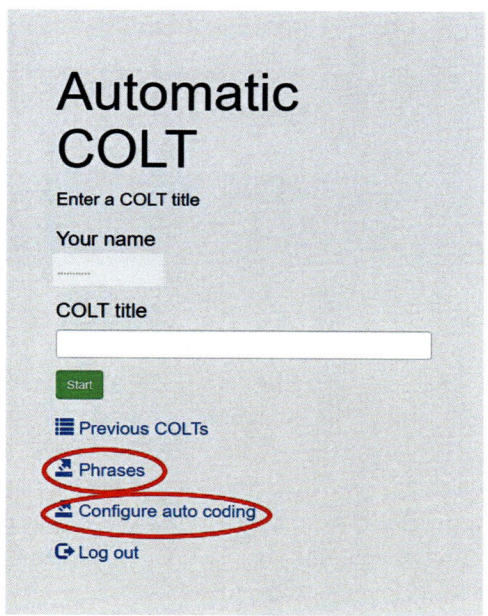

Figure 6.24 Phrases and configuration auto coding

information can be added to "Phrases". Then the AI system gives priority to this information over the pattern matching rules when coding the corresponding activities. To use this database, enter a key phrase with its COLT feature and category and click on 'Save' (Figure 6.25). Teachers using AI coding (and other users) can also remove the entered phrase or download the list of phrases to a desktop to check the content of the list.

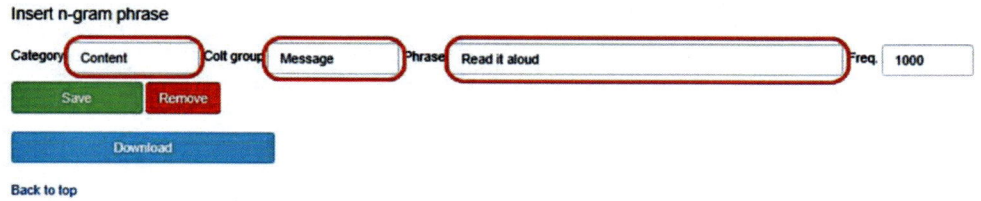

Figure 6.25 Phrases

"Configure auto coding" is the function that can change the hierarchically ordered key phrase information that the system uses to determine the transition of segments. Users can add their own key phrases, such as "Next you will", to signify the transition of episodes. They can also add key phrases, such as "This concludes" to signify the ending of a lesson (Figure 6.26).

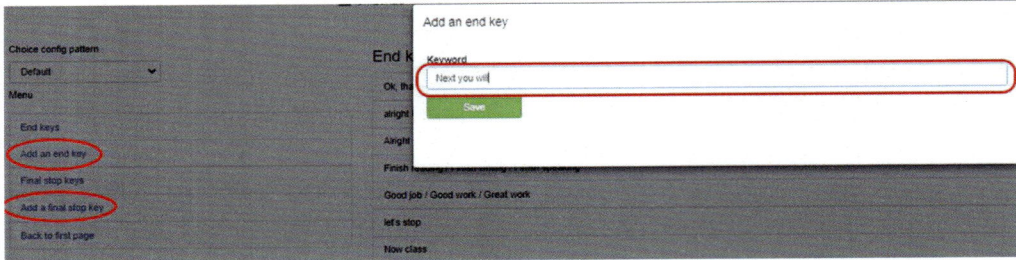

Figure 6.26 Configure auto coding

Recording and coding

When using Recording and coding, the procedure before starting coding is the same as for AI coding. When the class is ready to start, click "Recording and coding" and on the next page, click "REC" (Figure 6.27). Then click "Add" to make a new segment at the start of the lesson and at the end of an episode or activity. Code by selecting 11 or 1 for the COLT categories based on the teaching practices in the class. Click "STOP" when the class ends and then click OK in the opened dialogue box (Figure 6.28).

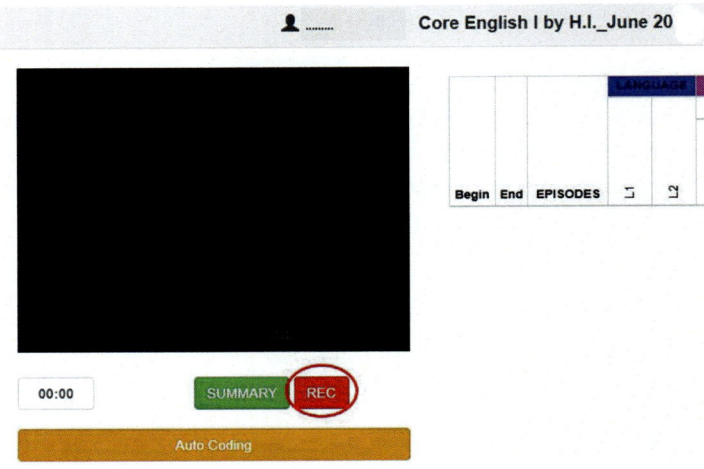

Figure 6.27 Recording and coding: Start

Uploading and coding

Clicking "Uploading and coding" will open the video upload dialogue box. On this screen, one can drag and drop a class video of less than 200 megabytes into the box and the uploading process will be completed in a minute or two (Figure 6.29). Click "Save" and then click either the " ▶ " play button on the video player for manual coding or AI coding for automatic coding (Figure 6.30). Refer to the AI coding and recording and coding sections for the procedures to follow.

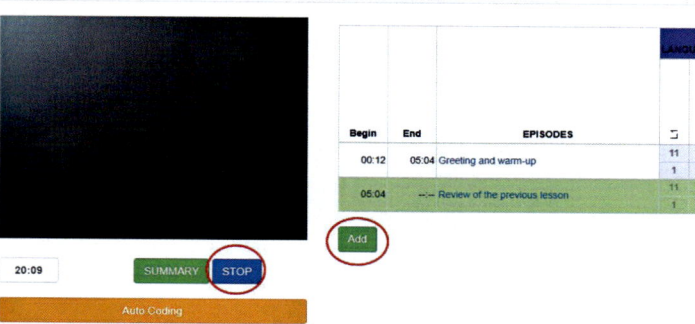

Figure 6.28 Recording and coding: Stop

Figure 6.29 Uploading a video file

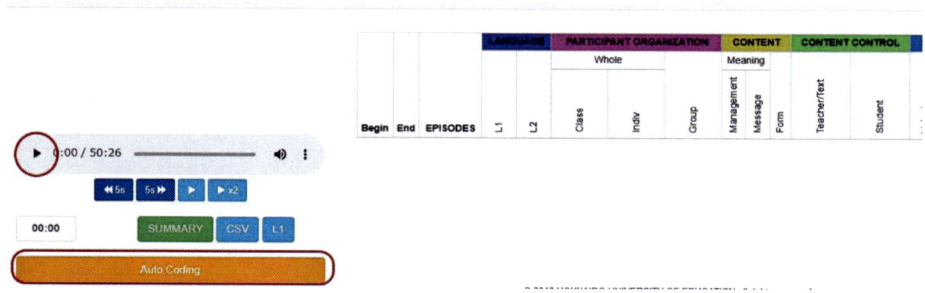

Figure 6.30 Uploading and coding

Coding without recording

When using Coding without recording, click the title to start the timer. This function can be used to code a video-taped lesson or a real-time classroom lesson. The procedure for coding is the same as for Recording and coding (Figure 6.31).

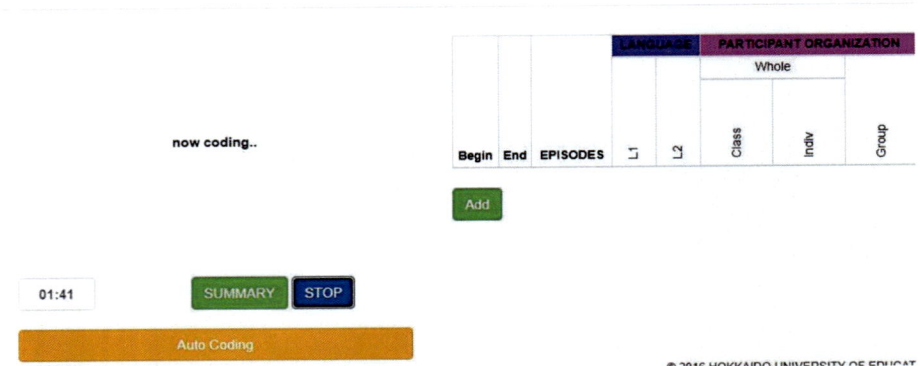

Figure 6.31 Coding without recording

Practice 10

Using the Coding without recording function on Automatic COLT, code the three activities shown in Figure 4.7 in Chapter 4. Remember that the coding categories used in Automatic COLT differ from those in the original COLT scheme. These are referred to as simplified COLT and are described in the Mobile COLT section above and displayed in Figure 6.16.

Start by creating a new COLT table for your own use. A new segment for coding is created each time the "Add" button is clicked. You can change the start and end time of the created segments later. For the purposes of this activity, we have indicated that A3 continued for five minutes. After coding the activities, click the "SUMMARY" button to view a summary of the coding and the global score. Check your coding results with the Answer Key.

Reflections on Digital COLT

All the COLT digital systems have their advantages in terms of conciseness and coding efficiency. With CollaVOD/COLAV-E, the opportunity to share and discuss coding results online is a significant improvement. However, it should be noted that CollaVOD/COLAV-E still depend on manual coding as did Mobile COLT and other comparable functions on Automatic COLT (e.g., Recording and coding). While the AI function on Automatic COLT omits manual coding, it is dependent on the development and use of databases and the creation of language pattern rules, which may not accurately match the instructional practices. Thus, AI coding is not perfect in terms of reliability and is a work in progress. More time is required to create a sufficiently large database to assist with greater AI coding reliability. As more users access Automatic COLT for their analysis of classroom data, it will contribute to the improvement of the system.

Overall, these digital COLT systems have significant potential for facilitating reflections on instructional practices by teachers. To date, this has been the focus of research using the digital versions and results indicate that they are a useful addition to the toolbox for the professional development of teachers. There is little doubt that digital COLT Part A, which provides online access, data sharing, and immediate results will help to open a new way of studying language teaching both as part of teacher training in educational institutions and in the development of language teachers' pedagogical practices in their classrooms.

The digital and technological advances with COLT Part A and the numeric version of COLT Part B (Chapter 5) also include enhancements that will improve methodological rigor when using the observation scheme for different research purposes. For example, the more efficient digital coding procedures, quick access to results and data synthesis facilitate the process of establishing inter-rater reliability. Furthermore, the availability of digital COLT creates an opportunity for replication research of existing studies that have used the original version of the COLT scheme to investigate a wide range of questions about L2 teaching and learning and relationships between the two.

The next chapter presents 12 summaries of published research that has been carried out using COLT Part A and/or B in diverse L2 educational contexts. This final chapter of the book concludes with two research briefs that point to ongoing and future work with digital COLT.

Acknowledgements

This chapter was written by Hiroki Ishizuka with editorial guidance and assistance from Nina Spada.

CHAPTER 7

Using COLT in research

This chapter consists of 12 research summaries that describe how COLT has been used for different research purposes in diverse L2 educational contexts. This includes research that: (1) describes and compares instructional practices in L2 classrooms and programs; (2) investigates the effects of different types of instruction on L2 learning and (3) documents the pedagogical development and reflective practice of teachers in professional development programs. In some of the research either COLT Part A or Part B was used and in others, both parts of the scheme were employed. The summaries are written by the original researcher/s and based on a publication of the work referenced at the end of each one.

The chapter is divided into three sections. The first presents six of the research summaries that were included in the first edition of the book. The second section contains six new research summaries: three that describe the use of the original version of COLT and three that describe the use of digital COLT. The final section includes two research briefs outlining plans for future work using digital COLT. Relevant publications cited in the summaries and briefs are included in the References at the end of the book.

Research summaries (1st edition)

Use of COLT Part A

The first two research summaries in this section report on the use of COLT Part A to describe differences in the instructional practices in English language classes in school-based programs in Canada and in Greece. The third summary describes how COLT Part A was used in research to investigate the relationship between teaching and learning in an adult English language program in Canada. The last summary describes how COLT Part A was revised and adapted for use in English language programs in Spain. An important feature of this work is the rationale and development of a system for the classification of activity types.

Observing with COLT in intensive ESL classrooms in Quebec, Canada
Nina Spada

In a classroom observation study of experimental intensive ESL programs in Quebec primary schools, the COLT scheme was used to describe the instructional practices and procedures in several classrooms. In these intensive programs, young francophone learners receive five full days of ESL instruction every week for five months of the school year. In the remaining five months, students return to their regular French language subject-matter classes (e.g., science, social studies). In the intensive ESL classes, no subject-matter instruction in the regular school curriculum is provided. Instead, students learn English through a variety of topics and themes appropriate to their age level and interests. Intensive ESL differs considerably from the regular ESL programs at the primary level which provide only 120 minutes a week of English language instruction.

The intensive programs were developed in accordance with the Quebec Ministry of Education's philosophy of communicative language teaching. When we began descriptive research in these programs, however, little was known about how teachers and students interacted in these classrooms, what materials were used, and the types of activities students engaged in. Because the programs were experimental in nature, no official curriculum existed, and individual school boards had developed and implemented their programs independently. Thus, one of the main focuses of our initial research was to systematically observe the type of instruction provided in these programs to determine whether and to what extent they differed. If the programs were found to differ, we (along with the teachers and school board administrators) were interested to know whether the instructional differences affected learning outcomes.

Eight intensive program classes were observed four times over a five-month period resulting in a total of thirty-two observation visits. These were full-day observation periods lasting approximately five hours each. During these visits an observer sat at the back of the classroom and coded for the features on Part A of the COLT scheme. At the same time, we audio-recorded the classes. The Part A analysis enabled us to determine whether there were any differences among classes at the level of Participant organization, Content, Student modality and Materials use. The results indicated that classes were very similar to each other.

In keeping with the Ministry of Education's guidelines, instruction was highly communicative in nature. That is, there was no explicit instruction in grammar and virtually no corrective feedback on form was provided. Instead, the emphasis was on the expression of meaning in primarily fluency-based activities. Instruction alternated between teacher-centred and student-centred activities and the emphasis was on speaking and listening.

Although the classroom data indicated high levels of similarity across the intensive program classes, there were indications that some intensive program teachers spent more time on form-focused instruction and providing corrective feedback than others (Spada 1990a, 1990b). This led to a series of quasi-experimental studies which focused on more detailed analyses of the instructional behaviour in relationship to learning outcomes. Some of these results are presented later in this chapter (see also Spada & Lightbown 1993; White, Spada, Lightbown, & Ranta 1991; White 1991).

Using Part A to obtain an initial 'macro-level' analysis of the classroom behaviours was useful. It permitted us to get a global sense of the type of instruction provided in these classrooms and at the same time enabled us to identify areas in which some teachers differed. These areas could then he explored in a more detailed Part B analysis. Part A also has the advantage of being relatively easy to use and does not require much time in the training of research assistants. The categories which presented the most difficulty were those under Other topics. In this study, we used a binary system to describe topics other than language. This included a distinction between 'familiar/core' topics and ones which were 'novel/elaborated'. We made this binary distinction because in the original COLT scheme, the tripartite system used to distinguish among topics (i.e., narrow, limited, and broad), was found to be problematic since most of the coding decisions fell into the middle category. This was due to difficulties in adequately defining distinctions between narrow and broad. Our attempts to resolve this with the binary system of 'familiar and novel' helped to resolve some of the problems, but unfortunately not all of them; the coders reported some difficulties in making these decisions. Other topics remains a high inference category on the COLT scheme and is a good example of why it is important to establish inter-rater reliability.

Lightbown, P.M. & Spada, N. (1994). An innovative program for primary ESL in Quebec. *TESOL Quarterly*, 28, 563–579.

Communicative language teaching in Greek high schools[38]
Vasiliki Zotou & Rosamond Mitchell

The study of a foreign language (normally English or French) is an integral part of the high school curriculum in Greece. During the 1980s, substantial efforts were made to promote the principles of communicative language teaching in this setting, for example through curriculum development projects – such as that leading to the production in 1987 of the 'Taskway English' materials (Dendrinou et al., 1987) for the junior high school – and a variety of in-service activities for teachers. However, little was known about the impact of this promotional activity on teachers' actual practices in the language classroom.

The project described in this summary was initiated by the first author while she was a doctoral student at the University of Southampton, England, to investigate current classroom practices in Greece from a 'communicative' perspective, and to make recommendations for the further strengthening of teacher preparation and professional development. The project is selectively outlined here, to provide a further example of the adaptation and use of the COLT observation system in a new setting. Readers interested in following up on the study in full detail are referred to Zotou (1993).

For the purposes of the study, 'effective' foreign language teaching was defined in a normative manner as the fullest implementation of communicative principles.[39] The researchers were concerned to discover the extent to which a group of Greek teachers of English as a foreign language (EFL), who were identified as 'effective' by such colleagues as advisers and head teachers, were conforming in their ongoing classroom practice to the instructional paradigm of communicative language teaching. They also aimed to link instructional patterns observed in the classroom with aspects of these teachers' professional biographies (e.g., their

---

38. This is a slightly reduced version of the summary published in the 1st edition of the COLT book.

39. The normative perspective on teacher effectiveness' compares a given exemplar of instruction with a model or conception of good teaching, derived from a theory or ideology. (Shulman, 1986).

experience of in-service training), and with students' attitudes to the foreign language learning process.

To achieve these different goals, the study involved the design and use of a range of data gathering instruments, including teacher interview schedules and student questionnaires. However, classroom observation would necessarily form a central element of the study. Clearly, given the intention to compare individual teachers' current practice with a normative model of effective teaching (rather than to explore classroom practice in a more open-ended way), systematic observation was an appropriate technique, and the researchers reviewed a number of possible instruments. We were aware of the COLT system from sources such as Allen, Fröhlich, & Spada (1984), Ullman & Geva (1984), and Spada (1987). After due consideration, COLT offered itself as the most suitable choice for this particular study, on several grounds:

–   Most importantly, COLT seemed to take generally agreed principles of communicative language teaching and organize them into a systematic set of coherent observational categories.
–   COLT was a well-developed system which appeared to be both 'learnable' and to offer good prospects for achieving reliability of coding.
–   COLT offered a basis for quantification and the development of distinctive behavioural profiles for teachers.
–   The fact that COLT had been applied in other contexts offered prospects for contrastive comparisons between the classroom practices of our Greek participants and the documented behaviour of other groups of teachers.

After some preliminary observations and trialing conducted with EFL classes in Southampton (both live and videotaped), a formal pilot study was conducted in two Greek high schools in spring 1989. Two English teachers were observed, and audio recorded working with eight different class groups for a total of seventy-two lessons, and the first author experimented with 'real time' coding using COLT in its original form. Using the pilot audio data, both authors conducted further coding in summer 1989 and became aware that, at least with this data corpus, they had difficulties in achieving acceptable levels of reliability with some aspects of the system. A few categories did not seem to 'fit' with Greek material, others seemed to need clarification/redefinition. (It also became clear at this point that the study should use COLT Part A only.)

Accordingly, we began the task of revision/elaboration of COLT Part A, to provide ourselves with an adapted set of coding conventions which could accommodate the specific characteristics of the Greek classroom material. The schedule for the fieldwork program demanded that Zotou return to Greece to collect the main study data before this task was fully complete. Thus, it was agreed that while she would conduct further 'real time' coding in the field, the main study classroom data would also be audio recorded so that field coding could be revised subsequently should this prove necessary.

During 1989–90, Zotou conducted the main field research in nine further schools in different areas of Greece (four high schools, and five senior high schools). Eleven teachers of English were selected to participate, based on positive professional judgements as to their 'effectiveness'. These teachers were observed, and audio recorded, teaching one or more different class groups. From the large number of recordings collected, a total of sixty-four lessons were selected as the final data corpus to be analyzed. (The 'norm' was a minimum of five lessons per teacher. Two teachers had, however, been observed working at two different levels, and for these individuals, five lessons at each level were analyzed.)

On Zotou's return to England, further fine-tuning of the analysis instrument was undertaken. Then a final definitive reliability study was carried out through joint coding of ten lessons from the main study corpus, using a modified set of category definitions based on those supplied by the COLT originators. (For the original version, see Allen, Fröhlich, & Spada, 1984; for our modified version, see Zotou, 1993). We coded four lessons together and through discussion reached agreement on coding definitions. We then coded the remaining six lessons separately, and compared the results, achieving an acceptable level of agreement overall. We then revised 'real time' codings of the remaining lessons in the main corpus in the light of the final fine-tuning of the instrument, and then converted data from the coding sheets into a form readable by a conventional statistical package.

The adapted coding sheet is referred to as COLTGr and the adaptations were limited. As in the original COLT Part A scheme (COLTCan), the coding unit is one minute of lesson time, and every third minute of the lesson is coded. Similarly, open-ended activity descriptions are entered in the same way (though retrospectively these were grouped for analysis purposes into a closed set of twenty-five activity types).

In COLTGr, *Participant Organization* categories are used as in the original scheme. Within the *Content* group of categories, the *Management, Language* and *Topic control* subgroups are virtually unchanged (apart from deletion of the *Implicit* language category). However, some changes were found necessary within the large *Other topics* subgroup of COLTCan. Some new categories were introduced, principally to reflect the fact that in these Greek classrooms, fictional texts of different kinds were frequently the focus of attention; other categories which we found difficult to distinguish reliably were also collapsed. Difficulties experienced initially in distinguishing among *Narrow, Limited* and *Broad* categories proved capable of being resolved by some sharpening of definitions and build-up of examples. The *Student modality* categories of COLTCan are used unchanged in COLTGr except for the addition of a *Practical activity* category. The *Materials* group of categories proved difficult to apply reliably at first, but this problem was largely resolved through some sharpening of definitions, with more explicit recommendations for the coding of different types of textbook materials (necessary because of the prominence of individual textbooks among materials in use in the classrooms observed) (see Zoutou, 1993 for the adapted COLTGr Part A scheme).

Thus, the modification of COLTCan for use with Greek high school data consisted partly in the provision of fuller and/or adapted definitions for individual categories, plus compilation of a reference set of examples. The main area of COLTCan within which actual modification of the proposed categories proved necessary was that of lesson *Content*. With hindsight, it seems hardly surprising that this domain should prove the most context-dependent, and the need to introduce modifications within it does not present any serious threat to the overall validity of the system in terms of the learning theory and pedagogic principles which COLT aims to operationalize.

Zotou (1993) used the data generated by COLTGr analysis to present a group portrait of these eleven teachers and the extent to which their teaching matched the desired 'communicative' profile. Based on this quantitative analysis, somewhat mixed conclusions had to be drawn on the different facets of the scheme, and in some respects, the persistence of traditional teacher-centred and form-centred instruction was evident.

As far as *Participant organization* was concerned, forms of organization other than whole-class work centring on the teacher were very rare; *Individual work* was found in only 12.4 per cent of observations, and *Group work* in 6.5 per cent. Similarly, as far as *Content* was concerned, the teachers were paying a good deal of attention to *Language topics*, with some explicit reference to grammatical form occurring within 26.8 percent of the total corpus of minutes coded. (On the other hand, explicit talk about other Language categories such as *Discourse* and *Function* was rare, occurring in less than 2 percent of coded time; thus, the kinds of talk about language which might be expected to increase in prominence in a 'communicative' approach remained marginal.) *Topic control* rested virtually always with the teacher; and the materials in use, normally one or other of a small range of textbooks, were typically used in *High control* mode (over 80 percent).

On the other hand, almost 60 per cent of all coded minutes involved one or more categories from within the *Other topics* subgroup within the *Content* domain; that is, there was a fundamental orientation towards meaning rather than towards language form. Moreover, quantitative analysis of the *Other topics* subgroup showed a strong bias towards *Broad topics* (30.2 per cent of observations overall were centred on such topics), as compared with *Limited* (24.3 per cent) and *Narrow* (only 7.7 per cent). This pattern within lesson *Content* constituted the strongest quantitative evidence found in the study of the influence of 'communicative' ideas on teachers' classroom practice. A distinctive feature of these Greek lessons was that many of these meaning-oriented episodes centred around fiction of one kind or another, much of it to be found in the textbooks in use (coded by us with the categories Stories and Literature/Poetry/Art). Thus, Stories (*Broad*) plus Literature/Poetry/Art (*Broad*) provided 21.7 percent of all codings.

Another feature of the lessons which arguably showed a positive communicative orientation was the strong bias within the *Student modality* domain towards listening and speaking (each coded positively for over 90 percent of all observations). Finally, while the absence of COLT Part B made precise quantification impossible, the lesson tapes provided ample evidence of the teachers' ability and willingness to run their lessons largely through the medium of the target language, English, especially at senior high school level.

In addition to the group profile briefly summarised above, the COLT-derived data allowed us to make several within-group comparisons, and to identify a subgroup of five teachers whose profile was substantially more congruent with communicative principles (greater use of group work, less talk about grammar, greater spread of *Broad* content topics, etc.,). The 'professional biographies' of these teachers, documented through interviews, could then be scrutinized to search for factors which appeared to predispose this particular subgroup to innovation/greater 'effectiveness' in communicative terms.

While the attempt to apply COLT Part A in this new setting involved substantial work in such areas as the (re)development of coding definitions, as well as investment of researchers' time in training and in the achievement of adequate reliability, we felt this effort to have been well worthwhile. Eventually we could produce an overview of Greek EFL teachers' classroom practices which we believe to be both reliable and valid (in so far as construct validity can be claimed for the 'communicative' principles operationalized in COLT). Furthermore, the instrument allowed us to distinguish between teachers who were more and less 'effective', from a normative CLT perspective. We realized that COLT offered the potential to do even more than was possible within the practical constraints of this particular study (e.g., we could have conducted formal statistical analyses of relationships between the classroom teaching profiles of particular teachers and the attitudes of their students, as documented through our questionnaires).

We inevitably rediscovered the limitations associated with all systematic instruments of this type: COLT Part A told us, for example, that group work was rare, but could not tell us why this is so without the support from other kinds of data. The instrument is also blind to issues of quality at a more micro level: it could tell us that group work was done, but not whether it was done well! (Here, perhaps, COLT Part B could have made a contribution, had we not quailed before the many methodological problems involved in learning and using it.) But overall, our experience with COLT reaffirmed our view that (a) systematic observation has a continuing justified place in classroom research as a valid approach for the description of classroom processes; and (b) the research community has much to gain from collaboration in the use and development of such instruments over time, in different settings. Thank you, Canada!

Zotou, V. (1993). Effective foreign language teaching: A Greek case study (Unpublished doctoral dissertation). University of South Hampton.

Examining process-product relationships in adult ESL classes
Nina Spada

This summary describes how COLT Part A was used to investigate relationships between instructional processes and learning outcomes in an adult communicative ESL program. The specific research questions were:

1. Would there be differences in the kind of instruction that learners in this communicative program received?
2. Would differences in instruction contribute to variation in learners' improvement in proficiency?

To investigate these questions, three intermediate-level ESL classes were observed, and the learners' English language abilities were measured. The classes were drawn from an English-speaking university in Canada and forty-eight adults were tested. These adults were from many different countries and came to Canada to take the intensive ESL course to be accepted into English-speaking universities in North America. They attended school five days a week for five hours a day over a six-week instructional period.

Several proficiency measures were used at pre-test and post-test administrations to assess the learners' proficiency in the first and the last week of classes. The first test was the listening section of the Comprehensive English Language Test (CELT).[40] Additional reading, writing, and 'talking' tests, which were developed by teachers in the intensive ESL program, were also administered to the subjects. As well, the grammar section of the Michigan test of English language proficiency[41] was administered along with a multiple-choice discourse test and a multiple-choice sociolinguistic test.

To measure classroom behaviours, Part A of the COLT scheme was used. Each of the three intermediate classes was observed for five hours a day, once a week for four weeks by one observer. The percentage of time each class spent on each of the categories of Part A and their sub-components was measured. These quantitative data were then compared to determine whether there were significant differences in instruction among the three classes. Additional qualitative data were collected within the category Activity type. These were examined for differences in the kinds of activities provided in the classes and the way in which they were carried out.

The results from the classroom observation data revealed that there were differences in the kind of instruction learners in these classes received. The quantitative analysis revealed that, although all three classes were communicatively based and the focus was primarily on meaning, one of the classes (class A) was more form-oriented and the two others (classes B and C) were more function-oriented. Furthermore, the qualitative analysis indicated that teachers differed in the way in which they implemented various activities. For example, in the listening activities in Classes B and C, both teachers spent more time preparing learners for the task through pre-listening activities. They also provided opportunities for learners to interrupt and ask questions while they were listening to the passage. The teacher in class A tended to give the students a list of comprehension questions which they read silently to themselves, then played the listening passage twice while the students answered the questions.

---

40. *Comprehensive English language test for speakers of English as a second language.* (1970). McGraw Hill.
41. *Michigan test of English language proficiency.* (1977). English Language Institute, Ann Arbor, Michigan.

The question as to whether there were differences in the learners' L2 proficiency in relationship to the instructional variation revealed the following. Learners in Class A did better (although not significantly) on the written grammar test and learners in Classes B and C appeared to be more accurate in the oral production task. The learners in Classes B and C performed significantly better on the listening measure than the learners in Class A.

The benefits of supplementing the quantitative data obtained with Part A of COLT with more detailed qualitative analyses were particularly striking in this study. It enabled the researcher to interpret the results with more confidence and led to several hypotheses about the role of form-based instruction within communicative language teaching. These hypotheses continue to be investigated in process-product research in different L2 learning environments.

doi Spada, N. (1987). Relationships between instructional differences and learning outcomes: A process-product study of communicative language teaching. *Applied Linguistics, 8*, 137–161.

COLT: Observations and Activities[42]

Marisol Valcárcel, Craig Chaudron, Mercedes Verdú & Julio Roca

Since 1987 the Spanish Education Authorities have been trying to launch a new Curriculum for the Teaching of English in Compulsory Education (8–16-year-olds), based on communicative principles. To develop procedures for evaluating Spanish intermediate teachers of English trained in communicative language teaching, both by means of classroom observation and measures of student achievement, we adopted the general format of the COLT scheme with several characteristics and principal dimensions coded across 'activity' units. We used this, along with several additions and modifications, as a 'real time' observational instrument. In doing so, we attempted to combine elements of both Parts A and B of the COLT scheme. In this summary, we will describe the development of the system; the dimensions retained and changed from the COLT scheme, including our assessment of reliability in coding dimensions; and finally, the system for description of 'activities' that we evolved over the first years.

Over a three-year period, our observation scheme was developed by our research team and used initially to observe and code events in classroom teaching by six teachers in grades 7 through 9, over two years of teaching. As in the COLT scheme, the unit of analysis was the Activity and factors such as *Time* per activity, *Participant organization* (a combination of *Addressor, Addressee,* and *Audience,* in which audio-visual materials or an outside visitor could also be one or more of the participants), and Skill(s) employed were identified simi-

42. The authors gratefully acknowledge the support of the Comité Conjunto Hispano Norteamericano para la Cooperación Cultural y Educativa: Madrid; the Universidad de Murcia and the Center for Second Language Research, Social Science Research Institute: University of Hawaii. Members of the research team initially included Rosario Albuquerque and Juana Marin.

larly. Other comparable dimensions coded, usually with two or three levels, were minimal or extended material *Text length*, teacher and student *Length of verbal interaction*, and teacher and student *Use of language* (in which we added *Mixed to L1 and L2*).

Modifications and additions of dimensions included *Turn control* (understood as student control over turn-taking: low, medium, or high); whether or not a real Context was provided for the activity discourse; low, medium, or high *Authenticity of language use*; degree of control over topic and product outcome (by the teacher); *Relation to L1* (by translation or reference); *Teacher feedback* (whether none, or on form or message); overall *Degree of interaction; Student comprehensibility*; and degree of *Student responsiveness*. Each of these added codes, we believed, captured important aspects of communicative language teaching, while several of the omissions and modifications of the COLT scheme reduced the number of decisions about activities that did not bear heavily on the degree of communicativeness. For instance, the large number of distinctions (twenty) within the COLT's *Topic* category were reduced to only four (*Managerial, Focus on form, Focus on function* and *Other*), and the COLT distinction between *Giving (predictable/unpredictable)* and *Requesting (pseudo/genuine)* information by the teacher or student was changed to two decisions, about the predictability and genuineness of information being exchanged, regardless of the specific giving or requesting nature of the activity. A further noticeable difference between the original and our adapted version of COLT omits the detail in teacher or student incorporation of utterances; primarily because we planned to independently evaluate them, and many other aspects of the discourse based on discourse 'act' coding of transcripts when necessary. The activity unit of analysis is not compatible with this level of detail.

An important aspect of our research was to determine the reliability of coding using our instrument. The independent decisions of three raters were compared pairwise for nineteen dimensions on the activities employed by two teachers over two lessons each, using Cohen's kappa, a conservative measure of agreement. The median agreements for the three pairings of raters fell below 75 per cent (*Student turn control, Authenticity of language use, Degree of interaction*). Seven dimensions had between 80 percent and 90 percent average agreement, and four had 90 percent or greater. Still more encouraging was the result that our coding of *Activity types* for thirty-seven activities ranged between 82 per cent and 88 per cent for the three pairs of raters, with 76 per cent (28) of these activities showing perfect agreement among the raters, and a further 21 per cent (8) being agreed on by at least two raters.

Our development of a system of activity types is, to our minds, one of the crucial contributions of our work to the development of such observation instruments, both for research and for teacher training purposes (Chaudron, 1991; Valcárcel et al., 1991). The COLT system developers explicitly avoided developing a set of identifiable activities, leaving the category 'open-ended', and thereby open to arbitrary descriptions. The lack of classification of activity types is a regrettable loss of information about classroom practices since there can thus be no assessment of the overall amount of more or less communicative behaviours evident in portions of classroom lessons. Only a summary, per teacher's class, of overall amount of time devoted to a given aspect of communicative behaviour is possible and, if in fact certain types or sequences of activities across language classes and programs proved to be more or less communicative, there is no way for the researchers to convey information to other researchers or back to the teachers involved about the commonalties or distinctions.

We, on the other hand, following the extensive language methodology literature on exercise typologies and tasks, attempted to isolate a more finite set of possibilities. Furthermore, we were able to use them quite successfully to demonstrate the changes over the course of a lesson in type, duration, and sequence of activities. Appendix 1 provides a brief description of the currently developed system of activity types. This system is a revision of an earlier one which appeared in Crookes & Chaudron (1991). We are awaiting future developments and focused research in the comparison of our descriptions with other analyses of student classroom behaviour and learning, and teacher in-service development. (See Appendix 1 at the end of this chapter for the activity classification system).

Crookes, G. & Chaudron, C. (2005). Guidelines for language classroom instruction (3rd ed.). In M. Celce-Murcia. (Ed.), *Teaching English as a second or foreign language.* (pp.46–66). Newbury House.

Use of COLT Part A and B

Below two researchers describe how COLT Part A and B were used in studies to investigate relationships between instructional input and learning outcomes. Both studies took place in French language classrooms in secondary schools – one in Canada and the other in Australia.

Core French process-product study
Patrick Allen

The aim of the study was to relate instructional differences in the Ontario core French program at the grade 11 level to differences in the communicative competence of the students. Eight classes, all from the metropolitan Toronto area, were preselected with the help of school board personnel to represent a range of L2 teaching practices. Early in the school year the students were given a series of pre-tests of French proficiency: (a) a multiple-choice grammar test; (b) two written production tasks (a formal request letter and an informal note) which were scored for both discourse and sociolinguistic features; (c) a multiple-choice listening comprehension test requiring the global comprehension of a series of recorded texts; (d) an informal oral interview administered to a subsample of students from each class and scored for proficiency in grammar, discourse, and sociolinguistics. During the school year each class was visited four times for observation with the COLT instrument. Part A was filled out during class time. Part B coding was done after the observation on a time-sampling basis, using transcription and/or audio recordings of the observed class.

At the end of the school year the classes were post tested with the same tests, and those students who were interviewed at the time of pretesting were reinterviewed.

Based on the Part A and Part B categories of the observation scheme, it was possible to rank-order the eight classes on a bi-polar composite scale from 'most experiential' to 'most analytic'. We grouped the COLT features into binary oppositions (experiential versus analytic, or 'high' versus 'low' communicative features) in order to arrive at a score which would permit ranking of the classes. We took the total percentage of time spent on each of the experiential features and added the figures together. This gave us two classes in the 'high' communicative group and six classes in the 'low' communicative group (the mean score being used as the dividing line). To give some idea of what the labels 'experiential' and 'analytic' meant in terms of classroom behaviour it may be useful to consider some examples. In the two most experiential classes, there was significantly more topic control by students, more extended written text produced by the students, more sustained speech by students, more reaction (by both teacher and students) to message rather than form, more topic expansion by students, and more use of student-made materials than in the other classes. These two classes were labelled type E classes, in contrast to the remaining type A classes, where significantly more analytic features were in evidence, including a higher proportion of topic control by teachers, minimal written texts by students, student utterances of minimal length, student reaction to form rather than message, and restricted choice of linguistic items by students.

It was predicted that the type A classes would score significantly higher on both written and oral grammatical accuracy measures than the type E classes, but that the type E classes would score higher on all other proficiency measures, including discourse and sociolinguistic measures, and scores on global listening comprehension. However, based on the post-test scores adjusted for differences in pre-test scores, no significant differences were found between the type E and type A classes, although a near-significant difference emerged in favour of the type A classes on the grammar multiple choice test. When the two type E classes were compared to the two most analytic type A classes (labelled type A*), the type A* classes did significantly better on the grammar multiple-choice test (and specifically on agreement rules), but few other significant differences were found. The next step was to find out whether there were some classroom features which were more important than others for the development of second language proficiency. At this point, we decided to perform a detailed correlational analysis relating the use of all the individual observation variables to L2 proficiency outcomes. The purpose of this analysis was to explore the empirical relationships between COLT categories and proficiency measures, without any a priori assumptions about their relative communicative value.

In our comparison of COLT categories and performance measures, we looked first at the relationship between adjusted post-test scores and individual COLT categories, and then at the correlations between adjusted post-test scores and various combinations of categories. Taking the individual categories first, we found that the profile of a successful classroom which emerged from COLT Parts A and B was as follows: the teacher did relatively more talking to the class as a whole than did individual students; relatively more time was spent on classroom management; more time was spent on form-focused activities than on general discussion; the students themselves spent relatively little time speaking; and visual aids and L2 materials were used relatively often.

The analysis based on combined COLT categories showed that extended writing, information gap, reaction to message, and topic incorporation were positively related to improvement, while sustained speech by students, predictable content/display request, reaction to form, and general discussion with limited or broad range of reference were negatively related. In the case of *Participant organization, Topic control* by teacher or student, and use of '*authentic*' L1 or *adapted* materials, the correlations with performance measures were generally low, indicating that these aspects of classroom treatment were relatively neutral with regard to improvement. It should be emphasized that few of the correlations were statistically significant. However, our purpose was to look at all the patterns that seemed to show consistency, in order to identify possible relationships for future study (see Allen, Carroll, Burtis, & Gaudino, 1987).

The process-product core French study was conducted as part of the Development of Bilingual Proficiency project and formed the third stage in a series of studies which included the development and validation of the original COLT observation scheme (Allen, Swain, Harley, & Cummins, 1990). Out of thirty-two observations (eight classes with four visits to each), twenty were carried out by the principal observer who had been previously trained on the validation study, and four were conducted by a second observer. On eight occasions the two observers worked together and discussed the observations and coding immediately after the class (inter-rater reliability measures were not used). No major problems were encountered either in the use of the observation scheme or in the subsequent coding. However, we felt that although the COLT observation scheme provided a great deal of useful information about classroom interaction, it did not enable us to pay sufficiently close attention to the exchange structure of discourse, particularly to the way in which conversations are jointly negotiated by means of various topic incorporation devices. In any future study, therefore, we recommended that the quantitative procedures based on COLT be supplemented by a more detailed qualitative analysis, with a view to obtaining additional information about the way meaning is co-constructed in the classroom.

doi   Allen, P. & Carroll, S. (1987). Evaluation of classroom processes in a Canadian core French programme. *Evaluation and Research, 1,* 49–61.

A study of communicative orientation and language learning outcomes in French in Australian secondary schools
Penny McKay

A study of the teaching and learning of French in junior secondary school classrooms in Queensland, Australia, sought answers to the following two research questions:

1. What is the nature of the communicative orientation of the junior secondary French classes observed?
2. Does communicative orientation make a difference to learner achievement in French?

The COLT scheme was used as an observation schedule for the detailed analysis of four French classes through years 9 and 10 in junior secondary schools, where students were 14 and 15 years of age. Each of the classes, in different schools in Brisbane, had started their study of French at the same time (in year 8, the first year of secondary school) and each class had had only one teacher throughout their study of French.

During the first year of the study (while the students were in year 9) six lessons were observed from each of the four classes. Using COLT Parts A and B, I was able to undertake a detailed process study to consider the first of the two research questions above. Since there is little detailed documentation of what happens in Australian secondary foreign language classes, this component of the study was important in itself as a means of helping us to gain a greater understanding of foreign language teaching in our secondary schools. The COLT analysis was carried out from full transcripts of the classes because it was often difficult to check back and return to the same spot on the recording for timing purposes, especially on Part B.

The scores on COLT A and B were used to rank the four classes by communicative orientation, following the methods used by Allen, Carroll, Burtis, and Gaudino (1987). The results of the year 9 process study were that, of the four year 9 classes, one class was highly communicative or meaning-focused (with a communicative score of 887), one was strongly form-focused (with a score of 470), and two classes sat in between (with scores of 694 and 693 respectively). The COLT scheme had been able to distinguish across the classes, using this type of calculation, with a wide range in the scores. However, this ranking system was not able to make a distinction between the teaching approaches in the two middle classes: one teacher focusing more on grammar, and the other more on patterns together with short communicative textbook-driven pair work activities. Yet these differences came through well in the COLT-based analysis of individual features of classroom interaction, and a detailed analysis of the differences in the classes in relation to the categories in COLT Part A and B was undertaken.

During the second year (year 10), only two of these classes were available for further observation because of teacher changes. The two remaining classes were still taught by the same teachers that the students had started French with at the beginning of secondary school; both teachers in these two remaining classes were native speakers of French. These classes were observed for five lessons each during the year. The communicative ranking scores of the two continuing classes remained into year 10. The score of the highly meaning-focused class remained high (with a communicative score of 885) while the second class, the more grammar-focused of the mid-scoring classes in year 9, became a little more communicative (with a score of 717). These scores were backed up again by the qualitative data from observations and interviews.

The year 9 classroom process data combined with the process data in year 10 for these two classes, became part of a process-product study for the year 10 classes, designed to answer the second research question. At the end of the year the students undertook tests in speaking (an interview rated by experienced teachers of French), listening and reading (two national Australian tests devised by the Australian Council of Educational Research), and writing (a teacher-developed test, rated by four experienced teachers of French). The classroom process data were correlated with the learning outcomes as measured by these tests.

It was hypothesized, amongst other things, that the students in more meaning-focused classes would score significantly better in speaking and listening because of their more meaning-focused classroom experiences. Briefly, the results of the tests showed that students in the highly meaning-focused class were not, in fact, significantly better in either of these skills. In addition, students in the more meaning-focused class were found to be significantly weaker in their reading and writing skills than the students in the second class (see McKay 1994, for more details).

The COLT scheme enabled me to undertake a detailed analysis of the interaction in the two classes, and to consider reasons why these results occurred. The analysis showed, for example, that in the meaning focused class, the students were 'fudging' a great deal and were not being pushed towards comprehensible output (Swain, 1985) by the teacher who would allow them to make only short one-word comments or responses. The analysis also showed that the second teacher had a clear focus on form but at the same time guided controlled communicative interaction in pair work. The differences between the classes were therefore complex. Overall, the results confirm the findings of other similar studies, that a highly communicative classroom is not as successful as the communicative literature originally suggested.

In the study I supplemented the scheme by doing an additional analysis of the focus on form in Part B. I felt that there was variation in the teachers' focus on form which needed to be recorded and analyzed. I made an additional check mark (using the *Reaction to form* column for this second purpose) to classify the turns into a range of possible categories in focus on form, including *Vocabulary, Grammar, Patterns* and *Pronunciation*, whenever there was attention to form in the turn. I nominated beforehand the kinds of turns which should be classified. My analysis was a useful addition to the COLT data for this study, showing, for example, that whenever the highly meaning-focused teacher did focus on form it was predominantly on vocabulary and pronunciation. Also, the focus on grammar in the more form-focused class was a very high proportion of all form focus. In both classes, focus on form was often integrated into activities, particularly in the more experiential class. Attention to this type of analysis would be a valuable addition in COLT Part B; guidelines from the developers would help to standardise and make comparable the findings from the analyses.

The need for this detailed coding conventions manual is a final comment I would like to make regarding the COLT scheme. The availability of a manual will be welcomed by people like me who have so far needed to become familiar with the scheme without training and with few people at hand who know the scheme in detail. Apart from the difficulties in learning how to use the scheme without detailed guidance, there is also the important issue of finding colleagues who have the expertise to act as co-raters to ensure inter-rater reliability.

McKay, P. (1994). Communicative orientation and language outcomes in Australian junior secondary foreign language classes (Unpublished doctoral dissertation). University of Queensland.

New research summaries

In the next two sections, six research summaries are included that were published several years after the publication of the first edition of this book. Three of them used the original version of COLT and the other three used different digital versions of the scheme. Like the summaries described above, they represent research that focuses on the use of COLT to describe pedagogical practices in different L2 educational contexts and to investigate relationships between L2 instructional input, interaction, and learning outcomes. These were the primary goals that motivated the development of the COLT observation scheme in the mid 1980s. Since then, COLT has been increasingly used for research in teacher education to explore the professional development and reflective practices of L2 instructors.

Original COLT

The three summaries below describe research using the original versions of Part A and B of the COLT scheme. The first two describe how COLT was used in teacher professional development programs – one in Turkey and the other in Mexico. The third research summary describes the use of COLT to investigate how differences in the communicative orientation of instruction in a French and a Japanese immersion program led L2 learners to respond to the same type of teachers' corrective feedback in different ways.

Using COLT in an EFL professional development program in Turkey
Ayse Akyel & Denis Ortaçtepe

Although communicative language teaching (CLT) is widely popular within English language education in Turkey, there are still schools, universities, and language teaching institutions that follow traditional approaches such as grammar translation or the audiolingual method (e.g., Coşkun, 2011; İnceçay & İnceçay, 2009; Kırkgöz, 2008). Even those programs that do claim to follow a communicative approach may not do so when it comes to teaching practices, materials development, curriculum design, testing, and teacher training purposes.

Our study, therefore, aimed to enhance Turkish English as a foreign language (EFL) teachers' knowledge and skills to enact CLT in their classrooms through an 8-month professional development program. In addition to focusing on the impact of the professional development on EFL teachers' practice, this study also related their reported and observed practice of CLT to teacher efficacy, which refers to teachers' belief in their capacity "to organize and execute courses of action required to successfully accomplish a specific teaching task in a particular context" (Tschannen-Moran et al., 1998, p. 233). The study addressed the following research questions:

1. What is the relationship between Turkish EFL teachers' efficacy and their self-reported practice of CLT in the classroom?
2. To what extent does the professional development program influence Turkish EFL teachers' self-reported and observed practice of CLT in the language classroom?

The eight schools from which the data came were in the process of updating their curriculum and English teachers' practices to make them more in line with the communicative approach. A collaboration, therefore, has been established with the language program directors of these K–12 schools and the English language teaching (ELT) department of a well-known university in Istanbul, Turkey. As a result of this collaboration, the faculty members in the ELT department would not only mentor the English teachers at these eight schools but also design a professional development program to address their needs and interests. After a 2-month needs assessment period of interviewing the teachers and the program coordinators; observing classes; and evaluating the textbooks, the results revealed that although the EFL students had been learning English since they were five years old, they had difficulties in using the target language in real-life like situations. The observed lessons mostly included grammar based, drill type activities, which were mechanical in nature, giving EFL students not many opportunities to use the language for meaningful purposes. In addition, the classes were highly teacher-centred, not allowing for active student learning through pair or group work. Therefore, the professional development (PD) program specifically focused on CLT to encourage EFL teachers to focus more on meaning-making activities, real-life like use of language (e.g., information gap activities), pair and group work, and the use of integrated skills. The PD program aimed to help EFL teachers understand CLT principles and strategies regarding the goals of language teaching, the kinds of classroom activities that best facilitate learning, and the roles of teachers and learners in the classroom (Brown, 1994; Celce-Murcia, 2001; Richards & Rodgers, 2004). Using instructional techniques and activities that engage learners in the negotiation of meaning and meaningful interaction, instead of activities that demand accurate repetition and memorization of sentences and grammatical patterns, was also at the centre of the professional development program.

As the coordinators of the PD program, we visited each school once a week over the 8-month period. During these visits, we observed language teachers in the mornings, and in the afternoons, we provided feedback to the observed teachers followed by a group discussion on the readings. Once a month, we held regular meetings with the English language program coordinators to discuss general problems and to offer possible solutions. Overall, the professional development program relied on the following principles in order to promote teachers' practice of CLT by (a) raising their awareness of past experiences, beliefs, practice and knowledge, (b) exposing them to new input through interactive seminars, workshops, and readings on CLT, and (c) engaging them in dialogue with colleagues and providing opportunities for collaborative reflection (Murray & Christison, 2011; Richard-Amato, 2003; Richards & Farrell, 2005).

Data were collected before and after the PD program using; (a) Teachers' Background Questionnaire, (b) English Teachers' Sense of Efficacy Scale (ESTES) (Chacon, 2005), (c) Communicative Orientation of Language Teaching (COLT): Observation Scheme (Spada & Fröhlich, 1995), and a questionnaire version of COLT (QCOLT). Among the 200 Turkish EFL teachers working in these eight schools, 50 teachers who taught the main course for the 7th, 8th and 9th grades attended the PD program. While all the participating teachers responded to the questionnaires, only 20 of them were observed due to time restrictions. Before the PD program began, each teacher was observed five times during a 40-minute English lesson by one of us, who sat at the back of the classroom and did not interact with the students at any time during the class. Every five minutes, we recorded what was happening during the lesson on the COLT Part A observation spreadsheet. Additional field notes were also taken and at the same time the entire lesson was audiotaped for later Part B coding. The same procedures were repeated after the end of the PD program.

All categories of the COLT Observation Scheme Part A except for 'the use of materials' were included in the study. This category was excluded because the study was carried out in an EFL setting where the teachers mostly used minimal texts and materials developed for 'non-native' speakers of the language. Following the suggestions of Spada and Fröhlich (1995), the coding for Part A was done in real time while the coding for Part B was conducted after the observations with the help of the audio recordings. The general coding procedures of Part B and Part A were followed in that check marks were placed in the appropriate features for the relevant categories within activities/episodes and whenever a teacher/student took a turn. Each activity and episode were timed so that a calculation of the percentage of time spent on the various COLT features could be determined (Spada & Fröhlich, 1995). At the end of each observation, we listened to the audio recordings and went over the data sheet for Part A first to ensure the validity and reliability of our coding. Once both of us agreed on all the items on Part A, we listened to the recordings one more time to code Part B. Both of us demonstrated agreement in our coding of Part A and B.

To assess the teachers' self-reported use of CLT in their lessons, we developed a questionnaire based on the features and categories of the COLT Observation Scheme and the previous literature on CLT (Bell, 2005; Brown, 2001; Larsen-Freeman, 2003; Richards & Rodgers, 2004). The Questionnaire of Communicative Orientation of Language Teaching Observation Scheme (QCOLT) consists of 50 items divided into two subscales: (a) Classroom events, and (b) Communicative features (see Ortaçtepe & Akyel, 2015 for more details).

In relation to the first research question, no significant relationship was found between teachers' efficacy and their self-reported practice of CLT. Similar to other research (e.g., Chacon, 2005), teacher efficacy did not seem to have a significant relationship with teachers' self-reported practice of teaching. A possible explanation for these results is that teachers may not be evaluating their teaching practices as grammar-oriented or communicative-oriented when they make decisions about their teacher efficacy.

In relation to the second research question, the findings indicated no significant change in teachers' self-reported practice of CLT. On the other hand, significant differences were observed in certain aspects of teachers' observed practice of CLT before and after the PD program. This was evident in the communicative orientation of classroom activities captured by COLT Part A as well as in the nature of the verbal interactions between teachers and students described in COLT Part B. With respect to the Part A findings, after the PD program, there was a statistically significant increase in teachers' use of group-work activities and a considerable decrease in the individual and whole-class activities (*Participant organization*). Teachers started to spend less time on management issues such as classroom procedure and discipline (*Content*) and preferred to engage students in activities that required the use of integrated skills rather than focusing only on one skill or on grammar and vocabulary in isolation (*Student modality*). There was also an increase in teacher-student joint control and students' control over the content (*Content control*).

Regarding the COLT Part B results, after the PD program, there was a decrease in teachers' use of L1 and L1 translation (*Target language*); there were more genuine questions asked to students to foster authentic communication in the classroom (*Information gap*), and a shift was observed from ultra-minimal to minimal speech (*Sustained speech*). That is, the EFL teachers did not give feedback just to indicate whether the student answer was right or wrong but tried to establish meaningful communication with the students. Additionally, after the PD program, the teachers reacted to students' utterances by providing less form-focused correction and more meaning-focused elaborative and clarification requests. No significant difference was found in the categories of message and form-focused repetition, paraphrase, comment, and expansion.

To summarize, after the PD program, there was less teacher control and more student involvement in classroom activities, more use of activities that encouraged students to use more than one mode of communication in English (i.e., integration of skills) through group work, and more focus on meaning rather than form. These changes suggest a shift from traditional grammar-based activities to more communicative ones because of the PD program which, in fact, aimed to improve these aspects of CLT in teachers' practices.

Overall, we found the COLT Observation scheme to be very helpful to analyze classroom observation data. It helps break down CLT into observable units/features and gives a general assessment of a lesson in terms of how communicative it is. The coding and analysis of Part B can be quite labour intensive, but we viewed the time spent for that section as an opportunity to immerse ourselves in the data and to really understand the dynamics of classroom interaction. We have been using COLT in our research methods courses since this study, as it helps novice researchers understand how the operationalization of a construct, in this case, a teaching approach, can be done via an observation scheme.

doi   Akyel, A., & Ortaçtepe, D. (2015). The effects of a professional development program on English as a foreign language teachers' efficacy and classroom practice. *TESOL Journal, 6*, 680–706.

Language attention in content-based instruction: The case of language instructors teaching content in a foreign language in Mexican higher education
Andrés Arias de la Cruz & Jesús Izquierdo

Content-Based Instruction (CBI) defined "as the integration of a particular content with language teaching aims" (Brinton, Snow, & Wesche, 2003, p. 2), continues to grow in popularity at all educational levels. In higher education, many universities offer CBI courses in their undergraduate and graduate programs. In most cases, content specialist teachers are appointed to teach these courses without any kind of language training support. Descriptive studies have revealed that, in these courses, students successfully achieve content learning (Friedenberg & Schneider, 2008; Rodgers, 2006). The learners, however, demonstrate limited language learning gains in areas such as grammar, vocabulary, syntax, and pronunciation (Tatzl, 2011; Myers, 2008). The observed limited language learning gains are hypothesized to result from the absence of attention to language. Content specialists explain that they disregard attention to language, because they do not see themselves as language teachers, but rather, as subject-matter specialists (Airey, 2012; Hincks, 2010; Unterberger, 2012). Moreover, they do not feel qualified to integrate language attention in their courses due to the absence of formal language teaching training.

These issues led the authors to enquire if teachers, with formal language teaching training, would exhibit attention to language while delivering subject-matter content in CBI courses. Thus, two research questions were addressed:

1. Does the instructional practice of language-trained instructors, who teach content through English to university Spanish-speaking learners, favor meaning-based over language-focused subject-matter instruction?
2. If attention is paid to language, which L2 features do these teachers address?

To answer the research questions, a classroom-based observational study was conducted. The observations were conducted following an unobtrusive approach (Mackey & Gass, 2005) in a university in the Southeast of Mexico. This university offers a BA in Modern Languages with some sheltered CBI courses (Brinton, Snow, & Wesche, 2003). In the study, 9 hours of regular classroom instruction from two lecturers, María and José, were analyzed. These lecturers taught *Culture of English-speaking Countries* and *L2 Material Development* accordingly. They had formal university education in language teaching and held international language proficiency certifications such as the Certificate in Advanced English (CAE) and the Test of English as a Foreign Language (TOEFL).

The research questions required the systematic description of the communicative orientation of instruction (i.e., focus on meaning, form, or meaning form) and the identification of features of language (e.g., vocabulary, grammar) that received attention in the CBI lessons. Part A of the Communicative Orientation of Language Teaching (COLT) observation scheme (Spada & Fröhlich, 1995) was selected for the observational analyses because in comparison to other available schemes, it provides a clear conceptual and operational definition of the instructional orientation of a language class with respect to language and meaning/content at a macro level (Spada & Fröhlich, 1995, p. 128). In the examination of classroom events at the level of activities and episodes in the current study, the researchers adhered to the definitions provided for the original COLT scheme: "an activity is typically marked by a change in the overall theme or content" (Spada & Fröhlich, 1995, p. 30). For the identification of episodes, the researchers considered that "episodes are characterized by any teaching/learning behaviour that is approximately a minute or longer" (Spada & Fröhlich, 1995, p. 33).

Following these operational definitions, the transcript of each lesson was broken down first into activities and then into episodes of approximately one minute. Then, transcript segments were entered into the "activities and episodes" column of the COLT scheme. To determine the communicative orientation of the lessons, the categories within the Content feature were of paramount importance, particularly Language and Other topics. The Other topics categories captured the extent to which the lessons focused on the content of the CBI courses (i.e., *Culture of English-speaking Countries* and *L2 Material Development*). The Language category identified the instructional episodes with respect to their specific focus (i.e., Form, Function, Discourse and Sociolinguistics). After the identification of the activities and episodes and their codification in the scheme, the researchers proceeded to carefully identify the features and categories reflected in each episode. To this end, from left to right on the COLT scheme Part A spreadsheet, the coders placed check marks into the appropriate box/es under each of the five major features for every episode.

Following inter-rater reliability principles (Mackey & Gass, 2005), the first author coded all the lessons. Due to the absence of expertise using COLT, at the beginning of the analysis stage, the first author required considerable time and care when coding the transcripts. To ensure consistency, the researcher regularly referred to the coding conventions and guidelines during the coding. The conciseness of the guidelines and examples provided in Spada & Fröhlich (1995) were very useful during this stage. Once the coding was finished, the first author met with the second author to verify the results. The researchers agreed on 96% of the coded activities and 88% of the episodes. To reach consensus over the coding disagreements, the researchers re-read and discussed the definition of each COLT category. During the reliability phase of the study, it was noticed that through the continuous use of COLT, the scheme became more user-friendly and increased understanding of the category definitions led to faster coding.

Upon completion of the reliability procedures, the next stage was relatively easy. During this stage, the authors calculated the frequency of occurrence of the Part A features and categories that revealed the communicative orientation of the lessons and the specific language features that were in focus. This simply involved counting the number of checkmarks under each of the relevant columns in Part A. In total, 20 activities and 277 episodes were recorded for the *Culture of English-Speaking Countries*. As for the *L2 Materials Development* course, 10 activities and 124 episodes were identified. Within these activities and episodes, the COLT coding revealed that both teachers showed systematic attention to content, with erratic attention to language. In 63% of the episodes, the course instructor of the *Culture of English-speaking Countries* course focused on content and in 37% of the episodes the instructor focused on language. Attention to language was mainly reactive and only when the pronunciation of words impeded the communication of ideas. The instructor of the *L2 Material Development* course also had a strong orientation to content. In 89% of the episodes, the course instructor focused on content, whereas the other episodes were focused on language. The most attended language feature was vocabulary. The course instructor limited himself to the provision of the words that the students needed to get their message across. Again, the analysis of the lessons revealed that attention to form was reactive. There was no evidence of proactive attention to language observed in either course.

Based on the COLT observational data, it was concluded that despite the teachers' formal education in L2 teaching and many years of language teaching experience, they exhibited a strong content-based orientation and a weak language-based orientation in their CBI lessons. When the teachers focused on language, this focus was unsystematic and most frequently in reaction to communication breakdowns that emerged from the use of incorrect vocabulary or pronunciation. As indicated in previous research, this lack of attention to language is unlikely to help learners restructure their ill-formed language production (Tatzl, 2011; Myers, 2008). Based on these results, the study makes two contributions to the domain of CBI. The first contribution relates to the necessity of a counter-balanced proactive focus on form (Lyster, 2007) in CBI. The evidence from this study indicates that when a focus on form occurred it was reactive. Given the limited language gains made by learners in CBI courses, there is an urgent need for more pre-planned or proactive focus on language. This study also illustrates that language teachers will not automatically pay attention to language when they teach CBI lessons. It seems likely that when teaching CBI courses, language teachers adopt a content-teacher identity. As content teachers, they prioritize meaning over form as content specialists do (e.g., Airey, 2012; Hincks, 2010; Unterberger, 2012) and disregard the language teaching training they have received. Thus, language teachers, who become subject-matter specialists, need educational assistance to bridge the pedagogical training and expertise of the two educational areas that are involved in CBI: content and language.

CBI constitutes an educational approach where language acquisition occurs as the students learn subject matter in the target language. Thereafter, the COLT scheme was selected for the analysis of CBI lessons, as it was created to observe language classrooms where the emphasis is on communication and to capture the degree to which the focus is on meaning/content and language. In our study, the COLT scheme made it easy "to obtain an overview of the structure of the class in terms of number and type of activities and episodes" (Spada

& Fröhlich, 1995, p.30). However, this distinction was not always easy to implement. First, the identification of the activities and episodes in Part A is challenging because they are naturally interwoven during a language lesson and their beginning and end are not always straightforward. To overcome this challenge, novice coders could consider the segmentation of the transcripts into one-minute fragments. Second, the classification of the activities and episodes across the meaning and language columns can be time-consuming and confusing for novice coders. Thus, they need a sound understanding of the definitions and examples in the scheme. Finally, inter-rater reliability is essential. It is recommended that, after a thorough reading and discussion of the COLT scheme features and categories at least two coders work independently and crosscheck their analysis results. When disagreement occurs, they should refer to the COLT scheme manual's definitions and examples. One of the benefits of the COLT scheme is that, once the coding has been verified, the frequency counts provide quantitative findings that can be interpreted in relation to the research questions under investigation. In the current study, the observation data were instrumental in identifying the particular and shared characteristics of the instructional orientation (i.e., form and content) and the specific aspects of language in focus during the CBI lessons.

doi   Arias, A., & Izquierdo, J. (2015). Language attention in content-based instruction: The case of language instructors teaching content in a foreign language in Mexican higher education. *Journal of Immersion and Content-based Language Education*, 3, 194–217.

Interactional feedback and instructional counterbalance
Roy Lyster & Hirohide Mori

This study compared patterns of corrective feedback (CF), uptake, and learner repair in two different instructional settings: French immersion (FI) for English-speaking children in the predominantly French-speaking Canadian province of Quebec and Japanese immersion (JI) for English-speaking children in the United States. The FI sample included four classrooms (i.e., three Grade 4 classrooms and one Grade 4/5 classroom) described in detail in Lyster & Ranta (1997). The data from the three JI classrooms are part of a larger classroom study described by Mori (2002); two were Grade 4 classes taught by the same teacher and the third was a Grade 5 class taught by a different teacher. The total dataset comprises 33 hr of classroom interaction, 18.3 hr in FI and 14.8 hr in JI.

The oral interaction in FI classes was audio-recorded and later transcribed and coded, whereas video-recordings were made of the JI classrooms and relevant episodes were then transcribed and coded. The six participating teachers continued with their regular immersion program, aware that the researchers were interested in observing classroom interaction but unaware of the research focus related to CF. We used an adapted version of the error treatment sequence identified in Lyster & Ranta (1997) to compare the distribution of different types of CF (i.e., recasts, explicit correction, and prompts) and learner responses (i.e., uptake, including learner repair) that occurred during the 33 hr of classroom interaction.

The development of Lyster and Ranta's (1997) coding categories, which are described next, was influenced by Doughty's (1994) error treatment categories and by the categories "reaction to form/meaning" and "incorporation of student utterances" in Part B of the COLT coding scheme (Spada & Fröhlich,1995).

A recast reformulates all or part of a student's utterance without the error and without verbally stating that an error occurred. Explicit correction also provides the correct form but, unlike recasts, clearly states that what the student had said was incorrect and may or may not include an explanation. In contrast, prompts do not provide the correct form and instead include a variety of signals that push learners to self-repair, including elicitations, metalinguistic clues, clarification requests, and teacher repetition of the error.

Learner uptake refers to the range of possible immediate learner responses to CF, including either (a) learner repair or (b) utterances still in need of repair. Learner repair entails the student's correct reformulation of an error, whereas learner responses still in need of repair include simple acknowledgments such as "yes," hesitations, off-target responses, partial repair, and occurrences of either the same or a different error (see Lyster & Ranta, 1997 for examples of the different types of CF and learner uptake).

Because our purpose was to contribute to a burgeoning awareness of contextual variables that influence classroom learners' attentional biases toward one type of CF over another, we used Part A of the COLT observation scheme (Spada & Fröhlich, 1995) to identify relevant instructional variables not captured by the analysis of the error treatment sequence alone. In the case of the FI classrooms, a nonparticipant observer coded classroom activities during the audio recordings using Part A of the COLT coding scheme. In the case of JI classrooms, a post-hoc analysis of a subset of video recordings of the JI classrooms was conducted using COLT Part A to enable a comparison of instructional variables between the FI and JI contexts. COLT Part A helped to assess the overall communicative orientation of each instructional setting and to provide explanatory support for any differences across settings with respect to observed patterns of CF and learner responses.

We summarize the results of this comparative study by answering our three research questions. The first research question asked what the distribution of different types of CF was in FI and JI classrooms. We found that teachers used CF in similar ways: Recasts constituted the greatest proportion of CF in both settings (54–65%), followed by prompts (26–38%), and then explicit correction (7–9%). The finding that immersion teachers in both settings behaved similarly in their CF choices – using recasts much more frequently than other types of CF – can be seen as well-tuned to the objectives of content-based L2 instruction, in which recasts play at least one of many possible roles. For example, recasts can serve to (a) provide positive or negative evidence, (b) maintain the flow of communication, (c) keep students' attention focused on content, and (d) scaffold classroom learners as they communicate about subject matter that requires communicative abilities that exceed their current developmental level (Lyster, 2002).

The second research question sought to identify the distribution of uptake and repair following different types of CF in FI and JI classrooms. Different patterns were observed in

FI and JI classrooms: Overall, JI students responded to CF more frequently (i.e., uptake) and more accurately (i.e., repair) than their FI counterparts. Moreover, the effects of CF type on uptake and repair were reversed in the two settings: The greatest proportion of uptake and repair in JI settings followed recasts (61% and 68%, respectively), whereas the greatest proportion of uptake and repair in FI settings followed prompts (62% and 53%, respectively). Recasts accounted for twice as much uptake than prompts did in JI classrooms, whereas prompts accounted for twice as much uptake than recasts did in FI classrooms. Thus, although no quantitative differences were detected in the teachers' choices of CF types across instructional settings, clear differences in learner responses were apparent.

The third research question asked what factors may have contributed to the observed similarities and differences in the occurrence of CF, uptake, and repair in FI and JI classrooms. The low proportion of learner repair after recasts in FI classrooms had previously been explained in terms of pragmatic ambivalence, owing to their frequent occurrence in confirmations, confirmation checks, or expansions, all intended to confirm or disconfirm the veracity of student utterances and thus obscuring their corrective potential (Lyster, 1998). However, JI students were exposed to the same functional range of recasts as FI students through content-based instruction and yet demonstrated higher rates of uptake and repair. In fact, recasts led to repair as effectively as explicit correction in JI classrooms, which strongly suggested that recasts explicitly served a corrective function in that setting.

We drew on the COLT analysis to answer the third research question. We found that the effectiveness of recasts in eliciting student uptake and repair in JI classrooms was partly due to at least two instructional design features with an analytic orientation: (a) the use of choral repetition and (b) an emphasis on speaking as a skill practiced in isolation through repetition and reading aloud. In other words, JI teachers tended to regularly integrate choral activities into their content-based instruction, providing target models and expecting students to respond with accurate repetition. We speculated that this served as a priming exercise that incited students to repeat recasts more in JI classrooms than in FI classrooms, where no such instructional strategies were detected by the COLT scheme.

Results of the error treatment analysis together with the COLT analysis led us to propose two possible explanations for the instructional differences between the FI and JI classrooms. First, differences in language structure and typology are greater between Japanese and English than between French and English. The relationship between French and English as cognate languages that share similar syntactic structures and writing systems arguably creates propitious conditions for less focus on language form, whereas the fact that Japanese and English are noncognate languages with completely different syntactic structures and different writing systems inevitably orients JI students and teachers toward more focus on form.

Second, the FI classrooms were in a typical L2 setting; French is the official language of Quebec and widely used in the Montreal area, thus giving FI students possibilities for exposure to French outside of the classroom. Conversely, the JI classrooms were in a typical foreign language setting; Japanese in the United States is a much less commonly used language, giving JI students negligible exposure to Japanese outside of the classroom. These differences in social setting might have affected communicative orientations in specific ways, setting the stage for the presence of choral repetition and oral production practice in isolation in JI classrooms and their absence in FI classrooms.

The COLT scheme thus identified specific instructional options with an analytic focus (i.e., attention to language) that were integrated into the predominantly experiential backdrop (i.e., attention to content) of the JI settings but not the FI settings. Although JI teachers did not draw on a structural syllabus to support their language instruction, they were adept at integrating analytic teaching strategies to support their content-based lessons. In the case of FI teachers, their recasts were not as effective as those of their JI counterparts at eliciting learner repair, although the prompts used by FI teachers were as effective at eliciting learner repair as those of JI teachers. The FI teachers tended to use recasts with more of a conversational purpose than a didactic one and to use prompts for didactic rather than conversational purposes (see Sheen & Ellis, 2011; van Lier, 1988). As overt signals that draw learners' attention to interlanguage forms, prompts were equally effective in both FI and JI settings, but much more so than recasts in FI classrooms. To further explain these findings, we proposed the *counterbalance hypothesis*, which states that the effectiveness of any one type of CF in a given instructional context is commensurate with the extent to which it differs from the classroom's overall communicative orientation.

According to the COLT analysis, what distinguished the two settings most from one another was the emphasis in JI classrooms on choral repetition and oral production practice in isolation. These analytic features were particular to the JI classrooms, revealing a form-focused orientation resulting from specific characteristics of the target language – a typologically different, noncognate foreign language – that served to focus the attention of both teachers and students more on form than would a typologically similar, cognate L2, such as French. We drew on these differences to illustrate the counterbalance hypothesis and to explain differences detected in learner responses to CF across both settings.

First, the counterbalance hypothesis predicts that recasts are effective for learners in classroom settings in which the communicative orientation permits regular opportunities for controlled production practice with an emphasis on accuracy. Classroom activities that include choral and other types of repetition draw learners' attention toward form in ways that predispose them to notice the corrective function of recasts (i.e., to notice the gap between their nontarget output and the teacher's recast and to follow up with a repair move). In these classrooms, recasts have the potential to unambiguously play their double role as both corrective and pragmatic moves, as they draw attention to form on the one hand and confirm the veracity of the learner's utterance on the other. As discourse moves that are well suited to meaningful interaction, recasts enable learners in these classrooms to reorient their attentional resources toward meaning in ways that avert an overemphasis on form at the expense of meaning. This is important because learners who bias attentional resources toward linguistic form benefit from their ability to detect formal distinctions "but perhaps at the cost of failing to detect other components of input utterances" (Tomlin & Villa, 1994, p. 199).

Second, the counterbalance hypothesis predicts that prompts are effective for learners in classroom settings in which the communicative orientation does not favor opportunities for controlled production practice with an emphasis on accuracy. It is predicted that learners unaccustomed to any accuracy-based oral production practice will (a) detect prompts more easily than the covert signals they need to infer from recasts, (b) benefit from being overtly prompted to shift their attentional resources toward form and momentarily away from meaning, and (c) benefit from the opportunities to produce modified output in the form of self-repair after prompts.

To conclude, this study adopted two coding schemes to compare two different instructional settings (FI and JI) from 'microscopic' and 'macroscopic' perspectives: respectively, the error treatment sequence model and the COLT scheme (see Spada & Lyster, 1997). Using two coding schemes to support comparisons of instructional settings in this way proved particularly useful for explaining differences across the two settings and overcoming the limitations of observational studies that compare classrooms along a single dimension such as CF and thus lack other relevant descriptive data to support the comparison. Drawing on both instruments enabled us to propose the counterbalance hypothesis to help interpret our findings and to stimulate further research into the effectiveness of CF across a range of classroom settings.

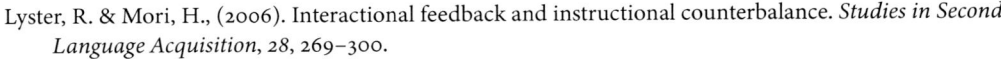

Lyster, R. & Mori, H., (2006). Interactional feedback and instructional counterbalance. *Studies in Second Language Acquisition, 28*, 269–300.

Digital COLT

Below are three summaries reporting research that was conducted using Digital COLT. Most of the work was conducted in Japan using COLT Part A in English language teacher education and professional development programs. The first summary describes how COLT Part A on the CollaVOD platform (see Chapter 6) was used as a reflection tool for high school teachers of English. In the second summary, Mobile COLT Part A (see Chapter 6) was used to document the pedagogical practices of four teachers of English in Japan overtime. The research summary also describes how the integration of AI Coding in Automatic COLT (see Chapter 6) and Moodle will be combined to investigate pre-service teacher training in French language classes in Canada. The third summary describes how numerical COLT Part B (see Chapter 5) was used to describe the communicative orientation of the verbal interactions of preservice Japanese English teachers in their teaching practicum.

Assessing the effectiveness of the COLT scheme as a reflection tool for high school teachers of English: A summary

Aiko Sano, Noriaki Katagiri, Yuko Sakai & Akinobu Shimura

Making English classrooms more communicative has been the focus of English education reformation over decades and it persists today. In Japan, a very short period is allocated for preservice English language teacher training, and novice teachers are often thrown into classrooms underprepared. The research described in this summary demonstrates how opportunities for in-service teachers to reflect on their teaching practices are invaluable, and how such reflections can become efficient and robust when supported by an objective framework that is theoretically driven. Using the Communicative Orientation of Language Teaching (COLT) observation scheme (Spada & Fröhlich, 1995) to observe and reflect on the language teaching practices in Japanese English classrooms, the following research questions were investigated:

1. How effective is the COLT scheme as a reflection tool for high school teachers of English?
2. How do teachers vary in the ways they reflect on their teaching using the COLT scheme?

Three in-service non-native English teachers, two experienced and one novice, from three different high schools in Japan participated in this study. First, two to three classes of each participant were observed and recorded on video. The recorded classes were then analyzed using COLT Part A (Spada & Fröhlich, 1995) to investigate how communicatively oriented they were. To accomplish this, we used the online CollaVOD system developed by Ishizuka and Yorozuya (2014). As described in Chapter 6, COLT Part A has been integrated into the CollaVOD platform to conduct semi-automatic analyses of video-recorded lessons. The teachers were also interviewed first with respect to their beliefs about language teaching in relation to the main features and categories in COLT Part A. They were then asked to reflect on their teaching performances while viewing the results of the COLT analyses based on their teaching. All the interviews were video recorded and transcribed with the participants' consent. The recorded and transcribed interviews were qualitatively analyzed with coding schemes inspired by the procedures of Grounded Theory Approach (Strauss & Corbin, 1997) to avoid subjective interpretation of the data by researchers.

COLT Part A: The analysis of the instructional practices of the three teachers revealed individual differences in their teaching styles. In terms of *Participant Organization*, the amount of time each teacher spent on *Class, Group Work,* and *Individual Work* were tallied and compared. They were then analyzed through cross-tabulation using Fisher's exact test to determine if the differences were statistically significant. The results indicated that T1(Teacher 1) spent less time on *Group Work* and more time on *Individual Work*. T2 spent much less time on *Class,* and much more time on *Group Work,* and very little on *Individual Work*. T3, the novice teacher, spent much more time on *Class,* and much less time on *Group Work*. In terms of *Content*, the amount of time each teacher spent on *Management, Language,* and *Meaning* were tallied and compared. T1 and T3 spent much of their teaching time on *Language*, while T2 presented a strikingly different trend of spending little time on *Language* and more time on *Meaning*. As for *Content Control*, T1 and T3 presented a similar pattern of spending more time with the content controlled by *Teacher/Text* while T2 spent more time controlled by *Teacher/Text/Students*. In terms of *Student Modality*, the students in T1's classes spent more time reading and writing compared to the others. Students in T3's classes were not given any opportunities to read in those particular classes and spent far more time listening to the teacher. As for the *Types of materials*, only T1 made use of *Audio Materials*. Both T1 and T3 used more *Minimal Text* than *Extended Text*, while T2 was the opposite and made use of *Extended Texts*. Furthermore, T2 tended to spend less time using instructional materials when compared with the others. The three teachers also showed different preferences in terms of the *Source of Materials* as well. Only T1 made use of authentic materials, or *L2-NS*. For more details of the COLT Part A findings and information regarding which comparisons were statistically significant, see Sano, Katagiri, Sakai, & Shimura (2017).

Teacher Beliefs: The analysis of the teacher interviews revealed that T1 presented a strong belief in student-centred teaching, because she considered it to be both more effective and motivating. Collaborative learning was ideal in her view, and thus she stated a preference for a limited amount of *Individual Work*. She also believed that grammar should not be taught out of context, and that meaning focused activities were more important than a focus on language forms. In terms of *Student Modality*, she was a proponent of a well-balanced curriculum with an emphasis on output-related activities. As for *Content Control*, she expressed a slight concern about giving too much control to students and commented that it might only be possible with advanced learners. T2 had similar beliefs to T1, especially in terms of the benefits of student-centred learning. Therefore, T2 tried to limit the amount of teacher talk and strived to maintain an ideal balance of *Individual Work, Group Work* and *Class* teaching. Again, like T1, T2 placed less emphasis on accuracy and grammar teaching. T2 had a stronger emphasis on teaching speaking compared to T1, and less emphasis on writing in terms of *Student Modality*. Another subtle difference between T1 and T2 was that T2 sought to increase *Content Control* by the students more than T1. The novice teacher, T3 had a similar but more flexible view on teaching compared to the other two. Although T3 stated that giving more *Content Control* to students was important especially to enhance their motivation, T3 viewed the teacher as the most important actor in the class. T3 was also slightly different from the other two with respect to language focused teaching; while the experienced teachers presented strong beliefs against grammar teaching, T3 believed in blending language focused learning intentionally in meaning focused activities. The three teachers were then asked to view the results of the COLT analysis of their teaching practices, and to reflect on how these related to their beliefs. These findings are presented in the next section.

Teacher Reflections: There were many instances where the teachers realized that there were discrepancies between what they believed and what they actually did in their teaching. For example, T1 emphasized a strong preference for group work in her classes. However, when discovering that only 17% of her class time was devoted to group work activities, she realized that reality did not reflect her ideals and noted that she needed to give more opportunities for her students to engage in group work in the future. T2 likewise came to the realization he was talking much more than he had intended when the COLT Part A data indicated he was teaching to the whole class for 31% to 53% of the time. A similar realization was reported by T1 with respect to *Content Control*. The COLT analysis revealed that in one of her classes, 100% of the content was controlled by the text and herself. Even though she had expressed the view that only advanced students would benefit from greater control of the instructional content, when she saw the COLT findings, it forced her into thinking about giving more control over content to her students during the lesson. In terms of *Student Modality*, both T1 and T3 came to realize that, in contrast to their intentions, little time was spent with students speaking. On seeing that students were engaged in listening for over 70% of the time in both of his classes, T3 realized that such heavy concentration of listening had to be changed.

Interestingly, not all the seemingly conflicting findings were considered problematic by the teachers. One such example was observed with T1, who spent nearly two thirds of her class teaching *Form*, which contradicted her belief that teaching form was pointless. However, she did not find it to be a conflict since in that particular class the focus was on vocabulary. This suggests that T1 does not view the teaching of vocabulary in the same way as teaching grammar given the greater emphasis on meaning in vocabulary instruction. The continued use of COLT Part A analyses for self-reflection may provide T1 with more insight into this distinction and reinforce the pedagogical choices she makes. Using this analytical tool to objectify ones' teaching practice was also effective in altering beliefs. For example, T2 expressed a strong belief in giving content control to students and stated that classes controlled by the teacher was not ideal. However, when he was presented with the results of the COLT analyses indicating that nearly 90% of class content in one of his classes was controlled by students, he commented that maybe it was too much. Finally, the COLT Part A analyses also gave a sense of self-assurance. For example, when T3 discovered that he gave his students control of the content for over 40% of his class, he was satisfied with these results and aimed to improve on this at a later stage. This suggests that making use of analytic tools such as COLT for teacher self-reflection, gives more autonomy to teachers in improving their teaching practices because they can evaluate their practices based on their present teaching levels.

To conclude, using the COLT Part A observation scheme on CollaVOD was an effective reflection tool for high school teachers of English in Japan because of its objectivity, the ease of its use, and the visual representation of the results. The process of reflecting on their teaching practices through the lens of COLT, led these three teachers to realize that some aspects of their teaching practices contradicted their beliefs. Making use of COLT succeeded in altering some of their beliefs, indicating its robustness as a teacher education tool. It also empowered the teachers, assuring them that some of their teacher beliefs are being implemented in their practices. Overall, it was shown in this study that using COLT as a self-reflection tool is a powerful approach to teacher training because it gives more control of professional development to the teachers themselves. Using COLT Part A on CollaVOD enables teachers, both experienced and novice, to choose a particular aspect of their teaching practice for improvement, to reflect on their beliefs in relation to their practice, and to gain more control over their progress.

Sano, A., Katagiri, N., Sakai, Y., & Shimura, A. (2017). Assessing the effectiveness of the COLT scheme as a reflection tool for high school teachers of English. *JACET International Convention Selected Papers*, 4, 85–113.

Providing quantitative data with AI Mobile COLT to support the reflection process in language teaching and pre-service teacher training
Hiroki Ishizuka & Martine Pellerin

This summary describes how Part A of the Communicative Orientation of Language Teaching (COLT) observation scheme (Spada & Fröhlich, 1995) has been integrated into a portable and digital platform to facilitate real-time analysis of classroom teaching using a Windows tablet. This is referred to as Mobile COLT (see Chapter 6). Another version of Mobile COLT incorporates artificial intelligence (A.I.) into the platform and is referred to as AI Mobile COLT. Below we describe how Mobile COLT has been used in language teacher education in Japan and how AI Mobile COLT will be combined with a learning management system (LMS) (i.e., Moodle) for use in French language teacher education in Canada.

Various observation schemes, such as the Flanders System, the Jarvis System, and the Stirling Project System, have been developed and tested to assess activities qualitatively or quantitatively in language classrooms. One of the widely used schemes is COLT (Spada & Fröhlich, 1995), which describes and quantifies the communicative orientation of instruction with respect to classroom activities (Part A) and the verbal interactions that take place between students and teachers (Part B). This summary focuses on the COLT Part A categories, which measure Participant organization (class/group/individual work), Content (meaning/form), Content control (teacher/text/student), Student modality (reading/writing/listening/speaking), and Materials (extended/minimal, native/non-native).

COLT has demonstrated great potential as a facilitating tool for language teacher development. However, a key barrier to widespread use is that the manual coding procedures are time-consuming and complex. Thus, Ishizuka and Kibler (2018) developed Mobile COLT, a portable, half-automated version of COLT (Part A) that facilitates real-time class analysis using a Windows tablet. The two studies introduced below were conducted using Mobile COLT.

Research was carried out in English language classrooms in Japan to examine how Mobile COLT can help promote language teaching development. Study 1 involved the observation of three teachers at different school levels: elementary, junior high, and high school. Each teacher was visited four or five times, and their teaching was analyzed using Mobile COLT. The coding results were shown to the teacher with a graphic image along with oral feedback. Study 2 involved the observation of a single elementary school English teacher on two separate occasions within a two-month interval. The same quantitative feedback process in Study 1 was used. After the final visits, all the observed classes in each study were compared with respect to their features and communicative orientation.

In the COLT scheme, activities involving group work, meaning-focused content (management and topics), student-controlled content, discourse (i.e., extended text), and materials for native speakers are considered part of more communicative instruction. In both experiments, the participating teachers tried to change their teaching styles every time their language classes were observed. They attempted to improve the less communicative aspects of their classes. The results of their efforts were sometimes successful, and sometimes not. Figure 1 shows an example of the improvement of communicative indices of one participant teacher during the five observations (one year) in Study 1.

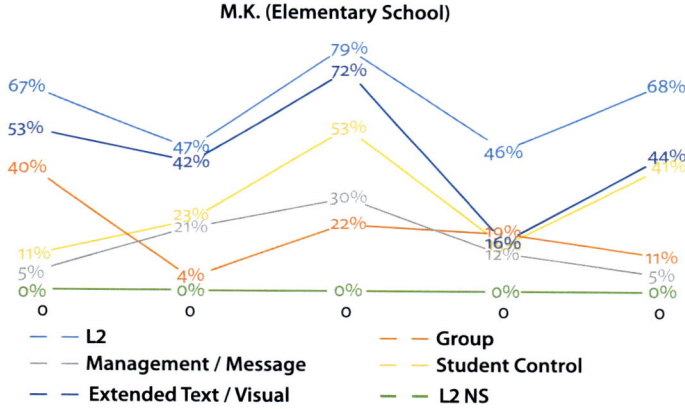

Figure 1. Development of COLT communicative features in the instruction of one teacher

Below Table 1 shows the results of the activities analysis conducted in English by an elementary school teacher in Study 2. Between the first and second observations, group work increased by 6%, and student control of the content increased by 19%. On the other hand, focus-on-meaning activities decreased by 12%, and the use of visual materials decreased by 18%.

The main outcomes that emerged from the two studies using Mobile COLT Part A are:

- the data that Mobile COLT provides to teachers can affect their teaching styles in a short span.
- Mobile COLT can help to identify instructional behaviours that teachers need to improve and to facilitate self-reflection.
- Mobile COLT can provide teachers with quantitative data about the features of their teaching styles.

Table 1. Analysis of the activities of an elementary teacher (Study 2)

COLT Categories	First visit		Second visit	
	Time	Rate	Time	Rate
Group	5:23	11%	8:18	17%
Student	5:53	12%	14:56	31%
Management / Message	2:55	57%	21:17	45%
Extended Text / Visual	1:51	55%	17:25	37%
L2-NS	0:00	0%	0:00	0%

More recently, A.I. has been incorporated into Mobile COLT and plans are underway to use AI Mobile COLT in a Japanese/Canadian collaborative project. This work is taking place within the context of research to explore the potential of digital applications for teacher education purposes (Pellerin, 2011; Pellerin et al., 2018). It is intended to document the evolution of the instructional practices of pre-service teachers enrolled in French language teaching programs in Canada by exploring the use of digital video recording. Moodle platform was used to support the storage and sharing of the video recordings. Access to the videos on the platform allows students to engage in self-reflection, and instructors and supervisors can provide feedback to the students regarding their teaching practices. However, the reflection and feedback available are based mainly on qualitative analysis of the videos. No quantitative data are generated through the platform. Access to quantitative data would contribute to building an evidence-based framework to better support the development of the teaching practices during the initial training of language teachers.

Thus, efforts have been made to explore the possibility of combining AI Mobile COLT with Moodle platform to create a standardized framework for the quantitative analysis of video data collected during classroom teaching. The specific aim is to explore how the AI Mobile COLT system can enhance the analysis of the video recordings of lessons taught by Canadian pre-service language teachers and posted on a Moodle platform to produce standardized feedback to improve the reflective process and enhance supervision during training. (For more information about AI Mobile COLT, referred to as AI Coding in the Automatic COLT system, see Chapter 6). We will first explore the feasibility of the project by testing how the segmenting and coding system used by AI Mobile COLT can be adapted in the context of Canadian French Immersion programs. This process will involve the following steps:

- AI Mobile COLT will need to be adapted for the French language.
- direct classroom observation in French immersion classrooms will need to be carried out to get acquainted with the unfolding language learning activities in an immersion approach to second language teaching.

– video recordings of the lessons taught by pre-service teachers during their practicum will need to be collected for the purpose of testing AI Mobile COLT embedded in Moodle.

Unfortunately, the COVID-19 pandemic forced us to suspend our project. With the onset of remote learning in March 2020, direct classroom observations became unfeasible for pre-service teachers and their supervisors. However, in 2021, we revived our research initiative, involving student teachers enrolled in a French-language teaching training program in a western province of Canada and doing their second year of teaching internship. The internships took place in primary schools in rural and remote regions and spanned six weeks, and data were collected throughout this period. The data analysis yielded fresh insights into the potential application of the AI Mobile COLT system for language teacher internships. It highlights the potential of AI Mobile COLT to enhance the quality and inclusivity of online supervision and mentorship, especially in the new educational context of a digital and A.I. era. For more details about this research see the Brief based on Pellerin & Ishizuka (2022) at the end of this chapter.

The integration of AI Mobile COLT analysis in pre-service language teacher training has great potential to provide improved follow-up on the progress of the pre-service teachers throughout their practicum. More specifically, the combination of AI Mobile COLT with Moodle could contribute to providing quantitative data built on an evidence-based framework to better support the development of teaching practices during initial training. Moreover, in the new era of COVID-19 and online and hybrid teaching, the integration of digital platforms (qualitative and quantitative) for pre-service teaching programs could promote innovative ways of online supervision and training for a new era.

doi Ishizuka, H., & Pellerin, M. (2020). Providing quantitative data with AI Mobile COLT to support the reflection process in language teaching and pre-service teacher training: A discussion. *EUROCALL 2020*, 125–131. Research-publishing.net.

Using COLT Part B to analyze preservice teacher classroom interactions
Noriaki Katagiri & Yukiko Ohashi

The study described in this summary focused on the English language use and communicative orientation of the verbal interactions of preservice Japanese English teachers in their teaching practicum (Katagiri & Ohashi, 2018). Since Japanese English education is situated in an environment where English is taught as foreign language, it was not until 2014 when the Ministry of Education, Culture, Sports, Science and Technology (MEXT) mandated that junior high school English teachers should teach their classes exclusively in English beginning in 2020. However, research carried out between 2012 and 2016 (MEXT, 2017) indicated that the English language proficiency of junior high school English teachers was quite low with only 32% reaching level B2 or higher as measured by the Common European Framework of Reference for Languages (Council of Europe, 2001, p. 24). Also, the use of English for more than half of the class period ranged from 72.3% of the time in Year 7 to 66.8% in Year 9 (MEXT, 2017).

The primary motivation for this research was to investigate how much L2 English pre-service teachers used, and to measure how communicatively oriented their verbal interactions were when teaching their English classes. The study also included an investigation of the teachers' use of L1 (Japanese) and Mix (L2 & L1), teachers' L2 lexical use, and communicative aspects of the learners' language. While some comparisons between the teachers' use of L2 and L1 are provided in this summary, the focus is on the teachers' use of English and the communicative orientation of their verbal interactions in the L2. For more details regarding other aspects of the teachers' and learners' language use, see Katagiri & Ohashi (2018)

We collected observation data from 14 preservice English teachers in Japanese classrooms where English is taught as a foreign language (EFL). This included 14 classroom interactions from the teachers when they engaged in their practicum at a local junior high school for five weeks. In the final week, the researchers recorded the preservice teachers' teaching demonstrations, which they expected would show their best teaching performance during the practicum. The complete recordings were transcribed and tabulated on the COLT Part B spreadsheet for analysis. One of the advantages of using COLT Part B is that it utilizes full transcripts of the classroom utterances of both teachers and students. That is, instead of using a "time-sampling procedure" that would "fragment the data" (Spada & Fröhlich, 1995, p. 66), full transcripts include all the teacher and student utterances and the verbal interactions between them. However, using Part B can be time consuming. The numerical version of COLT Part B was developed to reduce some of the time and to make it more efficient (Katagiri & Kawai, 2015). Using this version, the transcripts of the 14 preservice teachers were aligned on the COLT Part B spreadsheet and the utterances were coded using the numeric system. For more information about preparing transcripts for coding with the numeric system see Katagiri & Kawai (2015).

The numeric system takes advantage of the Microsoft Excel frequency function on the spreadsheet. As seen in Figure 1, the individual turns are on the far left of the spreadsheet and the coding for both individual and combined Part B features are on the right. Only the teacher turns are coded in Figure 1. The numbers that correspond to each coding category are listed under "Coding number". For example, #1 refers to L1 and #2 to L2; #3 refers to pseudo requests and #4 to genuine requests for information. The numerically coded results in each column are counted using the Microsoft Excel spreadsheet frequency function to display the occurrences for each category. The guidelines and details for the coding procedures using numeric COLT Part B are provided in Chapter 5.

Next, we display the numerically quantified coding results and summarize the analyses of them. Table 1 shows the results of the verbal interactions of the 14 preservice English teachers' features and categories. The coding number column at the far left is followed by six column heads corresponding to the COLT Part B features. Under each column head the exclusive categories with frequency counts are listed. This enables, for example, a comparison of the teachers' target language use with their use of the L1 and/or a combination of the

L1 & L2 (i.e., Mix). As indicated, the total number of English L2 turns was 2641 in the target language use category, and as for the information gap category, 1456 turns were coded as giving predictable information. The number of Japanese L1 turns was slightly higher (2758) and consisted primarily of giving predictable information. The number of requests for information in the L2 was significantly lower but the proportion of pseudo to genuine questions was similar. The teachers' language consisted of primarily minimal utterances with considerably fewer instances of sustained speech.

Table 1. COLT Part B coding 6 features with categories and verbal interaction count

			Teacher verbal interaction					
Coding number	Off task	Target language use	Information gap		Sustained speech	Reaction to form/ message	Incorporation of student utterances	
1	Off task	L1 2,758	Giving Info. Predict.	2,142	Minimal 5,178	Form 2,388	Correction	1,629
2	–	L2 2,641	Giving Info. Unpredictable	1,456	Sustained 700	Message 904	Repetition	288
3	–	Mix 659	Request Info. Pseudo request	408	–	–	Paraphrase	27
4	–	–	Request Info. Genuine request	331	–	–	Comment	607
5	–	–	–		–	–	Expansion	39
6	–	–	–		–	–	Clarification request	20
7	–	–	–		–	–	Elaboration	53

Note. L1 = Japanese language; L2 = English language; Mix = mixture of L1 and L2; Info. = information; Predict. = Predictable (Adapted from Katagiri & Ohashi, 2018, p. 93)

The combined COLT Part B features presented in Table 2, provide a more comprehensive picture of the teachers' verbal interactions. This table shows the frequency of the co-occurrence of different combinations of Part B features represented in the teachers' speech. The six-digit numbers in the far-left column represent the coding labels for the Part B features displayed in the far-right column (e.g., 2=L2; 3=pseudo request). As can be seen, the most frequently occurring utterances (n = 599) were those coded as L2/Giving Info. Predict/ Minimal (211000) and the least frequently occurring utterances (n = 53) were those characterized as L2/Message/Comment (200204). Confirming the results presented in Table 1, the preservice teachers interacted in English and Japanese to a similar degree with eight combined utterances in the L1 (40.0%), and nine in the L2 utterances (45.0%), with only three combined Mix utterances (15.0%).

TEACHER VERBAL INTERACTION

Coding category definitions (by coding number):

Coding number	Off task	Target language	Information gap	Sustained speech	Reaction to form/message	Incorporation of student utterances
1	Off task	L1	Giving Info. Predict.	Minimal	Form	Correction*
2	---	L2	Giving Info. Unpredict.	Sustained	Message	Repetition
3	---	---	Request Info. Pseudo requ.	---	---	Paraphrase
4	---	---	Request Info. Genuine requ.	---	---	Comment
5	---	---	---	---	---	Expansion
6	---	---	---	---	---	Clarif. request
7	---	---	---	---	---	Elab. request

Numerical coding of utterances:

(Instructor) / Utterances (Teacher and student speech)	Teacher coding representation	Off task	Target language	Information gap	Sustained speech	Reaction to form/message	Incorporation of student utterances
\<JT> Good morning, everyone.\</JT>	211000		2	1	1	0	0
\<STS> Good morning, Miss. Nishino, and Mr. Cameron, and Ms. Shimizu.\</STS>							
\<ALT> Good morning.\</ALT>	211000		2	1	1	0	0
\<STS> Good morning.\</STS>							
\<ALT> How are you?\</ALT>	221000		2	2	1	0	0
\<ST> I'm fine.\</ST>							
\<ST> I'm hungry.\</ST>							
\<ALT> Hungry.\</ALT>	201207		2	0	1	2	7
\<JT> \<J>Mada nijikanme dayo.\</J>\</JT>	101205		1	0	1	2	5
\<ALT> What's for lunch?\</ALT>	221005		2	2	1	0	5
\<ST> Curry rice!							
\<ST> Egg curry rice!							

Figure 1. Numerical coding sample on the spreadsheet aligned with the transcripts. (Adapted from Katagiri & Ohashi, 2018, p. 86)

Table 2. Teacher verbal interaction count

COLT Part B numerical coding ($N=262$)	Frequency ($N=6{,}059$)	Rank	COLT Part B literal coding
211000	599	1	L2/Giving Info. Predict/Minimal
121000	597	2	L1/Giving Info. Unpredict/Minimal
111000	595	3	L1/Giving Info. Predict./Minimal
101000	549	4	L1/Minimal
201000	474	5	L2/Minimal
221000	384	6	L2/Giving Info. Unpredict./Minimal
201204	121	7	L2/Minimal/Message/Comment
241000	116	8	L2/Request Info. Genuine requ./Minimal
231000	112	9	L2/Request Info. Pseudo requ./Minimal
321000	105	10	Mix/Giving Info. Unpredict./Minimal
131000	102	11	L1/Request Info. Pseudo requ./Minimal
311000	101	12	Mix/Giving Info. Predict./Minimal
101200	97	13	L1/Minimal/Message
301000	97	13	Mix/Minimal
222000	96	15	L2/Giving Info. Unpredict./Sustained
122000	77	16	L1/Giving Infro. Unpredict./Sustained
101204	75	17	L1/Minimal/Message/Comment
112000	68	18	L1/Giving Info. Predict./Sustained
202000	55	19	L2/Sustained
200204	53	20	L2/Message/Comment

Note. L1 = Japanese language; L2 = English language; Mix = mixture of L1 and L2; Info. = Information; Predict. = Predictable; Unpredict. = Unpredictable; requ. = request (Adapted from Katagiri & Ohashi, 2018, p. 94)

When we observe the combined coding results in relation to the use of L1, L2 or Mix, we see that among the top 20 coding patterns the information gap feature such as giving information and requesting information dominates the verbal interaction patterns despite the language used. Statistical testing confirmed that the preservice teachers engaged in significantly more *giving information* interactions than *requesting information*. This implies that the preservice teachers were more likely to provide instructions and to give answers to the questions they asked in their teaching demonstrations. Again, consistent with the results presented in Table 1, the preservice teachers' speech contained significantly more interactions giving predictable information than unpredictable information. This also suggests that the preservice teachers were more likely to provide answers to the questions to confirm the content of the instruction. Regarding the *requesting information* category, there was no statistical difference between their use of *pseudo requests* and *genuine requests* in the L1, L2 or Mix.

The use of the L2 differed from the L1 in certain combinations of the Part B features. For example, while the preservice teachers used significantly fewer requests for information than giving information, they appeared to incorporate more genuine requests in the L2 whether they were minimal or sustained. That is, the preservice teachers tended to depend on the L1 when "Giving Info. Unpredict/Minimal," and to use the L2 to initiate interactions coded as "Request Info. Genuine requ."

The results revealed that the preservice teachers used the L1 and the L2 to a similar degree in their teaching. This points to a need for greater use of the L2 in the classroom. The finding that more genuine questions were asked by the preservice teachers in the L2 than the L1 suggests a greater orientation toward communicative language use when using the target language. Nonetheless, greater use of genuine questions is needed to conduct more communicative English lessons. It would also be preferable for the preservice teachers to control the interactions to be more message oriented. This too would contribute to more communicative English lessons. The preservice teachers' preferred use of *form-based* interactions to *message-based* interactions supports the dominance of *giving predictable information* over asking *genuine* questions. If preservice teachers engage learners in more message-oriented interactions, this would likely result in more communicative English lessons. Overall, the numerical COLT Part B coding revealed that the preservice teachers tended to exhibit slightly more communicative language use in the L2 compared with the L1. Nonetheless, the overall pattern of their verbal interactions in the L2 indicates that improvements can be made in the communicative orientation of their linguistic interactions with students.

To conclude, this research was made possible firstly, with the use of full transcriptions of the preservice teacher utterances coded with the COLT Part B scheme. Most importantly, converting the original Part B coding procedures to a numerical system enabled a more efficient method of coding and quantifying the results. The numerical system also permits more in-depth analyses of the COLT Part B data, for example, the calculation of combined co-occurring categories. Indeed, the numerical conversion of COLT Part B permits faster, more efficient, and varied analyses.

Katagiri, N., & Ohashi, Y. (2018). Non-native preservice English teachers lexical usage and interactional patterns in transcriptions coded on COLT Part B scheme. *JACET International Convention Selected Papers, 5,* 80–110.

Future research with COLT

In the final section are two research briefs that describe ongoing and future work with digital COLT. The first addresses the potential of A.I. for automatic Part B coding pointing to several challenges and complexities that come with it. The second brief describes a small-scale study reporting the successful use of automatic Part A coding results in combination with online interviews and discussion data in a French language teacher preparation program.

Prospects for Automatic COLT Part B Coding
Noriaki Katagiri

This short article discusses the prospect of developing semi-automatic and in the future, perhaps fully automated COLT Part B coding using artificial intelligence (A.I.). The recent advancement of A.I. that enabled automated speech recognition (ASR), has the potential to access classroom transcriptions coded with COLT Part B numerical coding to 'learn' how to automatically code others. The goal of this article is to describe the outlook of integrating ASR transcriptions and numerical COLT Part B coding with A.I. machine learning.

In Chapter 5 and in the Katagiri and Ohashi summary included in this chapter, the numerical system developed for coding the teacher and student interactions using COLT Part B is described. This system has the advantage of providing faster and more expansive calculations of the frequency of occurrence of individual and combined Part B categories based on full transcripts of classroom interaction. Nonetheless, using Part B remains time-consuming, and there are at least two issues to address to speed up the process. One is transcribing classroom speech in less time, and the other is more rapid coding of the interactions. The following two sections discuss the issue of shrinking the transcription time and the challenges of using AI-based coding.

Since the development of the first digital computers in the 1940s, A.I. has come to the point where it can do better than human beings in the fields of at least image recognition, reading comprehension, and language understanding (Roser, 2022). In 2015 Microsoft introduced automated speech recognition (ASR) in transcribing speech on videos on SharePoint, and in 2021 Google incorporated ASR into Google Chrome, which displays live English captions while playing audio/visual content. According to Hollands et al. (2022), the English ASR word error ratios (WERs) for Microsoft and Google were 4.9% and 5.1%, respectively. Considering the low level of error, ASR technology has the potential to significantly reduce the workload of human transcribers. For example, in contrast to the "two working days" (O'Keeffe et al., 2007, p. 6), it takes to transcribe the teacher and learner speech in one 50-minute-long lesson, the length of time using ASR can be less than three hours (Katagiri, 2023). Of course, to obtain ASR with less WER, it is essential to record classes with high sound clarity using directional microphones. Thus, faster and hopefully more accurate ASR is the first step toward COLT Part B automaticity in the future. With the assistance of ASR, it will be possible to obtain classroom transcriptions of teacher-student verbal interactions much faster. This will result in a larger pool of classroom data, which will provide more resources for teacher education, reflection, and research. We anticipate accomplishing this task in the not-too-distant future. The second challenge, which relates to the A.I. coding of the transcribed data, will take considerably more time and is discussed below.

The availability of numerically coded transcriptions of teacher and student utterances using the COLT Part B categories, should make it possible to build a database for machine learning to determine the probable coding for utterances. That is, having A.I. learn the matching of verbal interactions with COLT Part B coding would create a system that can predict possible interaction coding results both locally (i.e., separately for each coding category) and globally (i.e., with combined categories). It is important to note that the matching of utterances with COLT Part B coding does not imply that one utterance corresponds to one specific coding set because the same coding can be used with many different utterances. For example, in the case of numerical coding, "241000, which represents "L2/Request info. Genuine requ./Minimal," Katagiri and Ohashi (2018) observed 116 utterances coded in the same way (e.g. "Do you like math? Raise your hand," "What do you want to be in your future?" and "Why do you think so?"). In addition, teacher utterances and student utterances use different coding categories. This complexity makes it important to select the most appropriate machine learning model.

The dataset will contain transcriptions with coding completed, and transcriptions before coding for two reasons: (1) transcriptions come first, followed by coding, and (2) transcriptions and their coding are not one-to-one matching. Thus, semi-supervised learning may be more suitable because the algorithm utilizes labeled and unlabeled datasets (Zhu & Goldberg, 2009). Other models may also exist. Whichever model is used, a large number of transcriptions is needed before we can determine which one is more suitable for Automatic COLT Part B coding. We are also not sure at this stage how many class transcriptions with and without coded data will be necessary for the semi-supervised machine learning to yield feasible results. However, since we now know that we have ASR to obtain quicker class transcriptions followed by enough COLT Part B coding results, we can be optimistic about achieving a simultaneous COLT Part B coding system in the future.

Using Automatic AI COLT coding analysis system in pre-service language teacher training[43]
Martine Pellerin & Hiroki Ishizuka

The COVID-19 pandemic has impacted the shortage of qualified and trained teachers nation-wide (UNESCO, 2020). The pandemic crisis has also demonstrated that initial teacher training needs to be reformed (Nations Unies, 2020) by fostering innovation in pedagogical coaching and supervision mechanisms to better respond to the shortage of qualified teachers in rural and remote areas. This includes the potential of new digital technologies for language teacher education purposes (Pellerin, 2018).

43. Part of this work was supported by the Japanese Grant-in-Aid for Scientific Research, Kule Dialogue Grants from University of Alberta Canada and from the Association of Canadian Francophonie Colleges and Universities (AUFC).

This brief describes a research project in which Automatic COLT (Part A), an artificial intelligence application, was used in the observation, analysis, and reflection on teaching practices during the internships of preservice French teachers (Pellerin & Ishizuka, 2022). The research was conducted in a western province of Canada. It involved three student teachers enrolled in a French-language teaching training program, and two qualified supervisors (experienced teachers and school administrators) responsible for the trainees during the internship. The internships took place in primary schools in rural and remote regions and lasted six weeks.

The research utilized Automatic COLT (Part A), the LMS platform Moodle as well as the ZOOM videoconferencing tool. As described in Chapter 6, Automatic COLT uses data collected from various types of English language classes and Microsoft speech recognition data to identify teachers' utterances which are then coded with COLT Part A using coding patterns embedded in the server. One of the major challenges of this research project was to build the French version of Automatic COLT. This included copying the English version to a new server and translating it into French as well as collecting data from 30 French language activities in classroom to include phrases unique to French language classes in the database.

The data collected for this study consisted of two main sources: (1) PDF documents containing Automatic COLT analysis results of audio recordings of classroom lessons conducted during the internships, and (2) transcripts of individual interviews conducted with the three trainees. The results indicated that the use of Automatic COLT combined with the Moodle LMS platform and the ZOOM video conferencing tool were effective mechanisms for the online pedagogical coaching and supervision of teacher trainees. First, it allowed trainees to engage in a process of reflection about their evolving practice during their internship. Some of the insights they gained are evident in the following quotes: 'I got to reflect on my own practices within the classroom a lot more while using Automatic COLT than I got to in my first practicum without it." (trainee #3). 'It definitely made me realize that I was maybe talking too much in some lessons that I should be asking more questions… so that was one way that I improved my lessons for the next ones incorporating more questioning within it…' (trainee #2). Second, access to the quantitative data generated by Automatic COLT allowed the supervisor during the video conferencing sessions to use the outcomes of quantitative data to provide feedback and specific pedagogical coaching to the students regarding their teaching practices.

The possibilities offered by the combination of the Automatic COLT system with the video conferencing tool and the LMS platform allowed for meaningful interaction between the teacher trainees and the supervisors resulting in high-quality, online supervision and pedagogical mentorship to better support the development of the teaching practices during the internship. Digital advancements like these hold great potential for educational institutions and teacher training programs not only in Canada but in other countries in the world, particularly in rural and remote areas.

References

Airey, J. (2012). "I don't teach language" The linguistic attitudes of physics lectures in Sweden. *AILA Review*, 25, 64–79.

Allen, P. (1983). A three-level curriculum model for second language education. *Canadian Modern Language Review*, 40, 23–43.

Allen, P., Bialystok, E., Cummins, J., & Mougeon, R. (1982). *The development of bilingual proficiency* (An interim report on the first year of research). Ontario Institute for Studies in Education, University of Toronto.

Allen, P., & Carroll, S. (1987). Evaluation of classroom processes in a Canadian core French programme. *Evaluation and Research*, 1, 49–61.

Allen, P., & Carroll, S. (1988). Analytic and experimental dimensions in core French classrooms. *Canadian Modern Language Review*, 45, 43–64.

Allen, P., Carroll, S., Burtis, J., & Gaudino, V. (1987). The core French observation study. In B. Harley, P. Allen, J. Cummins, & M. Swain. (Eds.), *The development of bilingual proficiency: Final report. Vol. II: Classroom treatment* (Unpublished report). Ontario Institute for Studies in Education, University of Toronto.

Allen, P., Fröhlich, M., & Spada, N. (1984). The communicative orientation of language teaching: An observation scheme. In J. Handscombe, R.A. Orem, & B. Taylor. (Eds.), *On TESOL: '83: The question of control* (pp. 231–251). TESOL. https://eric.ed.gov/?id=ED275155

Allen, P., Swain, M., Harley, B., & Cummins, J. (1990). Aspects of classroom treatment: Toward a more comprehensive view of second language education. In B. Harley, P. Allen, J. Cummins, & M. Swain. (Eds.), *The development of second language proficiency* (pp. 57–81). Cambridge University Press.

Allwright, R.L. (1972). Prescription and description in the training of language teachers. In J. Qvistgaard, H. Schwartz, & H. Spang-Hanssen. (Eds.), *Applied linguistics: Problems and solutions* (pp. 155–166). AILA Proceedings.

Allwright, D. (1988). *Observation in the language classroom*. Longman.

Arias, A., & Izquierdo, J. (2015). Language attention in content-based instruction: The case of language instructors teaching content in a foreign language in Mexican higher education. *Journal of Immersion and Content-Based Language Education*, 3, 194–217.

Australian Council of Educational Research. (1991). Australian Language Certificates. French.

Bachman, L., & Palmer, A. (1981). A multi-trait-multimethod investigation into the construct validity of six tests of speaking and reading. In A. Palmer. (Ed.), *The construct validation of tests of communicative competence* (pp.141–163). TESOL. https://eric.ed.gov/?id=ED223114

Bell, T.R. (2005). Behaviours and attitudes of effective foreign language teachers: Results of a questionnaire study. *Foreign Language Annals*, 38, 259–270.

Breen, M., & Candlin, C. (1980). The essentials of a communicative curriculum in language teaching. *Applied Linguistics*, 1, 1–47.

Brinton, D., Snow, M., & Wesche, M. (2003). *Content-based second language instruction* (2nd ed.). University of Michigan Press.

Brown, H.D. (2001). *Teaching by principles: An interactive approach to language pedagogy*. Longman.

Brumfit, C. (1984). *Communicative methodology in language teaching: The roles of fluency and accuracy*. Cambridge University Press.

Canale, M., & Swain, M. (1980). Theoretical bases for communicative approaches to second language teaching and testing. *Applied Linguistics*, 1, 1–47.

Celce-Murcia, M. (2001). Language teaching approaches: An overview. In M. Celce-Murcia. (Ed.), *Teaching English as a second or foreign language* (pp. 3–11). Heinle & Heinle.

Chacon, T.C. (2005). Teachers' perceived efficacy among English as a foreign language teachers in middle schools in Venezuela. *Teaching and Teacher Education, 21,* 257–272.

Chastain, K. (1969). The audiolingual habit theory versus cognitive code-learning theory: Some theoretical considerations. *International Review of Applied Linguistics, 7,* 97–106.

Chaudron, C. (1988). *Second language classrooms: Research on teaching and learning.* Cambridge University Press.

Chaudron, C. (1991). Activities in the classroom: A unit of analysis in classroom interaction for valid observation and analysis. In J. Drury & R. Wijesinha. (Eds.), *Aspects of teaching and learning English as a second language* (pp.14–33). Sri Lanka National Institute of Education.

Coskun, A. (2011). Investigation of the application of communicative language teaching in the English language classroom: A case study on teachers' attitudes in Turkey. *Journal of Linguistics and Language Teaching, 2,* 1–27. https://eric.ed.gov/?id=ED513910

Coulthard, M. (1977). *An introduction to discourse analysis.* Longman.

Council of Europe. (2001). Common European Framework of Reference for Languages: Learning, teaching, assessment. Retrieved on 2 February 2024 from https://rm.coe.int/1680459f97

Crookes, G., & Chaudron, C. (1991). Guidelines for classroom language teaching. In M. Celce-Murcia. (Ed.), *Teaching English as a second or foreign language* (pp. 46–67). Newbury House.

Dendrinou, V., Vikas, K., Marmaridou, S., Ouzounis, A., & Triandaphylou, T. (1987). *Taskway English – Vols 1, 2 and 3.* Greek Ministry of Education.

Dörnyei, Z. (2007). *Research methods in applied linguistics.* Oxford.

Doughty, C. (1994). Finetuning of feedback by competent speakers to language learners. In J. Alatis. (Ed.), *GURT 1993* (pp. 96–108). Georgetown University Press.

Doughty, C. (2003). Instructed SLA: Constraints, compensation, and enhancement. In C. Doughty & M. Long. (Eds.), *The handbook of second language acquisition* (pp. 256–310). Blackwell.

Edeihoff, C. (1981). Theme-oriented English teaching: Text varieties, media, skills, and project work. In C. Candlin. (Ed.), *The communicative teaching of English: Principles and an exercise typology* (pp. 49–62). Longman.

Ellis, R. (2001). Investigating form-focused instruction. *Language Learning, 51,* 1–46.

Ellis, R. (2012). *Language teaching research and language pedagogy.* John Wiley & Sons.

Fanselow, J. (1977). Beyond Rashomon – Conceptualizing and describing the teaching act. *TESOL Quarterly, 11,* 17–39.

Friedenberg, J., & Schneider, M. (2008). An experiment in sheltered sociology at the university level. In R. Wilkinson & V. Zegers. (Eds.), *Realizing content and language integration in higher education.* (pp.155–168). Maastricht University.

Fröhlich, M., Spada, N., & Allen, P. (1985). Differences in the communicative orientation of L2 classrooms. *TESOL Quarterly, 19,* 27–57.

Goo, J., Granena, G., Yilmaz, Y., & Novella, M. (2015). Implicit and explicit instruction in L2 learning. In P. Rebuschat. (Ed.), *Implicit and explicit learning of languages* (pp. 443–482). John Benjamins.

Guilloteaux, M., & Dörnyei, Z. (2008). Motivating language learners: A classroom-oriented investigation of the effects of motivational strategies on student motivation. *TESOL Quarterly, 19,* 55–77.

Harley, B., Allen, P., Cummins, J., & Swain, M. (Eds.), (1990). *The development of second language proficiency.* Cambridge University Press.

Hatch, E. (1978). Discourse analysis and second language acquisition. In E. Hatch. (Ed.), *Second language acquisition: A book of readings.* Newbury House. https://www.academia.edu/111752968/Second _language_acquisition_A_book_of_readings_Evelyn_Marcussen_Hatch_Ed_Rowley_Mass _Newbury_House_1978_Pp_x_488?uc-g-sw=109991318

Hincks, R. (2010). Speaking rate and information content in English lingua franca oral presentations. *English for Specific Purposes, 29,* 4–18.

Hollands, S., Blackburn, D., & Christensen, H. (2022). Evaluating the performance of state-of-the-art ASR systems on non-native English using corpora with extensive language background variation. *Interspeech 2022.*

Hymes, D. H. (1970). On communicative competence. In J. B. Pride & J. Holmes, (Eds.), *Sociolinguistics* (pp. 269–293). Penguin Books.

İnceçay, G., & İnceçay, V. (2009). Turkish university students' perceptions of communicative and non-communicative activities in EFL classroom. *Procedia – Social and Behavioral Sciences, 1,* 618–622.

Ishizuka, H., & Yorozuya, R. (2014). Collaborative VOD platform for classroom observation. In J. Viteli & M. Leikomaa. (Eds.), *Proceedings of EdMedia World Conference on Educational Multimedia, Hypermedia and Telecommunications, 2014* (pp. 2427–2432).

Ishizuka, H., & Kibler, R. (2018). Development of automatic language classroom analysis system. In *Proceedings of EdMedia: World Conference on Educational Media and Technology* (pp. 626–630). Association for the Advancement of Computing in Education (AACE). https://www.learntechlib.org /primary/p/184252/

Ishizuka, H., & Pellerin, M. (2020). Providing quantitative data with AI Mobile COLT to support the reflection process in language teaching and pre-service teacher training: a discussion. In K. M. Frederiksen, S. Larsen, L. Bradley, & S. Thouësny. (Eds.), *CALL for widening participation: Short papers from EUROCALL 2020* (pp. 125–131). Research-publishing.net.

Jarvis, G. A. (1968). A behavioural observation system for classroom foreign language skill acquisition. *Modern Language Journal, 52,* 335–341.

Johnson, K. (1982). *Communicative syllabus design and methodology.* Pergamon Press.

Kang, E. Y., Sok, S., & Han, Z. H. (2018). Thirty-five years of ISLA on form-focused instruction: A methodological synthesis. *Language Teaching Research, 23,* 403–427.

Katagiri, N. (2023). Web video text tracks to compile an English classroom transcript with bilingual speech. In *Proceedings of the 48th JASELE Annual Convention* (pp. 192–193).

Katagiri, N., & Kawai, G. (2015). Tabulating transcripts and coding on COLT Part B Scheme to quantify classroom interaction analysis categories. *HELES Journal, 14,* 23–41.

Katagiri, N., & Ohashi, Y. (2018). Non-native preservice English teachers' lexical usage and interactional patterns in transcriptions coded on COLT Part B scheme. *ACET International Convention Selected Papers, 5,* 80–110. Jacet. Retrieved on 2 February 2024 from http://www.jacet.org/SelectedPapers /JACET56_2017_SP_5.pdf

Kırkgöz, Y. (2008). A case study of teachers' implementation of curriculum innovation in English language teaching in Turkish primary education. *Teaching and Teacher Education, 24,* 1859–1875.

Krashen, S. (1981). *Second language acquisition and second language learning.* Oxford University Press.

Krashen, S. (1982). *Principles and practice in second language acquisition.* Pergamon Press.

Krashen, S. (1985). *The input hypothesis: Issues and implications.* Longman.

Krashen, S., & Seliger, H. (1975). The essential contribution of formal instruction in adult second language learning. *TESOL Quarterly, 9,* 173–183.

Larsen-Freeman, D. (2003). *Techniques and principles in language teaching* (2nd ed.). Oxford University Press.

doi Lightbown, P. M., & Spada, N. (1994). An innovative program for primary ESL in Quebec. *TESOL Quarterly, 28,* 563–579.

Lightbown, P. M., & Spada, N. (1993). *How languages are learned.* Oxford University Press.

Lightbown, P. M., & Spada, N., (2015). *How languages are learned* (5th ed.). Oxford University Press. https://elt.oup.com/catalogue/items/global/teacher_development/oxford_handbooks_for_language_teachers/9780194406291?cc=global&selLanguage=en&mode=hub

Littlewood, W. T. (1981). *Communicative language teaching: An introduction.* Cambridge University Press.

doi Long, M. H. (1980). Inside the 'black box': Methodological issues in classroom research on language learning. *Language Learning, 30,* 1–42.

doi Long, M. H. (1983). Native speaker/non-native speaker conversation and the negotiation of comprehensible input. *Applied Linguistics, 4,* 126–141.

doi Long, M. H. (1991). Focus on form: A design feature in language teaching methodology. In K. de Bot, D. Coste, R. Ginsberg, & C. Kramsch. (Eds.), *Foreign language research in cross-cultural perspective.* John Benjamins.

doi Lyster, R. (1998). Recasts, repetition, and ambiguity in L2 classroom discourse. *Studies in Second Language Acquisition, 20,* 51–81.

doi Lyster, R. (2002). Negotiation in immersion teacher-student interaction. *International Journal of Educational Research, 37,* 237–253.

doi Lyster, R. (2007). *Learning and teaching languages through content: A counterbalanced approach.* John Benjamins.

doi Lyster, R., & Ranta, L. (1997). Corrective feedback and learner uptake. *Studies in Second Language Acquisition, 19,* 37–66.

doi Lyster, R., & Mori, H. (2006). Interactional feedback and instructional counterbalance. *Studies in Second Language Acquisition, 28,* 269–300.

Mackey, A., & Gass, S. (2005). *Second language research methodology and design.* Routledge.

doi McKay, P. (1994). Communicative orientation and language outcomes in Australian junior secondary foreign language classes (Unpublished doctoral dissertation). University of Queensland.

McKay, S. (2006). *Researching second language classrooms.* Lawrence Erlbaum.

Ministry of Education, Culture, Sports, Science and Technology (MEXT), Japan. (2017). Heisei 28 nendo eigo kyoiku jisshi jokyo chosa (chugakko) no kekka [*Results of English language education progress report on junior high schools*]. Retrieved on 2 February 2024 from https://www.mext.go.jp/component/a_menu/education/detail/icsFiles/afieldfile/2017/04/07/1384236_03.pdf

doi Mitchell, R. (1985). Process research in second language classrooms. *Language Teaching, 18,* 330–352.

Mori, H. (2002). Error treatment sequences in Japanese immersion classroom interactions at different grade levels (Unpublished doctoral dissertation). University of California, Los Angeles.

Moskowitz, G. (1970). *The foreign language teacher interacts.* Minneapolis Association for Productive Teaching.

Munby, J. (1978). *Communicative syllabus design.* Cambridge University Press.

Murray, D. E., & Christison, M. (2011). *What English language teachers need to know. Vol. 1: Understanding learning.* Routledge.

Myers, M. (2008). Code-switching in content learning. In R. Wilkinson & V. Zegers. (Eds.), *Realizing content and language integration in higher education* (pp. 43–52). Maastricht University.

Nations Unies. (2020). Note de synthèse: L'éducation en temps de COVID-19 et après. Retrieved on 2 February 2024 from https://www.un.org/sites/un2.un.org/files/2020/09/policy_brief_-_education_during_covid-19_and_beyond_french.pdf

doi   Newmark, L., & Riebel, D. A. (1968). Necessity and sufficiency in language learning. *International Review of Applied Linguistics, 6*, 145–164.

doi   Norris, J., & Ortega, L. (2000). Effectiveness of L2 instruction: A research synthesis and quantitative meta-analysis. *Language Learning, 50*, 417–528.

doi   O'Keeffe, A., McCarthy, M., & Carter, R. (2007). *From corpus to classroom: Language use and language teaching.* Cambridge University Press.

Pellerin, M. (2011). The use of the open-source e-portfolio system Mahara to support the notion of digital documentation and the development of electronic-portfolio with pre-service language teachers. In T. Bastiaens & M. Ebner. (Eds.), *Proceedings of ED-MEDIA 2011--World Conference on Educational Multimedia, Hypermedia & Telecommunications* (pp. 523–528). Association for the Advancement of Computing in Education (AACE). https://www.learntechlib.org/p/37916/

Pellerin, M. (2018). Affordances of new mobile technologies: Promoting learner agency, autonomy, and self-regulated learning. *Journal of Interactive Learning Research, 29*, 335–350. https://api .semanticscholar.org/CorpusID:229293993

Pellerin, M., Branch-Mueller, J., Nicholas, P., & Wei, W. (2018). The integration of e-portfolios in higher education, and students' perceptions. *Journal of Interactive Learning Research, 29*, 529–544. https:// learntechlib.org/primary/p/181351/

Pellerin, M., & Ishizuka, H. (2022). Rethinking language teacher supervision and pedagogical coaching for a new digital era with AI COLT system, online platform, and videoconferencing tool. Paper presented at the 3rd Asia Education Technology Symposium (AETS 2022).

doi   Pica, T. (1987). The selective impact of classroom instruction on second-language acquisition. *Applied Linguistics, 6*, 214–222.

doi   Politzer, R. L. (1970). Some reflections on 'good' and 'bad' language teaching behaviours. *Language Learning, 20*, 31–43.

Prabhu, N. S. (1979). The teaching of English and notions about communication. In J. C. Richards. (Ed.), *Applications of linguistics to language teaching – RELC Anthology 6.* Singapore University Press.

Richard-Amato, P. (2003). *Making it happen: From interactive to participatory language teaching.* Pearson.

doi   Richards, J., & Farrell, T. (2005). *Professional development for language teachers: Strategies for teacher learning.* Cambridge University Press.

Richards, J., & Rodgers, T. S. (2004). *Approaches and methods in language teaching* (2nd ed.). Cambridge University Press.

doi   Rodgers, D. (2006). Developing content and form: Encouraging evidence from Italian content-based instruction. *The Modern Language Journal, 90*, 373–386.

Roser, M. (2022). The brief history of artificial intelligence: The world has changed fast – What might be next? *Our World in Data.* https://ourworldindata.org/brief-history-of-ai

Sano, A., Katagiri, N., Sakai, Y., & Shimura, A. (2017). Assessing the effectiveness of the COLT scheme as a reflection tool for high school teachers of English. *JACET International Convention Selected Papers, 4*, 85–113. https://www.jacet.org/SelectedPapers/JACET55_2016_SP_4.pdf

Savignon, S. (1972). *Communicative competence: An experiment in foreign language teaching.* Philadelphia Center for Curriculum Development.

Scherer, G., & Wertheimer, F. (1964). *A psycholinguistic experiment in foreign-language teaching.* McGraw-Hill.

Shulman, L. S. (1986). Paradigms and research programs in the study of teaching: A contemporary perspective. In M. Wittrock. (Ed.), *Third handbook of research on teaching* (pp. 3–36) Macmillan.

Sheen, Y., & Ellis, R. (2011). Corrective feedback in language teaching. In E. Hinkel. (Ed.), *Handbook of research in second language teaching and learning* (Vol. 2, pp. 593–610). Routledge. https://www.taylorfrancis.com/chapters/edit/10.4324/9780203836507-41/corrective-feedback-language-teaching-younghee-sheen-rod-ellis

Smith, P. D. (1969). The Pennsylvania foreign language research project: Teaching proficiency and class achievement in two modern languages. *Foreign Language Annals, 3*, 194–207.

Spada, N. (1987). Relationships between instructional differences and learning outcomes: A process-product study of communicative language teaching. *Applied Linguistics, 8*, 137–161.

Spada, N. (1990a). Observing classroom behaviours and learning outcomes in different second language programs. In J. C. Richards & D. Nunan. (Eds.), *Second language teacher education* (pp. 292–310). Cambridge University Press.

Spada, N. (1990b). A look at the research process in classroom observation: A case study. In C. Brumfit & R. Mitchell. (Eds.), *Research in the language classroom, ELT Documents: 133* (pp. 81–93). Modern English Publications in association with the British Council.

Spada, N. (1997). Form-focused instruction and second language acquisition: A review of classroom and laboratory research. *Language Teaching 30*, 73–87.

Spada, N. (2011). Beyond form-focused instruction: Reflections on past, present, and future research. *Language Teaching, 44*, 225–236.

Spada, N. (2019). Classroom observation research. In J. Schwieter & A. Benati. (Eds.), *The Cambridge handbook of language learning* (pp.186–207). Cambridge University Press.

Spada, N., & Frölich, M. (1995). *The communicative orientation of language teaching observation scheme (COLT): Coding conventions and applications.* Macquarie University.

Spada, N., & Fröhlich, M. (1995). *The communicative orientation of language teaching observation scheme (COLT): Coding conventions and applications.* MacMillan.

Spada, N., & Lyster, R. (1997). Macroscopic and microscopic views of L2 classrooms. *TESOL Quarterly, 31*, 787–795.

Spada, N., & Tomita, Y. (2010). Interactions between type of instruction and type of language feature: A meta-analysis. *Language Learning, 60*, 263–308.

Stern, H. (1983). *Fundamental concepts of language teaching.* Oxford University Press.

Strauss, A., & Corbin, J. M. (1997). *Grounded theory in practice.* Sage.

Swain, M. (1985). Communicative competence: Some roles of comprehensible input and comprehensible output in its development. In S. M. Gass & C. G. Madden. (Eds.), *Input in second language acquisition* (pp. 235–253). Newbury House.

Tatzl, D. (2011). English-medium masters' programmes at an Austrian university of applied sciences: Attitudes, experiences, and challenges. *Journal of English for Academic Purposes, 10*, 250–270.

Tomlin, R., & Villa, V. (1994). Attention in cognitive science and second language acquisition. *Studies in Second Language Acquisition, 16*, 183–203.

Tschannen-Moran, M., Woolfolk Hoy, A., & Hoy, W. K. (1998). Teacher efficacy: Its meaning and measurement. *Review of Educational Research, 68*, 202–248.

Ullman, R. & Geva, E. (1984). Approaches to observation in second language classes. In P. Allen & M. Swain. (Eds.), *Language issues and education policies: ELT Documents, 119* (pp.113–128). Pergamon.

UNESCO. (2020). Éducation et COVID-19: Réponse de l'UNESCO. Notes thématiques du Secteur de l'Éducation. *Note thématique no 2.2-avril 2020.* Retrieved on 2 February 2024 from https://unesdoc.unesco.org/ark:/48223/pf0000373338_fre

doi Unterberger, B. (2012). English-medium programmes at Austrian business faculty: A status quo survey on national trends and a case study on programme design and delivery. *AILA Review, 25,* 80–100.

Valcárcel, M., Verdú, M. Roca, J., & Chaudron, C. (1991). Classroom activity types, tasks, and sequencing. Paper presented at the 25th Annual TESOL Convention, New York, 26 March.

van Lier, L. (1988). *The classroom and the language learner.* Longman.

doi van Lier, L. (1997). Observation from an ecological perspective. *TESOL Quarterly, 31,* 783–787.

doi Watson-Gegeo, K. A. (1997). Classroom ethnography. In N. Hornberger & D. Corson. (Eds.), *Encyclopedia of language and education* (Vol. 8, pp. 135–144). Kluwer.

doi White, L. (1991). Adverb placement in second language acquisition: Some effects of positive and negative evidence in the classroom. *Second Language Research, 7,* 133–161.

doi White, L., Spada, N., Lightbown, P. M., & Ranta, L. (1991). Input enhancement and L2 question formation. *Applied Linguistics, 12,* 416–432.

Widdowson, H. G. (1978). *Teaching language as communication.* Oxford University Press.

Wilkins, D. A. (1976). *Notional syllabuses.* Oxford University Press.

Yalden, J. (1983). *The communicative syllabus: Evolution, design, and implementation.* Pergamon.

doi Zhu, X., & Goldberg, A. B. (2009). Introduction to semi-supervised learning. *Synthesis Lectures on Artificial Intelligence and Machine Learning, 3,* 1–130.

Zotou, V. (1993). Effective foreign language teaching: A Greek case study (Unpublished doctoral dissertation). University of Southampton.

Appendix A

The activity system: Classification

Following Edeihoff's classification of learning phases from the learner's point of view (1981, p. 57), we have tried to fit our selection of activities within the four phases:

Information and motivation phase
Input/Content phase (Organizing/Selecting information phase)
Working phase (Practise phase)
Transfer phase (Application phase)

In the first phase the aim is to arouse the learners' interest and experience and relevant language knowledge by confronting them with some novel, yet not totally unfamiliar experience. In the second phase the learners are involved in deepening their understanding of both theme and language by close attention to the detail of content and language, making conscious links to what they already know. In the Working phase individual linguistic and thematic difficulties can be isolated and examined in depth. Learners focus on particular examples of the theme and the characteristics of language used. The working phase prepares the way for the Transfer phase where the new knowledge and the refined communicative abilities of the learner can be put to active use. The main objective of this phase is to provide a place where the various preparatory activities can contribute to a more communicative task, with the emphasis on genuine and authentic communication.

Information and motivation phase activities

1. *Warm up*: mime, dance, song, jokes, play, etc.; this activity has the purpose of getting the students stimulated, relaxed, motivated, attentive, or otherwise engaged and ready for the classroom lesson; it is not necessarily related to the target language.
2. *Setting*: focussing in on lesson topic; either verbal or non-verbal evocation of the context that is relevant to the lesson point; teacher directs attention to the upcoming topic by way of questioning, miming, picture presentation, or possibly tape recording of noise and people.
3. *Brainstorm*: a special form of preparation for the lesson, like setting, which involves free, undirected contributions by the students and teacher on a given topic, to generate multiple associations without linking them; no explicit analysis or interpretation is given by the teacher.

4. *Story telling*: oral presentation of a story or an event on the part of the teacher as lengthy practice, although not necessarily lesson-based; it implies the use of extended discourse; it usually aims at maintaining attention or motivation, and it often implies an aim of entertainment.

5. *A propos*: conversation and other socially oriented interaction/speech by teacher, students or even visitors on general real-life topics; typically authentic and genuine.

Organizing and selecting information and content phase activities

6. *Organizational*: managerial structuring of lesson or class activities; includes reprimanding of students and other disciplinary action, organization of class furniture and seating, general procedures for class interaction and performance, structure and purpose of lesson etc.,

7. *Content explanation*: explanation of lesson content and grammar or other rules and points – phonology, grammar, lexis, sociolinguistics or whatever is being 'taught'.

8. *Role play demonstration*: use of selected students or teacher to illustrate the procedure(s) to be applied in the lesson segment to follow; it includes brief illustrations of language or other content to be incorporated.

9. *Recognition*: students identifying a specific target form, function, definition, rule or other lesson-related item, either from an oral or visual mode, but without producing language as response (e.g., checking off items, drawing symbols, rearranging pictures, matching of utterances with pictures, underlying significant information from a text, etc.).

10. *Language modelling*: presentation of new language, by the teacher, through isolated sentences with the help of visuals, drawings on blackboard, realia, miming etc., or making use of recorded material; it involves students' participation in the form of repetition, display question and answer, translation, etc.; it usually aims at checking correct pronunciation, meaning comprehension and syntax construction.

11. *Dialogue/Narrative presentation*: reading or listening passage, in the form of dialogue, narration, song or other, for passive reception (i.e., students get familiarised with the text without being asked to perform any task related to the content); it usually implies listening to a tape or teacher reading aloud and students following with or without the text.

12. *Question-answer display*: controlled activity involving prompting of students' responses by means of display questions (i.e., teacher or questioner already knows the response, or has a very limited set of expectations for the appropriate response); it is distinguished from Referential questions by means of the likelihood of the questioner knowing, and the speaker being aware of the questioner knowing, the response.

13. *Review*: teacher-led review of previous week/month! or other period as a formal summary and type of test of students' recall and performance.

Focus/Working phase activities

14. *Translation*: student or teacher provision of LI and L2 translations of a given text.
15. *Dictation*: students writing down orally presented text.
16. *Copying*: students writing down text presented visually.
17. *Reading aloud*: student/s reading aloud from a given text; it is distinguished from dialogue presentation in that the focus is on pronunciation and rhythm.
18. *Drill*: typical language activity involving fixed patterns of teacher and student responding and prompting, usually with repetition, substitution, and other mechanical alterations; typically, with little meaning attached.
19. *Dialogue/Narrative recitation*: students reciting a passage or dialogue which they have previously learned or prepared, either in unison or individually.
20. *Cued narrative/dialogue:* students building up a dialogue or a piece of narrative following cues from miming, cue-cards, pictures, flow charts, key functional requests or other stimuli related to narrative or dialogue (e.g., filling empty bubbles, cued-dialogues, completing a dialogue or a text, discourse chains, etc.)
21. *Drill meaningful*: language activity involving exchange of a limited number of fixed patterns of interaction; distinguished from Mechanical drills in that students must make a choice with respect to the meaning conveyed.
22. *Preparation*: students planning the subsequent activity (in pairs, individually or in groups) by means of rehearsing, making notes, or simply thinking.
23. *Identification*: students picking out significant items of information from an oral or visual mode and producing an oral or written response (i.e., they identify specific target forms, particular speech functions or any other relevant information related to the text by means of filling in columns, diagrams, taking notes, answering questions (display), etc., about factual information)
24. *Games*: an organized language activity that has a particular task or objective and a set of rules which involves an element of competition between players (i.e., board games, hangman, bingo, etc.); it usually implies an aim of entertainment and relaxation.
25. *Question-answer referential*: activity involving prompting of responses by means of referential questions (i.e., the questioner does not know beforehand the response information); distinguished from Information exchange in that the information obtained is not meant to achieve a task or solve a problem.
26. *Checking*: teacher guiding the correction of students' previous activity or homework, providing feedback as an activity rather than within another activity.
27. *Wrap-up*: brief teacher or student produced summary of point or items that have been practised or learned.

Transfer/Application phase activities

28. *Information transfer*: students extracting information from a text (oral or written) which they apply to another mode (e.g., visual –> written; oral –> written etc.,); it implies some transformation of the information by means of filling out diagrams, graphs, answering questions etc., while listening or reading. Distinguished from *Identification* in that students are expected to reinterpret the content of information.

29. *Information exchange*: activity involving one-way or two-way communication as in information gap exercises, when one or both parties must obtain some information from the other to achieve some goal; distinguished from *Meaningful drill* in that the pattern of exchange is not limited to a fixed set or order of structures; also distinguished from *Information transfer* in that the information is not reinterpreted; and distinguished from *Referential questions* in that obtaining the information is critical for the resolution of task.

30. *Role-play*: students acting out some specified roles and functions in a relatively free way; distinguished from *Cued dialogues* by the fact that cuing is provided only minimally at the beginning, and not during, the activity.

31. *Report*: prepared oral exposition of students' previous work (books read, stories, project work, etc.,) and elaborated on according to students' own interpretation; it can also be students' reports on information obtained from previous activity as long as that can be considered as preparation (i.e., students report back with the help of data obtained during the activity).

32. *Narration*: students' lengthy exposition of something which they have seen (film, video program, event, etc.), read (news, books, etc.) or experienced (events, story, etc.) and narrated in their own words and without previous preparation; distinguished from *Cued-narrative* because lack of immediate stimulus.

33. *Discussion*: debate or other form of group discussion of specified topic, with or without specified sides/positions prearranged.

34. *Composition*: written development of ideas, story, dialogues, or other exposition; it is akin to Report but in the written mode.

35. *Problem solving*: students are asked to work in an activity in which a problem and some limitations on means are established to resolve it; it requires cooperative action on the part of participants, in small or large groups, in order to reach a solution; only one outcome – sometimes among other possible solutions – is allowed per group.

36. *Drama*: planned dramatic rendition of play, skit, etc.

37. *Simulation*: activity involving complex interaction between groups and individuals based on simulation of real-life actions and experiences.

Borderline activity

38. *Testing*: formal testing procedures to evaluate students' progress; (this activity is considered borderline because it could be included in any phase, depending on the content to be tested)

Note: It must be pointed out that the phases above offer an idealized picture of the learning-teaching process and in reality, both the phases and the activities are interdependent and interact with each other and are not sequenced one after the other.

Answer key

Chapter 4

Practice 1: Giving predictable or unpredictable information

1. Both answers are coded as *Giving predictable information* since both the teacher and the student(s) know the main stores in this town in Quebec, Canada.
2. All three answers are coded as *Giving unpredictable information* since the teacher does not know what the student is going to say.
3. Since this is a review of the book borrowing procedure used in this class, both responses are coded as *Giving predictable information*.
4. The student answer: 'Spaghetti or fish chips' is coded as *Giving unpredictable information* if we assume that the teacher does not know the meal plan of the cafeteria. If, however, the teacher knows that the meal on Tuesdays is always spaghetti or fish and chips, the student response would be coded as *Giving predictable information*. In a case like this, one may wish to verify it with the teacher, particularly if there are many instances like this in the verbal interaction between teacher and students. If the coder has been in the classroom him/herself, it is often easier to decide whether a response provides predictable or unpredictable information, since the context and extralinguistic information (e.g. gestures) may provide a clue.

Practice 2: Requesting information: pseudo or genuine requests

1. Both teacher questions are *Genuine requests for information* since the teacher does not know the answers in advance.
2. The first 3 questions are *Genuine requests*. It could be argued that the teacher may have asked the substitute teacher what she did with the class. If that were the case, the requests would be coded as *Pseudo requests*. This could be verified with the teacher. The last three questions are Pseudo requests because the teacher knows what games are typically played in class.

Practice 3: Incorporation of student utterances – repetition, comment or paraphrase in connection with correction

1. correction + repetition
2. correction + comment
3. correction (only correction is checked off when metalinguistic information is provided or requested in response to an error).

4. correction + repetition
5. correction (only)
6. correction + paraphrase
7. correction + comment

Practice 4: Incorporation of student utterances – expansion, clarification request or elaboration request

1. clarification request
2. clarification request
3. elaboration request
4. two elaboration requests
5. expansion

Practice 5: Form restriction – restricted or unrestricted

1. restricted (because the students are requested to use the form 'I ate...')
2. restricted (because the students are practising the present continuous form -ing)
3. unrestricted (all three responses, since there is no expectation to use a particular linguistic form)
4. unrestricted

Practice 6: Part B Coding – Transcript 4

Situation: Students tell class what 'bugs' them. They have written 'What bugs me' on a card or piece of paper which they hold up while speaking.

Teacher & student speech	Coding
St: It bugs me when a bee string me.	L2/Unpred.info/Unrestr./Min.
T: Oh, when a bee stings me.	L2/Form-Corr.+Para./Min.
S1: Stings me.	D.I./L2/Form-Rep./Restr./Ultram.
T: Do you get stung often? Does that happen often? The stinging many times?	L2/Mess. Elab.Req./Sust.
S1: Yeah	L2/Unpred Info/Unrestr/Ultram.
T: Often?// (T turns to students who aren't paying attention) OK Chantal Luc, you may begin working on a	L2/Mess.-Clarif.Req.// L2/Off task[1]/Min.

research project, hey? (*T turns her attention back to* '*What bugs me*')	
S2: It bugs me (*inaudible*) and my sister put on my clothes.	L2/Unpred.Info/Unrestr./Min
T: Ah! She ... borrows your clothes?// When you're older, you may appreciate it because you can switch clothes, maybe.// Monique ... this is yours, I will check ... OK. It's good.	L2/Mess.-Para.² // >L2/Mess.-Exp.// L2/Offtask³/Sust.
S3: It bugs me when I'm sick and my brother doesn't help me my, my brother, cause he ... me...	L2/Unpred.lnfo/Unrestr./Min.
T: OK. You know, when ... (*inaudible*) sick, you're sick at home in bed and you say, oh, to your brother your sister: Would you please get me a drink of water?' ... Ah! Drop dead!',you know, 'Go play in the traffic!' You know, it's not very nice. Jean!	L2/Mess.-Exp/Sust.
S4: It bug me to have ...	L2/Unpred.Info/Unrestr./Min.
T: It bugs me. It bugzz me.	L2/Form-Corr.+Para/Min.

1. It is not clear whether this aside to the two students should be coded as *Off task* or as giving Unpredictable information (managerial and/or disciplinary, since the two students are not paying attention). It depends on whether *Off task* is strictly reserved for episodes that are non-curriculum related, such as an announcement over the PA system. It was decided to code this utterance as *Off task* since the teacher is temporarily turning her attention away from the central task of discussing 'what bugs them' with the class.

2. This utterance could also possibly be coded as Form-Correction + Paraphrase, depending on whether the teacher is also focusing on Form and not just on trying to understand what the student had meant to say. This coding reflects the decision that the teacher was concentrating primarily on the message.

3. It is difficult to determine from the tape and transcripts whether these remarks are related to the task or not.

S4; It bugs me// when my brother takes my bicycle. Every day.	L2/Form-Rep.// L2/Unpred.Info/Unrestr/Min.
T: Every day?// Ah! Doesn't your bro.. (inaudible) his bicycle? Could his brother lend his bicycle? Uh, your. brother doesn't have a bicycle?	L2/Mess.-Clarif.Req.// L2/Mess.-Elab.Req./Sust.
S4: Yeah.! A new bicycle (*inaudible*) bicycle.	L2/Unpred.Info/Unres/Min.
T: Ah, well. Talk to your morn and dad about it. Maybe negotiate a new bicycle for your brother.	L2/Mess.-Exp./Min.
S5: (inaudible)	D.I./ uncodable
T: He has a new bicycle.// But his brother needs a new one too?	Uncodable Incorporation//[4] L2/Mess.-Elab.Req./Min.
S5: Yes.	L2/Unpred.Info/Unrestri./Ultram.
T: Hey, whoa, just a minute!	L2/Mess.Clarif.Req./Min.
S6: Frédérique's brother has...	D.I./L2/Unpred.Info/Unrestr./Min.
T: Frédérique, who has a new bicycle? You or your brother?	L2/Gen.Req.[5] /Min.
S4: My brother.	L2/Unpred.Info/Unrestr./Ultram.
T: And you have an old one?	L2/Mess.-Clarif.Req./Min.
S4 (inaudible)	Uncodable
T: And your brother takes your old one?	L2/Mess.-Clarif.Req./Min.
S4: ... clutch ... (inaudible) bicycle.	L2/Unpred./Info/Urestr./Min.
T: His bicycle!// Ah! How old is your brother?	Uncodable[6]// L2/Mess.-Elab.Req./Min.

---

4. Since the preceding student utterance was inaudible, the teacher's reaction "He has a new bicycle." is not codable although it's likely that it is a Message-related Repetition or Paraphrase.

5. Although the teacher is still trying to clarify who has a new bicycle, the question "Who has a new bicycle, you or your brother?" is addressed to the former student S4 and not to the previous student S6. Therefore, it has been coded as a Genuine request and not as a Clarification request.

6. Since the meaning of the student's response is not clear, the teacher's reaction cannot be coded.

S4: March 23.	L2/Unpred.Info/Unrest./Ultram.
T: His birthday?	L2/Mess.-Clarif.Req./Min.
S4: Yeah!	L2/Unpred. Info/Ultram.
T: And how old was he?	L2/Gen.Req/Min.
S4: Fourteen.	L2/Unpred.Info/Unrestr./Ultram.
T: Fourteen!! Well, why don't you tell your brother that when he takes your bike you will take his bike. And he may have more scratches than he figures for. OK?	L2/Mess.-Rep// L2/Mess.-Exp./Sust.

Chapter 5

Practice 7: Calculating content

Exclusive/primary focus		Combinations	
Procedure (3 min.)	10.00%	Form/Function (5 min.)	16.6%
Form (2 min.)	6.67%	Form/Function/Narrow (15 min.)	50.00%
Broad (5 min.)	16.67%		

Practice 8: Coding numeric strings

S1 It bugs me when a bee string me.	2222000
T: Oh, when a bee stings me.	201113
S1: Stings me.	2012102
T: Do you get stung often? Does that happen often?	241207
S1: Yeah.	2213200

Chapter 6

Practice 9: CollaVOD coding

Part A coding of class video and Global Score

An Example Answer Key

Communicative Orientation of Language Teaching Observation Scheme

School: A Junior High
reaches: Ms. Oda
Subject: English I

Grado(s): 7.
Lesson(min.): 14:35
Date: 27/9/2023

Observer: H. Ishizuka
Analyst: Hiroki Tshizuka
Page:

Time		ELAPSED TIME	ACTIVITY No.	EPISODES No.	ACTIVITIES & EPISODES	PARTICIPANT ORGANIZATION — Class (T↔S/C, S↔S/C, Choral)	Group (Same task, Different tasks)	Individual (Same task, Different tasks)	CONTENT — Management (Procedure, Discipline)	Language (Form, Function, Discourse, Sociolinguistic)	Other topics (Narrow, Broad)	CONTENT CONTROL (Teacher/Text, Teacher/Text/Stud., Student)	Listening	Speaking	Reading	Writing	MATERIALS Type — Other, Minimal Text, Extended Text, Audio, Visual	MATERIALS Source — L2-NNS, L2-NS, L2-NSA, Student-made
0	0	84	1	1	Greeting and Small talk	T↔S/C: 11 ; Choral: 1					Narrow: 11	Stud.: 11	Listen: 11	Speak: 1				
0	1	136	2	2	Pair Work — What did you do yesterday	T↔S/C: 1 ; Choral: 1 ; Same task (Group): 11			Procedure: 1		Narrow: 11	Stud.: 11	Listen: 11	Speak: 11				
0	3	97	3	3	Confirmation of the pair talk	T↔S/C: 11 ; Choral: 1			Procedure: 1		Narrow: 11	Teacher/Text: 11	Listen: 11	Speak: 1				
0	5	242	4	4	Review content of last lesson	T↔S/C: 11					Narrow: 11	Teacher/Text: 11	Listen: 11	Speak: 1				
0	9	57	5	5	Distributing handouts	T↔S/C: 11			Procedure: 11				Listen: 1	Speak: 1		Other: 11		
0	10	71	6	6	Taking notes while Listening to CD	T↔S/C: 11				Form: 11	Narrow: 11	Teacher/Text: 11	Listen: 11	Speak: 11		Writing: 11	Audio: 11	L2-NNS: 11
0	11	88	7	7	Repeating after CD	T↔S/C: 11 ; Choral: 11			Procedure: 1	Form: 11	Narrow: 1	Teacher/Text: 11	Listen: 11	Speak: 11 ; Read: 11			Extended Text: 11 ; Audio: 11	L2-NNS: 11
0	12	101	8	8	Role play in pairs	T↔S/C: 1 ; Same task (Group): 11			Procedure: 1	Form: 11	Narrow: 1	Teacher/Text: 11	Listen: 11	Speak: 11			Extended Text: 11 ; Visual: 11	L2-NNS: 11
Totals						6 0 1 ; 0 2 0 0 ; 0 0 0			1 0 3	0 0 0	6 0	6 2 0 7	6 3 1 1 1	1 0 2			

This has been coded as 1 because the primary focus in on Form (i.e. pronunciation).

Global Scoring: 9

group		min.	rate	Score
PATICIPANT ORGANIZATION	Group	03分57秒	27%	2
CONTENT	Management, Other Topics	11分27秒	78%	4
CONTENT CONTROL	Teacher/Text/Stud.,Student	01分14秒	8%	1
MATERIALS Type	Extended Text	00分28秒	3%	1
MATERIALS Source	L2NS,L2-NSA	00分00秒	0%	1

An Example Answer Key

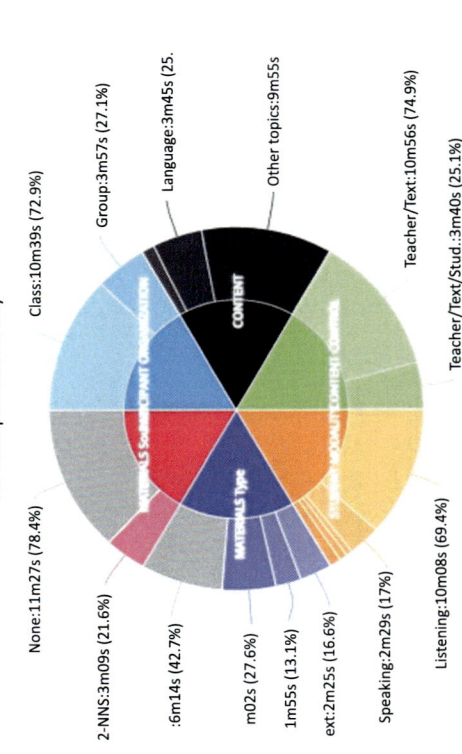

Class:10m39s (72.9%)

Group:3m57s (27.1%)

Language:3m45s (25.

Other topics:9m55s

Teacher/Text:10m56s (74.9%)

Teacher/Text/Stud.:3m40s (25.1%)

None:11m27s (78.4%)

2-NNS:3m09s (21.6%)

:6m14s (42.7%)

m02s (27.6%)

1m55s (13.1%)

ext:2m25s (16.6%)

Speaking:2m29s (17%)

Listening:10m08s (69.4%)

Practice 10: Automatic COLT – Coding without Recording

Part A coding of Figure 4.7 in Chapter 4

LANGUAGE	1. L1	0 sec	0:00	0%	
	1. L2	780 sec	13:00	100%	Almost all is done in the second language
PARTICIPANT ORGANIZATION	3. Class	780 sec	13:00	100%	Most of activities in whole class mode
	4. Indiv	0 sec	0:00	0%	No individual activities
	5. Group	0 sec	0:00	0%	No group work
CONTENT	6. Management	240 sec	4:00	30%	Some content related to classroom management
	7. Message	540 sec	9:00	69%	Mostly meaning focus
	8. Form	0 sec	0:00	0%	no form focus
CONTENT CONTROL	9. Teacher/Text	780 sec	13:00	100%	almost exclusively teacher/text control of speech or writing
	10. Student	0 sec	0:00	0%	No learner free speech or writing
STUDENT MODALITY	11. Listening	780 sec	13:00	100%	Almost exclusively listening activities
	12. Speaking	0 sec	0:00	0%	No speaking activity
	13. Reading	0 sec	0:00	0%	No reading activity
	14. Writing	0 sec	0:00	0%	No listening activity
MAT-TEXT	15. Minimal Text	0 sec	0:00	0%	No word-or sentence-level presentation
	16. Extended Text	0 sec	0:00	0%	No use of extended texts
MAT-AUDIO	17. Audio	0 sec	0:00	0%	No use of native audio
MAT-VISUAL	18. Visual	0 sec	0:00	0%	No use of visual information
MAT-SOURCE	19 L2-NNS	0 sec	0:00	0%	No use of reading materials for non native speakers
	20. L2-NS	0 sec	0:00	0%	No use of native speaker materials
	21. Student- made	0 sec	0:00	0%	No use of learner created materials

Summary of Part A coding

Author index

Subject index

Words in boldface type represent the major features within Part A and Part B of the COLT scheme. Words in italics represent the COLT categories and subcategories.